# HATRED, BIGOTRY, AND PREJUDICE

# Contemporary Issues

Series Editors: Robert M. Baird
Stuart E. Rosenbaum

## Other titles in this series:

# HATRED, BIGOTRY, AND PREJUDICE

## DEFINITIONS, CAUSES & SOLUTIONS

edited by
**Robert M. Baird &
Stuart E. Rosenbaum**

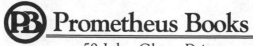 Prometheus Books

59 John Glenn Drive
Amherst, New York 14228-2197

Published 1999 by Prometheus Books

Inquiries should be addressed to
Prometheus Books, 59 John Glenn Drive, Amherst, New York 14228–2197.
VOICE: 716–691–0133, ext. 207.
FAX: 716–564–2711.
WWW.PROMETHEUSBOOKS.COM

03 02 01 00 99    5 4 3 2 1

Library of Congress Cataloging-in-Publication Data

Hatred, bigotry, and prejudice : definitions, causes, and solutions / edited by Robert M.
    Baird and Stuart E. Rosenbaum.
        p.    cm. — (Contemporary issues)
    Includes bibliographical references.
    ISBN 1–57392–748–1 (pa. : alk. paper)
    1. Prejudices. 2. Hate. 3. Toleration. I. Baird, Robert M., 1937–        .
II. Rosenbaum, Stuart E. III. Series: Contemporary issues (Amherst, N.Y.)
BF575.P9B54    1999
303.3'85—dc21
                                                                99–37902
                                                                CIP

Printed in the United States of America on acid-free paper

# Contents

6    Contents

# Introduction

Dallas, TX: Three men ran up to two gay men eating in a park and began beating them. During the attack, the assailants called the victims "queers" and "fags." One of the victims, who was of Asian descent, also was called anti-Asian slurs. After the beating, the perpetrators stood the victims up against a wall and shot them "execution style," killing one of the men and wounding the other.[1]

Springfield, Missouri: Members of the Ku Klux Klan harassed and threatened a gay male couple after one of the men testified in support of a proposed local hate crimes ordinance. Robed Klan members regularly paraded outside their home, smashed the windows of their car, threw eggs and tomatoes at their house, and drove trucks through their yard, tearing up the lawn. The gay men finally moved to another town.[2]

James Byrd. Matthew Shepard. Barnett Slepian. The names of these three men became common coin in America at the end of 1998. These men were murder victims, and their deaths became poignant reminders that hatred, along with the cruelty and barbarism that accompany it, remain integral to America's democratic culture. James Byrd was a forty-nine-year-old black man who lived in Jasper, Texas. Three white men—John William King, Shawn Allen Berry, and Lawrence Russel Brewer—are charged with Byrd's murder. King, Berry, and Brewer allegedly chained Byrd to the back of a pickup truck and dragged him behind the truck until his body came apart. Jasper County District Attorney, Guy

James Gray said that "James Byrd at the time he was chained at the back of the pickup truck was alive. . . . Not only was he alive, he was conscious at that time, and he was using his elbows and his body in every way he could to keep his head and shoulders away from the pavement." Gray told how Byrd's body, "swinging out right and left like a boat pulling a skier," slammed into a culvert, shearing off Byrd's head and shoulder. Gray also noted that "they chose to take that body and leave that body in front of a black cemetery, as some form of a message."[3] Byrd's death was a murder; it apparently was also a hate crime. In early 1999, John William King was sentenced to death for his role in the crime; trials of the other two defendants were pending.

Matthew Shepard and Barnett Slepian were also murdered; they were also apparently victims of hate. Shepard was a gay University of Wyoming student who "came on" to two men in a bar, according to the report of a girlfriend of one of the two. Shepard was found the next morning beaten and tied to a fence post on the Wyoming prairie. Slepian was a Jewish obstetrician who performed abortions in Buffalo, New York. Slepian was shot with a high-powered rifle through his kitchen window, in the presence of his wife and children, just after returning from synagogue on a Friday night.

Hatred is as close to us as our own skin. We all know what it is to seethe with passion against another human being, to hate. From our earliest years we have experienced attractions and repulsions to others that transcend reason and thought. We all know, from "inside," what hatred is.

Fortunately, everyday life customarily insulates us from our hatreds and their consequences by the inertia of routine. When a colleague, business associate, or a relative angers us, we are normally able to carry on without striking, shouting, or planning for revenge; we "let bygones be bygones," and we do so as a matter of course, perhaps as a matter of principle or even of simple respect for normalcy and routine.

Occasionally, however, our passions, our angers, or our hatreds "get out of hand"; they make demands on us that cannot be controlled by our commitment to routine. On these occasions we "lose control" and our passions overcome us; we do strike, we do shout, we do lust after revenge. Husbands or wives behave abusively, even murderously, toward one another; parents strike their own children; and friends may murder or permanently injure one another. On these unfortunate occasions, the object of our anger or hatred is a particular individual.

These same negative passions occasionally move us to abusive or injurious behavior toward groups of people, groups we feel negatively toward not because of anything they have done to us but simply because they are the groups they are. Catholics may resent Protestants; Christians may resent Jews; Arabs may harbor animosity toward Israelis; Indians may think badly of Pakistanis; Asians may resent Westerners; Swedes may sneer at Norwegians; and Hispanics may have contempt for Caucasians, as the latter may resent African Americans. Serbs and Kosovars live in constant fear of, and animosity toward, each other. And since all these hatreds and animosities have targets who are individuals, they result in murder, in terrorist acts, and in incivilities of various kinds directed toward individuals. The flexibility and ingenuity with which humans wield negative passions against groups of others sometimes seems unlimited.

When we harbor negative passions "impersonally" against groups rather than against individuals who have deliberately or inadvertently offended us, then we are prone to intolerance and hate. We become sources of bigotry and prejudice, and we are liable to abuse or injure others not because of anything they have done but merely because they have some characteristic—race or gender or nationality or sexuality—beyond their own choosing. When Ku Klux Klan members wear white robes and masks they effectively symbolize this "impersonal" character of their attitude toward African Americans; thus masked, they act not as individuals but as "whites" against "blacks." Nevertheless, when Klan members act in white disguise they remain fully capable of inflicting profound injury on the individuals ("blacks") they target, and their hatred becomes palpable. Targets of hate are always individuals. Not only targeted individuals but also their families and their communities inevitably suffer when individuals are victims of hate. So it was with James Byrd, Matthew Shepard, and Barnett Slepian.

Fyodor Dostoeyvsky captures the intensity of the hatreds that can arise out of bigotry and prejudice in his description of crimes committed by Turks and Circassians against the Slavs in Bulgaria:

> They burn villages, murder, outrage women and children, they nail their prisoners by the ears to the fences, leave them so till morning, and in the morning they hang them—all sorts of things you can't imagine. People talk sometimes of bestial cruelty, but that's a great injustice and insult to the beasts; a beast can never be so cruel as a man, so artistically cruel. The tiger only tears and gnaws, that's all he can do. He would never think of nailing people by the ears, even if he were able to do it. These Turks took a pleasure in torturing children, too; cutting the unborn child from the mother's womb, and tossing babies up in the air and catching them on the points of their bayonets before their mother's eyes. Doing it before the mother's eyes was what gave zest to the amusement.

As an account of what hatred might inflict on individuals just because they are members of a group, Dostoeyvsky's description may seem extreme; still, we recognize the mentality he describes and we recognize instances in Nazi treatment of Jews, in conflicts between Catholics and Protestants in Northern Ireland, and in tension among racial groups in Yugoslavia, in America, in South Africa, and in most other parts of the world. Frequently, this odious mentality remains in the background, disguised by the routine of everyday life, but occasionally it springs out of hiding and molests or torments the otherwise innocent and, more rarely, injures or even destroys them.

The Los Angeles riots of 1992 are a well-publicized example of the same mentality at work. Millions of American citizens watched incredulously as Caucasian members of the Los Angeles Police Department brutally beat Rodney King, an African American who lay helplessly on the ground futilely trying to fend off their blows. The criminal charges brought against the police officers for unprofessional conduct and excessive use of force were tried in suburban Simi Valley by a jury entirely Caucasian except for one Hispanic member. On April 29, 1992, when the jury returned their verdict, those same millions of Americans were stunned by the apparent injustice of the jury's acquitting the officers. On April 29, 1992, the riots began in south central Los Angeles. Televised reports suggested the violence was racially motivated and directed against Caucasians and Hispanics, against anyone who happened not to be African American. In this complex situation, the mentality of prejudice and hatred seems operative in various ways. Would the police officers have similarly beaten a Caucasian guilty of the same offenses as Rodney King? Would the jury have returned an acquittal had Rodney King been Caucasian? Would the jury have returned an acquittal had there been a significant number of African Americans among them? Would the riots have occurred had the African Americans in Los Angeles not believed the beating and the verdict were conclusive evidence of "white" prejudice and bigotry against them?

The Los Angeles rioting was an especially dramatic example of the subtle, multiple, and complex ways prejudice and bigotry can result in passionate hatreds and attacks on others, but more ordinary phenomena of prejudice and bigotry seem somehow an inevitable part of our daily lives. Prejudice and bigotry of many sorts seem always to lurk just beneath the surface of our interactions with others as though seeking a moment of vulnerability through which to spring into our actions. The intergroup tensions we live with, and normally find ways of accommodating, seem always ready to lead us into ways of behaving we are always ready to condemn when we see them in others. The tensions expressed in the Los Angeles riots are only a few of the similar tensions also lurking beneath our surfaces.

Reliable statistics about the frequency of occurrence of hate crimes are difficult to get. In October, 1998, the FBI issued its statistics on hate crime. The report documented 8,049 hate crimes during calendar year 1997. This number of hate crimes reported by the FBI was down from 8,734 hate crimes during calendar year 1996. The Anti-Defamation League notes about the 1997 figure that 1,087 of the 8,049 total were directed against Jews and Jewish institutions, and that almost 80 percent of the total hate crimes were directed against people and property on the basis of religion. These FBI statistics were collected under the mandate of the Hate Crime Statistics Act (HCSA) of 1990,[4] and are controversial partly because the number of reporting institutions declined between 1996 and 1997.

An earlier report of The National Gay and Lesbian Task Force Policy Institute, *Anti-Gay/Lesbian Violence, Victimization, and Defamation in 1991*, summarizes hate crimes documented by major metropolitan police departments against homosexual men and women. The five metropolitan areas surveyed reported a total of 1,822 incidents, a 31 percent increase over 1990's total of 1,389. Among incidents mentioned in the report is the attack by ten young men armed with wooden clubs and a knife on three gay men outside a Houston night club, resulting in the death of one and serious injury of another; another such incident was the stabbing death of a gay man in Wisconsin by an assailant who later told police, "I wanted to kill this fag. My whole life is devoted to killing faggots and child molesters. . . ." In addition to detailing some of these hate-motivated attacks against homosexuals, the report also takes note of other organizations' reports of increased violence. The Anti-Defamation League reported a record level of anti-Semitic incidents in 1991, and the American-Arab Anti-Discrimination Committee likewise reported a record level of incidents against Arab-Americans. These "impersonal" phenomena of bigotry, prejudice, and hatred operate in myriad dimensions of our lives and are becoming a growing social problem, one that threatens every human on our planet.

The threat, and perhaps the increasing frequency, of these hate crimes is now being reinforced by the internet. The World Wide Web offers opportunity unmatched by any previous medium for the expression of hate. The "Nuremburg Trials" website is suspected by many of encouraging the sort of attacks against abortion providers that took Barnett Slepian's life. Among other things, the site lists abortion providers and gives detailed information about them and their families. When abortion providers are "taken out," their names appear with lines drawn through them. Another such "hate" site belongs to The Westboro Baptist Church of Westboro, Kansas. The URL of the Westboro Baptist Church is http://www.godhatesfags.com. Members of the Westboro Baptist Church picketed Matthew Shepard's funeral in order to protest his lifestyle and to warn those present about God's hatred for fags. Such websites abound and are easy to find.

The nonprofit Jewish organization, The Anti-Defamation League, is dedicated to fighting against hatred and also against websites they judge to be hate sites. The ADL has even developed a "hate" filter for the internet so that parents can prevent children from visiting any of several hundred websites, including sites of the Ku Klux Klan, the Westboro Baptist Church, and the Aryan Nations.

The internet is a vast new fertile region for the propagation of hate, and controversy about censoring or blocking particular sites continues to build.

Our familiarity with the phenomena of hate, however great, does not help us understand them. Why are we sources of bigotry and prejudice against our fellow humans? This question seems especially urgent when we remember the universal proclamations of our reason, our morality, and our religions against bigotry and prejudice. How can our fear, suspicion, and hatred of different others survive our moral commitments to the Golden Rule, the Categorical Imperative, or the Principle of Utility, or our religious commitments to Jesus, Mohammed, Krishna, or the Buddha? All of our rational, moral, or religious commitments enjoin us to treat different others as our equals; they urge us to see those others as worthy of the same respect we accord ourselves and our friends. These normative commitments, whether of morality or of religion, uniformly counsel us against the bigotry and prejudice that so commonly infect our actions toward others. Nevertheless, we persist in those negative patterns of character and conduct. Why?

Explanations typically find such tendencies deeply rooted in human nature; they find humanity intrinsically or essentially inclined toward bigotry, prejudice, and hatred. About how or why this intrinsic tendency characterizes humanity different theorists may disagree, and usually they also disagree about the extent to which this intrinsic tendency might be overcome. An example of such "intrinsic-to-human-nature" thought is the fundamentalist theological view that humans are bigoted because they have inherited "original sin." According to this fundamentalist view, Adam and Eve were real people who willfully disobeyed God and consequently their progeny—all of humanity—are inherently sinful. The tendencies to bigotry, prejudice, and hatred are part of this inherent sinfulness and, on this fundamentalist view, are theological necessities; they are amenable to change only through salvation, a radical transformation in the souls of individuals wrought by personal realizations of sinful depravity and appeals for God's unwarranted mercy. Although deeply rooted in Western ways of thought, this theological explanation seems to many contemporary theorists too fundamentalist; it relies too heavily on narrow theological views that are either not plausible in themselves or are not compatible with contemporary worldviews. Although this fundamentalist view begs many important questions, it exemplifies well the kind of "essentialist" explanation many contemporary theorists find persuasive.

Another explanation that finds these tendencies deeply rooted in human nature is common among social psychologists. Because of various social pressures, we humans have a need to classify and categorize the people we encounter in order to manage our interactions with them. We have a need to simplify our interactions with others into efficient patterns. This essential simplification leads naturally to stereotyping as a means to the desired efficiency. The resultant stereotyping has as an unfortunate side effect the bigotry and prejudice that so frequently makes social relations with different others extremely difficult. How can these stereotypes, along with their unfortunate side effects, be altered? Putting the question differently, what is social psychology's analogue of salvation? Among contributors to the present volume, Elliot Aronson, and John Dovidio and Samuel Gaertner suggest answers. They argue that pervasive stereotypes must be directly challenged by experiences that contradict normally convenient classifications of others. More directly, they suggest we "rub elbows" with different others, engage in mutual projects with them, and get to know them. These kinds of challenges to pervasive stereotypes may open up new possibilities for interaction with others and leave behind the unfortunate side effects of bigotry and prejudice. In the concluding essay of this volume, Martin Marty describes a significant effort to challenge such stereotypes. Still, the question of how to challenge stereotypes on so massive a scale as to effect significant betterment of the social phenomena of bigotry and prejudice is a difficult one the authors may not adequately address. Nevertheless, many people regard their suggestions as largely exempt from the liability of question-begging that infects the theological explanation of the previous paragraph.

Another account seeks an explanation for the phenomena of bigotry and prejudice in the resources of evolutionary biology. On this biological account, humans, like all animals, are driven to maximize their own genetic participation in the future of their species, and to defend against violations of their own gene pool by intruders or outsiders. A natural extension of this biological drive is a tendency to protect the genetic integrity of one's own group, a tendency expressed in varieties of xenophobic behavior, including, for example, racism, nationalism, and homophobia. This drive, along with its associated xenophobic tendencies, expresses itself invariably, whether or not it is reasonable or even available to our awareness. Among contributors to this volume, Pierre van den Berghe and Edward Wilson appear to argue for this biological-deterministic perspective. Naturally attending this biological perspective is the unfortunate consequence that "salvation" is not a possibility; we may not alter these biological facts about ourselves, but must merely accept them as part of our scientific understanding of all biological organisms, including humans. As van den Berghe sees the matter, our tendencies toward bigotry and prejudice "have an underlying driving force of their own, which is ultimately the blunt, purposeless natural selection of genes that are reproductively successful." An unremittingly bleak view, this biological-deterministic perspective offers no hope that humanity might somehow transcend the genetically fixed xenophobias that systematically undermine prospects for intergroup solidarities. As the theological perspective mentioned previously may appear too "theological," too question-begging about controversial theological issues, likewise this biological perspective may appear too "scientistic," too question-begging about issues involving the nature of science, scientific understanding, and scientific explanation. However, both the theological and the biological perspectives, for all their apparent question-begging, have some currency and apparent plausibility among many people concerned to understand the phenomena of bigotry and prejudice.

A further account sees the explanation for our tendencies toward bigotry and prejudice in our "historicity," in our "situatedness," in the fact that we must have limited perspectives or prejudices because we are finite, limited, historical creatures. Brice Wachterhauser expresses this view in giving an account of the philosophical views of Hans Georg Gadamer. This historical-deterministic view may initially seem as pessimistic as the biological-deterministic view, but it does differ and it does offer hope. The hope it offers derives from the fact that it makes our unfortunate tendencies a function of historical contingencies rather than biological laws; it does not regard these historical contingencies as beyond deliberation, choice, or alteration. The essays in this volume by Cornel West and Richard Rorty offer significant and constructive suggestions about how to approach present historical contingencies in order to undermine pervasive xenophobic tendencies and to address related social issues. Only the biological perspective roots our tendencies toward bigotry and prejudice in implacable laws beyond choice or deliberation. Only the biological perspective denies us the hope offered by the social-psychological perspective and also by the historical-determinist perspective, and even by the fundamentalist perspective.

The essays that follow appear in seven sections. The lead essay in the volume, the entirety of Part One, is a lengthy excerpt from John Dewey's "Creative Democracy: The Task Before Us," an address Dewey delivered in 1939 at the celebration of his eightieth birthday. Dewey's commitment to the social and moral dimensions of the ideal of democracy are deeply embedded in American cultural ideology, and Dewey's account of those dimensions here is as acutely perceptive as any in the canon of American intellectual culture. The essays in Part Two are recent accounts of disturbing occurrences in the fabric of contemporary American society, including not only responses to the murders of James Byrd, Matthew Shepard, and Barnett Slepian, but also a response to the recent tragedy of Columbine High School, where two students apparently filled with hate and fear took the lives of twelve of their classmates and one teacher before turning their guns on themselves. The essays of Part Three focus on issues of hate-crime legislation. Part Four goes to the intellectual heart of the issue of hatred by seeking an account of the nature of hate, bigotry, and prejudice. The selection by Gordon Allport is taken from his widely influential classic work, *The Nature of Prejudice*, first published in 1954. The selection by Jean-Paul Sartre, "The Portrait of the

Anti-Semite," is another classic first published in 1946; Sartre's account of what prejudice is in the constitution of the self is timeless. Paula Rothenberg's account of bigotry and prejudice may be seen as "revisionist" by contrast with the more conventional account suggested by Abraham Kaplan.

The essays in Part Five express prominent current explanations for the persistence in our lives of prejudice and bigotry. Elliot Aronson's contribution expresses the social psychological explanation; Pierre van den Berghe's contribution expresses the biological-deterministic perspective; and Brice Wachterhauser's essay expresses the historical-determinist explanation. The essay by Edward Wilson is a contemporary reinforcement of van den Berghe's perspective; Wilson's biological determinism, however, seeks to avoid the defeatism that seems naturally to accompany van den Berghe's presentation of that perspective. The concluding essay of this section is by Richard Goldstein, who offers a contemporary journalistic account of a psychoanalytic explanation for hatred of homosexuals.

The essays of Part Six are efforts to evince the unreason and immorality of some phenomena of bigotry and prejudice. These essays by Peter Singer, Richard D. Mohr, and Martha Nussbaum may seem out of place in the context of a volume seeking definitions, causes, and solutions for the all-too-brute facts of bigotry and prejudice. However, we believe these essays are appropriate precisely because they do make quite clear from what seems to be a dispassionate purely moral perspective the unreason and immorality of common forms of bigotry and prejudice. As the ordinary phenomena of hatred and bigotry seem to make obvious, acknowledging their unreason and immorality may not reduce the intensity or frequency with which they occur; nevertheless, we believe that staring squarely at the fact of their unreason and immorality may be useful for those who are willing to follow the arguments of these selections.

The essays of Part Seven are suggestions about how we might overcome our bigotry and prejudice and work toward a solution of the social problems that arise from them. Since we are not all perfectly rational in ways assumed by the essays of Part Six, these suggestions may appeal more broadly than do those of Part Six. The essays by Elliot Aronson and by Samuel L. Gaertner and John F. Dovidio assume as background for their proposals the social psychological explanation expressed by Aronson's contribution to Part Five. Their ideas are good common sense supported by some extensive social-psychological research. The essays by Cornel West, Richard Rorty, and Martin Marty, while thoroughly consistent with the suggestions of Aronson, and Gaertner and Dovidio, are informed by the broader political, social, and religious perspectives required for seeking solutions in the context of the historical-determinist explanation for bigotry and prejudice.

Both the social-psychological and the historical-determinist explanations leave the solution to these problems in the human hands of those sufficiently well informed, sufficiently well intentioned, and appropriately situated to put in place policies and practices that might yield progress. The biological determinist explanation implies that nothing can be done, that thoughtfulness and wisdom are no better than thoughtlessness and ignorance; it puts human problems beyond human solution. The fundamentalist theological explanation is little better; it too fails to encourage thoughtfulness and wisdom in addressing these human problems.

The social psychological and the historical-determinist explanations admit that our religious, economic, and political institutions all make contributions to the kinds of people we are. These institutions shape us as tolerant or intolerant, as greedy or generous, as narrowly doctrinaire or broadly conversant with many perspectives. As we increase in thoughtfulness and wisdom, individuals may make contributions to those institutions that shape us; we may choose to shape them in such ways that they become more likely to turn out tolerant and generous individuals who are broadly conversant with many perspectives. In so far as thoughtfulness and wisdom enable us to shape our institutions in these positive ways, they are not only useful but indispensable to our hopes for a society free from bigotry, prejudice, and hatred. The concluding essays by Cornel West, Richard Rorty, and Martin Marty encourage us to alter current historical contingencies and to improve our social institutions. Each offers significant suggestions about how we may wield what wisdom we are able to muster in order to produce desirable improvements in our cultural institutions.

Whether or not we can agree with the specific suggestions of Cornel West, Richard Rorty, and Martin Marty, we can only affirm their shared conviction that thoughtfulness and wisdom are useful in addressing the issues of bigotry and prejudice. In sharing this conviction we naturally turn our backs, as do they, on the perspectives of biological-determinism and fundamentalism.

As usual, we hope this volume will be useful in the effort to bring thoughtfulness to bear on this issue of critical social importance.

NOTES

1. National Gay and Lesbian Task Force Policy Institute, *Anti-Gay/Lesbian Violence, Victimization, and Defamation in 1991* (Washington, D.C.), p. 16.

2. Ibid., p. 18.

3. Michael Graczyk, "Dragging Death Detailed at Trial," The Associated Press, reported in *The Waco Tribune Herald*, Tuesday, January 26, 1999.

4. The source of these statistics is the Anti-Defamation League Website: http://www.ADL.org

# Part One
# Our Community, Our Values

# 1

# Creative Democracy: The Task Before Us

## John Dewey

Democracy as a personal, an individual, way of life involves nothing fundamentally new. But when applied it puts a new practical meaning in old ideas. Put into effect it signifies that powerful present enemies of democracy can be successfully met only by the creation of personal attitudes in individual human beings; that we must get over our tendency to think that its defense can be found in any external means whatever, whether military or civil, if they are separated from individual attitudes so deep-seated as to constitute personal character.

Democracy is a way of life controlled by a working faith in the possibilities of human nature. Belief in the Common Man is a familiar article in the democratic creed. That belief is without basis and significance save as it means faith in the potentialities of human nature as that nature is exhibited in every human being irrespective of race, color, sex, birth, and family, of material or cultural wealth. This faith may be enacted in statutes, but it is only on paper unless it is put in force in the attitudes which human beings display to one another in all the incidents and relations of daily life. To denounce Naziism for intolerance, cruelty, and stimulation of hatred amounts to fostering insincerity if, in our personal relations to other persons, if, in our daily walk and conversation, we are moved by racial, color, or other class prejudice; indeed, by anything save a generous belief in their possibilities as human beings, a belief which brings with it the need for providing conditions which will enable these capacities to reach fulfilment. The democratic faith in human equality is belief that every human being,

From *The Collected Works of John Dewey: The Later Works, Volume 14.* Copyright © 1988 by the Board of Trustees, Southern Illinois University. Reprinted by permission of the publisher.

independent of the quantity or range of his personal endowment, has the right to equal opportunity with every other person for development of whatever gifts he has. The democratic belief in the principle of leadership is a generous one. It is universal. It is belief in the capacity of every person to lead his own life free from coercion and imposition by others provided right conditions are supplied.

Democracy is a way of personal life controlled not merely by faith in human nature in general but by faith in the capacity of human beings for intelligent judgment and action if proper conditions are furnished. I have been accused more than once and from opposed quarters of an undue, a utopian, faith in the possibilities of intelligence and in education as a correlate of intelligence. At all events, I did not invent this faith. I acquired it from my surroundings as far as those surroundings were animated by the democratic spirit. For what is the faith of democracy in the role of consultation, of conference, of persuasion, of discussion, in formation of public opinion, which in the long run is self-corrective, except faith in the capacity of the intelligence of the common man to respond with common sense to the free play of facts and ideas which are secured by effective guarantees of free inquiry, free assembly, and free communication? I am willing to leave to upholders of totalitarian states of the right and the left the view that faith in the capacities of intelligence is utopian. For the faith is so deeply embedded in the methods which are intrinsic to democracy that when a professed democrat denies the faith he convicts himself of treachery to his profession.

When I think of the conditions under which men and women are living in many foreign countries today, fear of espionage, with danger hanging over the meeting of friends for friendly conversation in private gatherings, I am inclined to believe that the heart and final guarantee of democracy is in free gatherings of neighbors on the street corner to discuss back and forth what is read in uncensored news of the day, and in gatherings of friends in the living rooms of houses and apartments to converse freely with one another. Intolerance, abuse, calling of names because of differences of opinion about religion or politics or business, as well as because of differences of race, color, wealth, or degree of culture are treason to the democratic way of life. For everything which bars freedom and fullness of communication sets up barriers that divide human beings into sets and cliques, into antagonistic sects and factions, and thereby undermines the democratic way of life. Merely legal guarantees of the civil liberties of free belief, free expression, free assembly are of little avail if in daily life freedom of communication, the give and take of ideas, facts, experiences, is choked by mutual suspicion, by abuse, by fear and hatred. These things destroy the essential condition of the democratic way of living even more effectually than open coercion which—as the example of totalitarian states proves—is effective only when it succeeds in breeding hate, suspicion, intolerance in the minds of individual human beings.

Finally, given the two conditions just mentioned, democracy as a way of life is controlled by personal faith in personal day-by-day working together with others. Democracy is the belief that even when needs and ends or consequences are different for each individual, the habit of amicable cooperation—which may include, as in sport, rivalry and competition—is itself a priceless addition to life. To take as far as possible every conflict which arises—and they are bound to arise—out of the atmosphere and medium of force, of violence as a means of settlement into that of discussion and of intelligence is to treat those who disagree even profoundly—with us as those from whom we may learn, and in so far, as friends. A genuinely democratic faith in peace is faith in the possibility of conducting disputes, controversies, and conflicts as cooperative undertakings in which both parties learn by giving the other a chance to express itself, instead of having one party conquer by forceful suppression of the other—a suppression which is none the less one of violence when it takes place by psychological means of ridicule, abuse, intimidation, instead of by overt imprisonment or in concentration camps. To cooperate by giving differences a chance to show themselves because of the belief that the expression of difference is not only a right of the other persons but is a means of enriching one's own life-experience, is inherent in the democratic personal way of life.

If what has been said is charged with being a set of moral commonplaces, my only reply is that that is just the point in saying them. For to get rid of the habit of thinking of democracy as something institutional and external and to acquire the habit of treating it as a way of personal life is to realize that democracy is a moral ideal and so far as it becomes a fact is a moral fact. It is to realize that democracy is a reality only as it is indeed a commonplace of living.

Since my adult years have been given to the pursuit of philosophy, I shall ask your indulgence if in concluding I state briefly the democratic faith in the formal terms of a philosophic position. So stated, democracy is belief in the ability of human experience to generate the aims and methods by which further experience will grow in ordered richness. Every other form of moral and social faith rests upon the idea that experience must be subjected at some point or other to some form of external control; to some "authority" alleged to exist outside the processes of experience. Democracy is the faith that the process of experience is more important than any special result attained, so that special results achieved are of ultimate value only as they are used to enrich and order the ongoing process. Since the process of experience is capable of being educative, faith in democracy is all one with faith in experience and education. All ends and values that are cut off from the ongoing process become arrests, fixations. They strive to fixate what has been gained instead of using it to open the road and point the way to new and better experiences.

If one asks what is meant by experience in this connection my reply is that it is that free interaction of individual human beings with surrounding conditions, especially the human surroundings, which develops and satisfies need and desire by increasing knowledge of things as they are. Knowledge of conditions as they are is the only solid ground for communication and sharing; all other communication means the subjection of some persons to the personal opinion of other persons. Need and desire—out of which grow purpose and direction of energy—go beyond what exists, and hence beyond knowledge, beyond science. They continually open the way into the unexplored and unattained future.

Democracy as compared with other ways of life is the sole way of living which believes wholeheartedly in the process of experience as end and as means; as that which is capable of generating the science which is the sole dependable authority for the direction of further experience and which releases emotions, needs and desires so as to call into being the things that have not existed in the past. For every way of life that fails in its democracy limits the contacts, the exchanges, the communications, the interactions by which experience is steadied while it is also enlarged and enriched. The task of this release and enrichment is one that has to be carried on day by day. Since it is one that can have no end till experience itself comes to an end, the task of democracy is forever that of creation of a freer and more humane experience in which all share and to which all contribute.

# Part Two
# Hate and Incivility

2

# Hate of the Union:
# Why Homophobia Has Become
# America's Favorite Pastime

## Michael Musto

Practically overnight, two weeks ago, America went from being perceived as an international oral-sex joke to one of the planet's biggest showplaces of homo hate. Oh, our bias for all-around bigotry had been cooking in the headlines for some time. From the alleged police brutalizing of Abner Louima to the death-by-dragging of James Byrd in Texas (followed by the Labor Day float mocking Byrd's plight) to the alarming rise in antigay and anti-Semitic expression, the stage had been set for ritualized loathing of the Other. The rage, the sickness, the violent streak in our country had reared its head, and it confirmed itself as our hideous star attraction on October 6, when twenty-one-year-old Matthew Shepard was robbed, tied to a fence, and viciously killed. (Aaron J. McKinney and Russell A. Henderson, who reportedly singled Shepard out for being gay, stand accused of the crime.) Monica who?

The Laramie, Wyoming, act has again shed a spotlight on the ugliness of irrational contempt, the bizarre allure of picking on societal outcasts because they're easy targets and available scapegoats. But it's also a reminder that, while hate seems to be more popular than ever, perhaps it's just more visible. Like presidential indiscretions, prejudice-based attacks have always existed, but a lot of times they weren't reported because officials and the media didn't know—or care—about them. Gay-bash victims rarely came forward to say, "They beat me because I'm queer," and the perpetrators knew they could count on them not to do so, the silence paving the way for more and more thrill assaults. Since that's changed to some extent—though there are still lots of holdouts—Shepard's alleged killers apparently made sure he *couldn't* come forward, leaving it to McKinney's girlfriend, Kristen Price, to recreate the tragedy for the public when cornered. Interestingly, Price *emphasized* the gay-bash element, claiming that McKinney had been outraged by "the thought of a gay guy approaching him and humiliating him" at a hangout—the old he-shouldn't-have-foisted-his-lifestyle alibi.

The McKinney gang might have actually drummed up this scenario as some kind of twisted justification. (In Wyoming, where there are no hate-crime laws, it couldn't hurt.) But if Price's account is actually true, the fury ignited in McKinney by Shepard's "flirting" calls to mind the way Scott Amedure's confession of love for Jonathan Schmitz on *The Jenny Jones Show* in '95 sparked Amedure's grisly murder. In both cases, the overtures were received as unbearably "humiliating" gestures, prompting one to wonder just how secure these thin-skinned thugs are in their own manhood. Shouldn't it be the rebuffed person who's mortified, not the guy saying, "No, thanks"? And in Shepard's case, what exactly constituted flirting, anyway? Saying, "Hi, my name's Matt" (though Price, in her secondhand version, insisted Shepard threw himself on McKinney)?

Raging insecurity's not the only catalyst for the anger at the heart of this heartlessness. Shepard's alleged killers are high-school dropouts who were clearly battling the most prevalent illness among young gay bashers: a sense of powerlessness. School didn't work out for them, and with their low-paying jobs and uncertain futures, the real world was probably seeming fairly hopeless, too. And bad happenings fueled the fire. As the *New York Times* reported, McKinney's mother died about five years ago, and—apparently being a professional blamer who needs to point fingers and aim punches—McKinney once yelled at her doctor in a bar for causing her death. The police say he and Henderson even picked a fight with two Hispanics as Shepard lay crucified and dying on the outskirts of town—though it somehow fails to comfort me to know that they're equal-opportunity haters.

Lately, hate crimes aren't just a reaction against gays' advances in bars, but against gays' advances in society, and the way the radical right has twisted those accomplishments as rewards for degeneracy. The more visible and protected we get, the more the righties are threatened, as if every forward step by gays in mass culture will mean an end to straight sitcoms. Goaded by the Trent Lotts, folks start longing for the good old days when you could treat gays like second-class citizens without any opposition. And what a few years ago percolated as a blame against the queer community for spreading AIDS—combined with a Bible-thumping, you-deserved-it mentality—has morphed into ire at gays for having survived the plague and carried on while continuing to demand special (read equal) rights. As their rage boils up, these full-time haters adhere to Jerry Springer's message: the answer to every disagreement is to poke your opponent's eyes out.

Last year, the National Coalition of Anti Violence Programs said it attributed an alarming rise in antigay violence "to the unprecedented national attention given to the 'coming out' of actress Ellen DeGeneres and her television character." The right condemned her, and the backlash devolved into a monosyllabic concept: bash. Ellen's inspiring openness—which has no doubt *saved* lives—has even made some gay people uncomfortable, like Sandra Bernhard, who's been romping through the media pegging Ellen and Anne Heche's relationship as "shtick"—as if her own sexual evasions haven't been exactly that. And columnist Liz Smith recently wrote that Heche revealed too much about her relationship with Ellen in an interview, and this kind of honesty could spell the end of gossip!

Meanwhile, minorities attack each other even more often than they do themselves, never noticing the irony inherent in trying to rise out of oppression by persecuting other downtrodden people. The doctrine of hatemonger Khallid Abdul Muhammad—who riles up African Americans with his distaste for Jews and gays—reminds us how one group can target another in the name of communal pride. I'm surprised Giuliani didn't welcome the Million Youth March for this very reason. (I guess his racism temporarily eclipsed his homophobia.) The mayor has certainly been astoundingly silent about the rise in local gay-bashing reports, as New York becomes a place where the supposed fringe is fringier and more disposable than ever. In the last few months, while living in my delusion that the gay life here is a carefree one, I've gotten no less than three "faggots" and one "*maricón*"—and believe me, I wasn't flirting. Plus I recently found myself in an altercation with a woman at a bookstore who volunteered that gays are offensive because they *choose* to be that way—as if anyone would elect to enter her homophobic world.

Perhaps the most startling statement to come out of this whole horrorshow was made by Shepard's own bereaved father, Dennis. According to Wyoming governor Jim Geringer, Dennis insisted through his grief, "We should not use Matt to further an agenda," nor should we "rush into just passing all kinds of new hate-crimes laws." I think Matthew would be screaming otherwise.

# 3

# Blight to Life:
# Antiabortion Extremists and
# Another Murdered Doctor

## Sharon Lerner

Just after Buffalo-based OB-GYN Barnett Slepian was killed by a sniper bullet last Friday night, the two other doctors who provide abortions in the Buffalo area went into seclusion in the hope of avoiding a similar fate. Slepian, fifty-one, was shot shortly after returning from synagogue, while his wife and one of his sons were in the room. No doubt all doctors who perform abortions around the country would like to retreat into safety from such violence, which shadows their every move.

If you provide abortions, or even publicly support them, it is not paranoid to assume "they"—an extremist faction of the antiabortion movement—are out to get you. For chilling validation of such fears, one need only glance at the Nuremberg Files (www.christiangallery.com/atrocity/), a website that posts personal information about doctors, nurses, security guards, clinic escorts, law enforcement officers who provide protection to abortion providers, owners or directors of abortion clinics, and even, as the site puts it, "judges and politicians who pass or uphold laws authorizing child-killing or oppressing pro-life activists."

The purpose of such a database is purportedly to gather evidence for eventual legal trials. (The abortion haters behind this project envision a tribunal that will try abortion-related activities as war crimes, the way the Allies did the Nazis after World War II.) Of course, the other—more obvious—aim of going public with home addresses, photos, license plate numbers, and even, as the site specifies, "names and birthdates of spouse(s), children, and friends" is to make life hellish—and perhaps shorter—for abortion supporters.

There is little doubt that such information can be put to violent use. The Nuremberg Files, which was started by the extremist American Coalition of Life Activists (though the group's name no longer appears on the site), suggests that antiabortion activists send letters to "your local baby butcher squad" with the following threat: "Those who slaughter God's children without affording them due process of law need to understand they are going to be held accountable. Everybody gets a payday someday."

The temptation may be to dismiss such bluster as mere wacko rhetoric. Clearly, these are not the prolifers who back antiabortion legislation in Congress and buy advertisements in the mainstream media. Such groups, including the National Right to Life Committee and the American Life League, routinely decry violence against abortion supporters and point out that the perpetrators often operate on their own. Indeed, John Salvi, the man convicted of killing two receptionists and a security guard at two abortion clinics in Massachusetts in '94, shot his victims during a schizophrenic mania.

But as fringe—or downright crazy—as such elements may be, they are established and influential elements of the antiabortion movement nonetheless. Before his final decline into clinical insanity and eventual suicide, Salvi, for instance, frequented antiabortion meetings and believed he was acting on behalf of the Catholic Church. The shooting even brought him hero status in some circles. ("Salvi deserves a medal" was how one New Hampshire-based antichoice zealot put it.)

Antiabortion fanatic Michael Griffin received similar support for murdering Dr. David Gunn in 1993. After the shooting, thirty-two people signed on to a statement endorsing "justifiable homicide." And these were not just random nuts but organizational leaders, editors, and clergymen who backed the proclamation that "whatever force is legitimate to defend the life of a born child is legitimate to defend the life of an unborn child."

Indeed, the frightening rings around Dr. Slepian's murder ripple outward whichever direction you look. There are four previous sniper attacks that bear an eerie resemblance to this latest one (all occurring in upstate New York or Canada around this time of year, the shots fired from similar positions with the same kind of rifle). Some theorize that an antiabortion terrorist—or terrorists—is staging the attacks in a twisted commemoration of Canada's remembrance day, which falls on November 11 and which some antiabortion activists refer to as "Remember the Unborn Children Day."

Then there's the fact that the Nuremberg site is not alone in its project of stalking abortion supporters. Life Dynamics, a Texas-based antiabortion group, has been setting up its own clearinghouse for information on abortion providers —including pictures and home addresses—in a project it calls "Spies for Life."

And consider the fact that one can access the Nuremberg Files through links from other, ostensibly more moderate, antiabortion sites on the Internet.

The result of these efforts is plain to see. Six people have been murdered in attacks on abortion clinics since 1990, and there have been fifteen attempted murders in that time. Just this year, a police officer moonlighting at the New Woman, All Women Health Care Clinic in Birmingham, Alabama, was killed in a bomb blast and a nurse at that clinic was severely wounded. There are also 150 incidents of arson against abortion providers on record as well as 39 clinic bombings and more than 100 cases of assault and battery.

But even these grisly tallies do not tell the whole story. They don't reflect the experience of Mary Smith, an abortion provider based in Denton, Texas, who has seen antiabortion flyers featuring her picture tacked up on trees throughout her small town. Protesters regularly picket Dr. Smith's church on Sundays and line her path to work. She fears for her children in school.

And they don't capture the inner turmoil of Richard Hausknecht, a New York City-based OB-GYN and occasional abortion provider who has spent years speaking out in support of the right to abortion. The local sheriff parked in Hausknecht's upstate driveway all weekend, in an effort to protect the doctor from abortion opponents who might be lurking outside his window. "I really had not given a great deal of thought to the fact that maybe I have been gambling with my life before," Hausknecht told the *Voice*. "But after this weekend, things are different. Is it going to modify what I do? You bet. If you can be shot inside your own home, then there's no place left to hide."

But if doctors are afraid—and they have every reason to be—some are also redoubling their devotion to the cause of abortion. Dr. Slepian's murder only "makes people more committed," says Vickie Breitbart, board member of the National Abortion Federation. Training to do abortions (which physicians must seek on their own, since it is not routinely provided in medical schools) now includes counseling workshops and group discussions about the violent occupational hazards.

NAF fosters such personal expressions while encouraging trainees to wear bulletproof vests and draw their curtains. But "once they've actually come in and done a series of procedures and seen what abortion means in the day-to-day lives of women, that strengthens their commitment," says Breitbart.

Dr. Slepian's commitment weathered years of challenges. He endured protests at his clinic, received some 200 death threats, and was endlessly picketed, even at his house on Hanukkah. Dr. Slepian tolerated such harassment, as he acknowledged in a letter published in a Buffalo newspaper in '94. "But," he wrote, "please don't feign surprise, dismay or certainly not innocence when a more volatile and less-restrained member of the group decides to react to their inflammatory rhetoric by shooting an abortion provider. They all share the blame."

# 4

# Firestarters:
# My Journey to Jasper

## David Grann

Jasper, Texas. Darrell Flinn wouldn't say it was an omen, exactly. But the fires did start right around the time those three white boys allegedly tied that Negro behind a pickup truck and dragged him for three miles down Huff Creek Road in nearby Jasper, Texas. They burned all night, sometimes for more than a week. Helicopters swept down, spraying water, though it didn't seem to do much good. It hadn't rained hard for more than two months, and all it took was a bolt of lightning, the flick of a cigarette, or a spark from an engine before another blaze broke out.

On this Tuesday, a teenager had lit a fire right there in Vidor, where Flinn lived, sending up flames from the yellow pine trees even as he sat out with his three little kids at Smith Lake to cool off in the sweltering heat. "It's so hot we can't even burn a cross," Flinn said, glancing at me. "There's a state ordinance against any loose fires."

That, of course, meant no cross-burning at this Saturday's rally, though it didn't much matter to Flinn. Everyone in the media would be there anyway. He'd already been on MSNBC, CNBC, CBS, *Hard Copy*. Even a reporter from Italy had called that morning. "How do you say nigger in Italian, 'negre'?" he mused aloud.

I didn't say anything, and watched as he took off his combat boots and T-shirt and exposed his belly to the sun. "What do you think's gonna happen in Jasper?" he asked. "You think those niggers with shotguns will show up?"

Reprinted by permission of *The New Republic* © 1998, The New Republic, Inc.

Looking up from my notebook, I shrugged and asked how many from his Klan would show up.

Flinn said he didn't like to make predictions because if he said forty, and only twenty showed up, it would seem like the event was a failure. "I estimate a hundred and forty," he said, suddenly throwing away his caution. He started to tick off the other groups, pausing after each for emphasis: Alabama White Knights . . . Missouri's New Order Knights . . . America's Invisible Empire . . . The American Knights . . . North Georgia White Knights. . . . Finally, Flinn got up to go in the lake. Tommy, his four-year-old son, was sitting on the shore with his feet crossed, shivering even in the heat. "You wanna go swimming out with daddy?" he said. The boy didn't move. "You got a fever?" he asked, touching his forehead. Flinn reached down and scooped some water on Tommy Bird's head to cool him off, then dove in himself

His oldest son was swimming nearby. "Come on over here, Brandon, and tell Mr. David what ya wanna be when you grow up."

"I dunno yet," he said, dipping his head underwater. "I'm only eight."

Flinn made a cone with his hands over his head, as if he were playing charades. "Tell Mr. David. He came all the way from Washington. It's okay. I told ya you could tell him."

Brandon studied his father's hands. "A fireman?"

"What else? What does daddy do in the nighttime?"

The boy squinted, then smiled. "A Klansman?"

"That's right," Flinn said, grinning at me, as if imparting some important lesson to both of us. Then, in one swift motion, he wrapped his arms around Brandon and dove into the water, kicking up his legs so that only a small tattoo of a dragon glimmered in the hot sun.

I got to Texas two weeks after James Byrd Jr. was dragged to his death for no other apparent reason than he was black, and after Jesse Jackson and the Rev. Al Sharpton and NAACP President Kweisi Mfume and California Congresswoman Maxine Waters and Transportation Secretary Rodney Slater had come to pay their respects, and after the president of the United States had sent his condolences, and after Dennis Rodman had offered to pay for Byrd's funeral, and after Don King had donated $100,000 to a memorial fund, and after the KKK had announced it would rally in Jasper to raise white people's pride, and after the New Black Panther Party and the Black Muslims had vowed to show up with shotguns to arm the black people of Jasper against the Klan.

I wasn't sure exactly why I was there, other than that everyone else from the media was there—convinced, perhaps, that the Old South was rising again, at least for an afternoon. Before I got to Jasper, though, I had stopped in Vidor, about an hour away, because that was where the old Klan still purportedly thrived and where Darrell Flinn, the imperial wizard of the Knights of the White Kamellia, had moved recently with his wife and three boys.

Vidor, it turned out, looked just the way it sounded: poor, grimy, and mean. The local grocery store posted a sign saying "No guns allowed," and the pawnshop across the street sold silver bracelets and secondhand AK-47s. Even though the city was named after King Vidor, the movie director who, in 1929, directed *Hallelujah,* the first Hollywood movie with an all-black cast, the population remained all white, save for a handful of families holed up in a small federal housing project across the train tracks—the "coon cage," Flinn called it. In 1993, when the first African American in more than six decades moved into Vidor under a government-enforced desegregation order, several Klansmen showed up in white sheets. Five years later, several blacks in the surrounding area told me they still don't stop here for gas at night, even though the hand-painted sign on Main Street saying "Nigger, Don't Let the Sun Set on You in Vidor" was taken down some thirty years ago.

While Flinn and I were swimming, city officials in Jasper—which is over 40 percent black—pleaded with the media and the black militants and the KKK not to turn their fishing town into another Vidor. We don't want hate groups here, black or white, said the county sheriff, a burly white man wearing a ten-gallon hat. Neither did the city's first black mayor nor, more importantly, the Byrd family.

But Flinn insisted the Klan would come anyway, which was not surprising. What was surprising was his professed reason why. "We want to condemn the killing, not endorse it," he said. "No one deserves to die like that."

At least in public, Flinn is trying to put a friendlier face on what's left of the hate movement. As the KKK's membership has dwindled to fewer than 5,000 across the country, Flinn, like David Duke before him, has sought to reinvent the Klan as simply one more victimized group demanding its rights. "We do not advocate violence anymore," he told me—unless, that is, "we are met with violence."

But, when I arrived at the SHAPE Community Center in southeast Houston the next night, a half-dozen Black Panthers and Muslims were already loading their weapons—shotguns and street sweepers and AR-15s—as they plotted strategy for Saturday's showdown in the town square. "The white man will confront something new in Jasper," proclaimed Quanell X, a twenty-seven-year-old former youth minister of the Nation of Islam and the current leader of the militant Black Muslims. "Well-trained, well-organized, and disciplined black men."

As Quanell stood, two guards clad in army fatigues toting twelve-gauge shotguns rushed to his side. Unlike his troops, the general carried none of the paraphernalia of war. He wore an Armani suit and a diamond-studded gold watch.

As he filed past me, one of the guards said, "Search the cracker before he gets in the car." I pulled my pad and pen out of my pocket and spread my arms.

Outside, we climbed into an onyx-colored Mercedes and headed for the Fox television studio, where Quanell would debate on-air the infamous Klansman, Michael Lowe. While we sped along the back streets of Houston, looking through the tinted windows at the black kids sitting on their porches smoking cigarettes in the 100-degree heat, I asked Quanell X why he felt compelled to go to Jasper if most people there didn't want him. "It's simple," he said. "We want to say to the KKK that your days of intimidating, harassing, and insti-gating violence against black people is all over. . . . We are willing and ready— *take this left here*—to fight the Klan by any means necessary. . . . That if you want a war—*here! here!*—we'll be damned if we won't give you one."

"What about the black pastors from Jasper who don't want you to come?" I asked.

"I don't give two cents about what some weak-kneed, handkerchief-head, Negro pastor thinks of me. I'm only interested in what God thinks of me."

If the Ku Klux Klan had learned that the best way to get attention was to advocate hatred camouflaged by kindness, then the Black Panthers and Muslims had learned that the best way to get attention was to advocate peace through vio-lence. At the television studio, where Quanell X had become a regular in the days after Byrd's killing, the militant leader disappeared into the bathroom and reemerged wearing a white bow tie.

While a technician connected his earpiece, Quanell and the rest of us could hear Lowe's trademark lisp, testing his mike from another studio in Texas. Then came another voice, the host's, even louder: "The KKK and a so-called group of black radicals are heading to a town where a black man was allegedly killed by white supremacists. Will there be more bloodshed? . . . Up next!" Quanell narrowed his eyes at the camera's white light. "Okay," said a producer in the control room. "Hold onto your shirts—and thank God they can't touch each other."

The next morning another fire broke out, this one right near Jasper. "It's supposed to get even hotter," said Flinn. I'd stopped by one last time for break-fast with the imperial wizard at Gary's Coffee Shop. There, Flinn introduced me to James, the current grand dragon of the Knights of the White Kamellia, who would only give me his first name. Unlike Flinn, James didn't look much like the new "improved" Klan: His hair and eyes were a muted yellow, his teeth brown and crooked, and tattoos were stenciled all along his arms. When I asked him if he'd bring a shotgun to the rally, he lit his second Marlboro of the morning and said, "I'll probably bring something just in case." Each time the talk took such a turn, Flinn nudged him with his elbow. Later, when I got up to leave, James looked suspiciously at my scribbled handwriting and asked, "What religion are you, anyway?" I didn't say anything. "You gotta be somethin'," he said, leaning across the table. I glanced at Flinn, then back at James, whose veins were tightening in his arms. I thought for a moment of my bar mitzvah. "Episcopalian," I said.

The town of Jasper woke up Friday morning to the sounds of gospel, to calls for unity and peace. "I don't need the Black Panthers to come speak for me as a black person," said Bobby Hudson, a tall, lanky preacher in a red satin shirt and white shoes. He stood outside Fowler's Garage, where James Byrd used to sit and sip beer and chew tobacco and while the days away with his friends. "This is not about this town. What transpired here is about three sick people," he said.

Byrd's old friends, all of whom were black, nodded. "Amen, brother. That's right."

But, outside the courthouse, the press was already gathering with their tripods and booms and satellite trucks. In the center of a nest of cameras, a black man from Houston, named Motapa, with blue and red and green and yellow pigments on his face handed out leaflets saying, "I will fast on air for three days." As the cameras focused on him, he exclaimed: "The blood of James Byrd is like the sacrament of Jesus Christ. It will spread all over America," while a friend of his waved a cane at me and predicted that, in twenty-four hours, "this is going to be bigger than the O. J. Simpson trial."

Except that something strange was happening in Jasper: While the hotels filled with visitors, most of the locals were fleeing town. Unlike the late 1950s and 1960s, when people rose up from within the very fabric of Southern society—blacks from the streets and the churches, the Klan from the local businesses and bars—Jasper's race war was being fueled entirely by outsiders, by a handful of atomized groups. On this Saturday morning, the journalists came in droves, from Paris and Tokyo and Bonn and New York and New Orleans. By 10:00 A.M., they vastly outnumbered the spectators and law enforcement officers and swarmed from one side of the square to the other, searching for angry white men or black men or *any* men to film. "This is a joke," said a journalist holding a mike. "Where's all the fuckin' bloodshed?" When a lone Klansman finally arrived with a young boy, carrying Confederate flags, an army of reporters surrounded him. "That's it," prodded one cameraman, "show us the tattoo. . . . Can you give us a side shot? . . . *Perfect.* . . . *Perfect.*" But, as the press pushed closer, the Klansman's teenage companion began to tremble. "Do you hate me?" shouted a black reporter. "No," the boy said sheepishly. "Then who do you hate?" He looked around at the cameras, searching for his friend. On the verge of tears, he blurted out, "Everybody."

After an hour of this, the press moved on, bored and listless. As I considered leaving, twenty-five Klansmen, led by Flinn, appeared in black and white robes, surrounded by a phalanx of police wearing riot gear. Then came the Panthers, toting rifles and chanting, "Black power." "We can take these bastards!" screamed one. "We can run over the damn police and take their asses!" There were no more than a handful of them, but, upon spotting the cameras, they began to charge—unleashing a stampede of more than 300 reporters. I chased after Quanell X in his ochre Armani suit and matching alligator shoes, shouting questions he couldn't hear. I climbed onto a bench for a better view. From there, I could see a Panther being filmed by a Klansman who was being filmed by the police—all of whom were being filmed by the media.

After a momentary retreat, the seven Panthers charged again. And again, I was running, pushing against the barricades to keep up with them. I saw a girl fall and a cameraman step on her.

Shaken, I made my way across the square, away from the crowd, which was still racing from side to side in a kind of unrehearsed theater. I found my car and drove through town, out into the country, past the local paper and the sheriff's station, until I stopped outside a small wooden house, where the Byrds lived. Two police guards stood outside. "How are things in town?" one guard asked, looking at my sweat-stained clothes.

"Not so good," I said, though the more I thought about it, the more I realized how little the chaos in the square had anything to do with the killing of James Byrd, or with anything real.

I asked for directions out to Huff Creek Road—an unmarked street on the outskirts of town. I crossed over a bridge straddling a trough of dust and passed several run-down houses, a Baptist church, and a cemetery. Finally, below a row of yellow pine trees, I pulled over and began to walk back toward town, past where they had allegedly beaten Byrd and tied his ankles to a chain. After a half-mile or so, I came upon an orange painted circle, then another, and another, marking where the police had found Byrd's severed head and torso and limbs. There was still blood encrusted in the dirt. The crime scene ran for two-and-a-half miles, and, as I neared the end, I felt the first drops of rain.

# 5

# School's Been Blown to Pieces: Everyday Terror in the Suburbs South of Denver

## Frank Kogan

Littleton, Colorado. They were eighteen and seventeen, it was almost the end of the school year, and you look forward at the end of the school year to freedom. Eighteen and life: the whole vista, the whole landscape, is opening in front of you. They saw nothing. They had utterly nothing to live for and they chose to die, and there was no meaning in their life and they tried to give meaning to their death, and they came up with a really stupid meaning, a live-action video game with victims who really bled and coundn't fight back. A sad painful story considering what must have been inside those two boys. However smart they were, they did not look inside themselves because looking at whatever was closing them off would have hurt too much. It hurt less to kill people and finally to kill themselves.

Or anyway, that's my pop-psych evaluation of two killers I'm never going to know anything about. (Andrew Palmer, analyzing it all from New Zealand: "Presume the dorky-looking one died a virgin." That might sum it up. Or not.) Eventually there will be a book, since one of the boys, Eric Harris, left so much paper behind; but I'm not going to read it, since killers are boring. I'd much rather know about a trench-coat kid who didn't kill anyone. Or about some jock, or skater, or freak. I'd rather know what Columbine High School was like on April 19, the day before the shooting, than read again what happened on April 20. And what Arapahoe High School is like, what Highlands Ranch High

School is like, what Littleton High School is like, what Cherry Creek High School is like.

"The people I don't want to walk past would be the jocks that are the good old boys," says Sonia Pai, senior at Cherry Creek. "There's a lot of abuse that goes on at our school, that no one talks about. Those guys are huge, they all play football; their girlfriends are maybe 100 pounds at the most, and I know there's a lot of abuse in all kinds of forms. I'm a peer counselor at school, you hear more about things that aren't talked about. A lot of sexual abuse happens, in all kinds of forms, and no one thinks anything of it."

The two killers, Eric Harris and Dylan Klebold, did do something useful, inadvertently. They talked about the normal terror of school life (not the terror they were committing but the terror they were claiming to avenge), and they talked about social divisions in suburbia, and they mentioned the name of a social class—jocks!—and said they were deliberately targeting that class and wanted to kill it. There's an apparent paradox: They seemed to be shooting indiscriminately and setting off bombs, simply wanting to kill as many people as they could; yet they also questioned people, shot some, spared others, depending on the answers. The killers yelled, "All the jocks stand up. We are going to kill you." They shot kids in sports hats. A gunman asked a girl if she believed in God and when she said "Yes!" he asked "Why?" and then not waiting for an answer he killed her. A gunman said, "We don't like niggers," and shot a black man in the face.

Actually, all of this is consistent; if (back to the pop psych) you're fending off your inner terror by terrorizing others. Anything that's a power trip works, even if it's deciding to spare people. And saying to someone "Give me a reason not to kill you" is a form of taunting and torture whether you kill the kid or not.

The press basically had a few hours to not only get a story but to become sociologists. The most damaging error was to describe the shooters as "goths," which is about as useful as describing Charles Manson as a hippie, and is going to put a lot of vulnerable outcast kids at risk. Same with the overemphasis on trench coats. Most newspeople seem to be accepting as cold fact that, because the killers wore trench coats (apparently not even that often, and not real trench coats), they belonged to "The Trench Coat Mafia," and that all their beliefs were shared by the other trench-coaters and that they shared all the other trench-coaters' tastes. Lou Kilzer and Lyn Bartels of the *Denver Rocky Mountain News* and Susan Greene of the *Denver Post* (an astonishing story published April 24), in work that seems unnoticed even by colleagues at their own papers, are reporting that the Trench Coat Mafia never considered the two killers members (so these two outcasts couldn't even crack the outcast group), that an oft-cited yearbook picture of the Mafia doesn't include either of them, and (in Greene's piece) that only one kid in the Mafia likes to listen to Marilyn Manson. (Perhaps the rest don't like the way Manson sings?)

Susan Greene is interviewing a kid—this is one of the kids who's in the Trench Coat Mafia—and what he's saying is that every day he's filled with utter fright, it's utter hell. The jocks on a daily basis, they're smashing him into lockers, they're calling him "faggot," he's riding his bike home from school and they're throwing soda cans and rocks out car windows at him, and sometimes they're sideswiping him with their cars.

This kid is not a scapegoater, not like the two killers. Susan Greene: "Not all jocks tormented him, the teen noted. But he said a handful of bullies held so much power that most of the school emulated them, or at least were too afraid to voice dissent." The killers were like him in one way; they were tormented, bullied—except, unlike him, they got to the point where the only important thing in their lives was to plan for the great day when, for a few hours, they could be even bigger terrorizers than the guys who'd terrorized them.

Go to any predominantly white suburban school in the last fifty years. You'll get a top-dog group, a high-status group, they're the kids involved in the activities, they're doing the proms, committees, student council, and so on, or are involved in sports. These people, depending on the year and place, are called socs (SO-shes, for socialites), debs, preppies, jocks.

And then you'll get a refusal group. They've refused the school; it's not their social life *at all*. They're off fighting or smoking or fooling around, and if they're concerned with school it's to disrupt it or ridicule it, or just endure it. These people are called (a great tradition of expressive derogatory poetry) rocks, greaseballs, hoods, greasers, grits, burnouts, dirtbags, stoners, jells, jelly heads, skaters.

You'll have different side groups, nerds, brains, some maybe following geeky roads to status: the drama club, the school newspaper. And you'll have loners, the unaffiliated, and the real losers. And you'll get some side refusal groups: rednecks, farmers. But everyone will be leaning one way or another, toward the preppies or toward the skaters, let's say, who seem to be the kings of the heap and the antiheap these days in the suburbs south of Denver.

Sometimes those in the weird artsy-fartsy area will assert themselves, suddenly become a refusal group that challenges everybody. These are the freaks, the punks.

The names aren't fair. They're stereotypes that don't necessarily really apply to anybody, but nonetheless people live in them, walk through them, are affected by them.

Somehow in political discourse and in journalism, these normal things, normal to every high school to some degree or another—terror, bullying, social stratification—are not known to exist. They don't belong in suburbia, though every politician and reporter must have gone to a school, must have been in such social stratification, must have been in the neighborhood of terror, whether they felt it or not, whether they noticed or not. (Great line from the *Denver Post*: "Teasing is not new.") Yet whenever these appear—terror and division—highlighted by some deadly event, they're such a surprise. How did *these* get here? Were they brought in by the music, by Marilyn Manson?

# 6

# Matthew's Passion

## Tony Kushner

When Trent Lott heard the news about the murder of Matthew Shepard, the first thoughts that flashed through his mind were all about spin. Trent Lott worried about how to keep his promise to the religious right, to speak out against the homosexual agenda, without seeming to endorse murder. Trent Lott endorses murder, of course; his party endorses murder, his party endorses discrimination against homosexuals and in doing so it endorses the ritual slaughter of homosexuals.

Democracy is a bloody business, demanding blood sacrifice. Every advance American democracy has made toward fulfilling the social contract, toward justice and equality and true liberty, every step forward has required offerings of pain and death. The American people demand this, we need to see the burnt bodies of the four little black girls, or their sad small coffins; we need to see the battered, disfigured face of the beaten housewife; we need to see the gay man literally crucified on a fence. We see the carnage and think, Oh, I guess things are still tough out there, for those people. We daydream a little: What does that feel like, to burn? To have your face smashed by your husband's fist? To be raped? To be dragged behind a truck till your body falls to pieces? To freeze tied to a fence on the Wyoming prairie, for eighteen hours, with the back of your head staved in? Americans perfected the horror film, let's not kid ourselves: These acts of butchery titillate, we glean the news to savor the unsavory details.

---

Tony Kushner, "Matthew's Passion." Reprinted with permission from the November 9, 1998, issue of *The Nation*.

And then, after we've drawn a few skin-prickling breaths of the aromas of torture and agony and madness, we shift a little in our comfortable chairs, a little embarrassed to have caught ourselves in the act of prurient sadism, a little worried that God has seen us also, a little worried that we have lazily misplaced our humanity, a little sad for the victims: Oh, gee, I guess I sort of think that shouldn't happen out there to those people, and something should be done. As long as I don't have to do it.

And having thought as much, having, in fact, been edified, changed a very little bit by the suffering we have seen, our humanity as well as our skin having been pricked, we turn our back on Matthew Shepard's crucifixion and return to our legitimate entertainments. When next the enfranchisement of homosexuals is discussed, Matthew Shepard's name will probably be invoked, and the murder of gay people will be deplored by decent people, straight and gay; and when the religious right shrills viciously about how the murder doesn't matter, as it has been doing since his death, decent people everywhere will find the religious right lacking human kindness, will find these Gary Bauers and Paul Weyrichs and Pat Robertsons un-Christian, repulsive, in fact. And a very minute increment toward decency will have been secured. But poor Matthew Shepard. Jesus, what a price!

Trent Lott endorses murder. He knows that discrimination kills. Pope John Paul II endorses murder. He, too, knows the price of discrimination, having declared anti-Semitism a sin, having just canonized a Jewish-born nun who died in Auschwitz. He knows that discrimination kills. But when the pope heard the news about Matthew Shepard, he, too, worried about spin. And so on the subject of gay bashing, the pope and his cardinals and his bishops and priests maintain their cynical political silence. Rigorously denouncing the abuse and murder of homosexuals would be a big sin against spin; denouncing the murder of homosexuals in such a way that it received even one-thousandth of the coverage his and his church's attacks on homosexuals routinely receive, this would be an act of decency the pope can't afford, for the pope knows: Behind this one murdered kid stand legions of kids whose lives are scarred by the bigotry this pope defends as sanctioned by God. None of these kids will ever be allowed to marry the person she or he loves, not while the pope and his church can prevent it; all of these kids are told, by the Holy Catholic Church, and by the Episcopalians and Lutherans and Baptists and Orthodox Jews: Your love is cursed by God. To speak out against murdering those who are discriminated against is to speak out against discrimination. To remain silent is to endorse murder.

A lot of people worry these days about the death of civil discourse. The pope, in his new encyclical, *Fides et Ratio* (Faith and Reason), laments the death of civil discourse and cites "ancient philosophers who proposed friendship as one of the most appropriate contexts for sound philosophical inquiry."

It's more than faintly ludicrous, this plea for friendship coming from the self-same pope who has tried so relentlessly to stamp out dissent in churches and Catholic universities, but let's follow the lead of the crazies who killed Matthew Shepard and take the pope at his word.

Friendship is the proper context for discussion. Fine and good. Take the gun away from the head, Your Holiness, and we can discuss the merits of homosexual sex, of homosexual marriage, of homosexual love, of monogamy versus promiscuity, of lesbian or gay couples raising kids, of condom distribution in the schools, of confidential counseling for teenagers, of sex education that addresses more than abstinence. We can discuss abortion, we can discuss anything you like. Just promise me two things, *friend*: First you won't beat my brains out with a pistol butt and leave me to die by the side of the road. Second, if someone else, someone a little less sane than you, feeling entitled to commit these terrible things against me because they understood you a little too literally, or were more willing than you to take your distaste for me and what I do to its most full-blooded conclusion, if someone else does violence against me, *friend*, won't you *please* make it your business to make a big public fuss about how badly I was treated? Won't you please make a point, *friend*, you who call yourself, and who are called, by millions of people, the Vicar on Earth of the very gentle Jesus, won't you please in the name of friendship announce that no one who deliberately inflicts suffering, whether by violence or by prejudice, on another human being, can be said to be acting in God's name? And announce it so that it is very clear that you include homosexuals when you refer to "human beings," and announce it so that the world hears you, really hears you, so that your announcement makes the news, as you are capable of doing when it suits your purposes? Won't you make this your purpose, too? And if you won't, if you won't take responsibility for the consequences of your militant promotion of discrimination, won't you excuse me if I think you are not a friend at all but rather a homicidal liar whose claim to spiritual and moral leadership is fatally compromised, is worth nothing more than . . . well, worth nothing more than the disgusting, opportunistic leadership of Trent Lott.

A lot of people worry these days about the death of civil discourse, and would say that I ought not call the pope a homicidal liar, nor (to be ecumenical about it) the orthodox rabbinate homicidal liars, nor Trent Lott a disgusting opportunistic hatemonger. But I worry a lot less about the death of civil discourse than I worry about being killed if, visiting the wrong town with my boyfriend, we forget ourselves so much as to betray, at the wrong moment in front of the wrong people, that we love one another. I worry much more about the recent death of the Maine antidiscrimination bill, and about the death of the New York hate-crimes bill, which will not pass because it includes sexual orientation. I worry more about the death of civil rights than civil discourse. I worry much more about the irreversible soul-deaths of lesbian, gay, bisexual, transgendered children growing up deliberately, malevolently isolated by the likes of Trent Lott and Newt Gingrich than I worry about the death of civil discourse. I mourn Matthew Shepard's actual death, caused by the unimpeachably civil "we hate the sin, not the sinner" hypocrisy of the religious right, endorsed by the political right, much more than I mourn the lost chance to be civil with someone who does not consider me fully a citizen, nor fully human. I mourn that cruel death more than the chance to be civil with those who sit idly by while theocrats, bullies, panderers, and hatemongers, and their crazed murderous children, destroy democracy and our civic life. Civic, not civil, discourse is what matters, and civic discourse mandates the assigning of blame.

If you are lesbian, gay, transgendered, bi, reading this, here's one good place to assign blame: The Human Rights Campaign's appalling, post-Shepard endorsement of Al D'Amato dedicates our resources to the perpetuation of a Republican majority in Congress. The HRC, ostensibly our voice in Washington, is in cahoots with fag-bashers and worse. If you are a heterosexual person, and you are reading this: Yeah yeah yeah, you've heard it all before, but if you have not called your Congressperson to demand passage of a hate-crimes bill that includes sexual orientation, and e-mailed every Congressperson, if you have not gotten up out of your comfortable chair to campaign for homosexual and all civil rights—*campaign*, not just passively support—may you think about this crucified man, and may you mourn, and may you burn with a moral citizen's shame. As one civilized person to another: *Matthew Shepard shouldn't have died. We should all burn with shame.*

# Part Three
# Hate-crime Legislation

# 7

# *R.A.V., Petitioner v. City of St. Paul, Minnesota*

JUSTICE SCALIA delivered the opinion of the Court.

In the predawn hours of June 21, 1990, petitioner and several other teen-agers allegedly assembled a crudely made cross by taping together broken chair legs. They then allegedly burned the cross inside the fenced yard of a black family that lived across the street from the house where petitioner was staying. Although this conduct could have been punished under any of a number of laws, one of the two provisions under which respondent city of St. Paul chose to charge petitioner (then a juvenile) was the St. Paul Bias-Motivated Crime Ordinance, which provides:

> Whoever places on public or private property a symbol, object, appellation, characterization or graffiti, including, but not limited to, a burning cross or Nazi swastika, which one knows or has reasonable grounds to know arouses anger, alarm, or resentment in others on the basis of race, color, creed, religion, or gender commits disorderly conduct and shall be guilty of a misdemeanor.

Petitioner moved to dismiss this count on the ground that the St. Paul ordinance was substantially overbroad and impermissibly content-based and therefore facially invalid under the First Amendment. The trial court granted this motion, but the Minnesota Supreme Court reversed. That court rejected petitioner's overbreadth claim because, as construed in prior

---

Case No. 90-7675, argued December 4, 1991, and decided June 22, 1992.

Minnesota cases, . . . the modifying phrase "arouses anger, alarm, or resentment in others" limited the reach of the ordinance to conduct that amounts to "fighting words," *i.e.*, "conduct that itself inflicts injury or tends to incite immediate violence. . . ." . . . The court also concluded that the ordinance was not impermissibly content-based because, in its view, "the ordinance is a narrowly tailored means toward accomplishing the compelling governmental interest in protecting the community against bias-motivated threats to public safety and order. . . ."

I

In construing the St. Paul ordinance, we are bound by the construction given to it by the Minnesota court. . . . Accordingly, we accept the Minnesota Supreme Court's authoritative statement that the ordinance reaches only those expressions that constitute "fighting words." . . . Assuming, *arguendo,* that all of the expression reached by the ordinance is proscribable under the "fighting words" doctrine, we nonetheless conclude that the ordinance is facially unconstitutional in that it prohibits otherwise permitted speech solely on the basis of the subjects the speech addresses.

The First Amendment generally prevents government from proscribing speech, . . . or even expressive conduct, because of disapproval of the ideas expressed. Content-based regulations are presumptively invalid. . . . From 1791 to the present, however, our society, like other free but civilized societies, has permitted restrictions upon the content of speech in a few limited areas, which are "of such slight social value as a step to truth that any benefit that may be derived from them is clearly outweighed by the social interest in order and morality." . . . We have recognized that "the freedom of speech" referred to by the First Amendment does not include a freedom to disregard these traditional limitations. . . . Our decisions since the 1960s have narrowed the scope of the traditional categorical exceptions for defamation, . . . and for obscenity, but a limited categorical approach has remained an important part of our First Amendment jurisprudence.

We have sometimes said that these categories of expression are "not within the area of constitutionally protected speech," . . . or that the "protection of the First Amendment does not extend" to them. . . . Such statements must be taken in context, however, and are no more literally true than is the occasionally repeated shorthand characterizing obscenity "as not being speech at all." . . . What they mean is that these areas of speech can, consistently with the First Amendment, be regulated *because of their constitutionally proscribable content* (obscenity, defamation, etc.)—not that they are categories of speech entirely invisible to the Constitution, so that they may be made the vehicles for content discrimination unrelated to their distinctively proscribable content. Thus, the government may proscribe libel; but it may not make the further content discrimination of proscribing *only* libel critical of the government. . . .

Our cases surely do not establish the proposition that the First Amendment imposes no obstacle whatsoever to regulation of particular instances of such proscribable expression, so that the government "may regulate [them] freely." . . . That would mean that a city council could enact an ordinance prohibiting only those legally obscene works that contain criticism of the city government or, indeed, that do not include endorsement of the city government. Such a simplistic, all-or-nothing-at-all approach to First Amendment protection is at odds with common sense and with our jurisprudence as well. It is not true that "fighting words" have at most a "*de minimis*" expressive content, . . . or that their content is *in all respects* "worthless and undeserving of constitutional protection" . . .; sometimes they are quite expressive indeed. We have not said that they constitute "*no* part of the expression of ideas," but only that they constitute "no *essential* part of any exposition of ideas." . . .

The proposition that a particular instance of speech can be proscribable on the basis of one feature (*e.g.,* obscenity) but not on the basis of another (*e.g.,* opposition to the city government) is commonplace, and has found application in many contexts. We have long held, for example, that nonverbal expressive activity can be banned because of the action it entails, but not because of the idea it expresses—so that burning a flag in violation of an ordinance against outdoor fires could be punishable, whereas burning a flag in violation of an ordinance against dishonoring the flag is not. . . . Similarly, we have upheld reasonable "time, place, or manner" restrictions, but only if they are "justified without reference to the content of the regulated speech." . . . And just as the power to proscribe particular speech on the basis of a noncontent element (*e.g.,* noise) does not entail the power to proscribe the same speech on the basis of a content element; so also, the power to proscribe it on the basis of *one* content element (*e.g.,* obscenity) does not entail the power to proscribe it on the basis of *other* content elements.

In other words, the exclusion of "fighting words" from the scope of the First Amendment simply means that, for purposes of that Amendment, the unprotected features of the words are, despite their verbal character, essentially a "nonspeech" element of communication. Fighting words are thus analogous to a noisy sound truck: Each is . . . a "mode of speech" . . .;

both can be used to convey an idea; but neither has, in and of itself, a claim upon the First Amendment. As with the sound truck, however, so also with fighting words: The government may not regulate use based on hostility—or favoritism—toward the underlying message expressed. . . .

Even the prohibition against content discrimination that we assert the First Amendment requires is not absolute. It applies differently in the context of proscribable speech than in the area of fully protected speech. The rationale of the general prohibition, after all, is that content discrimination "raise[es] the specter that the Government may effectively drive certain ideas or viewpoints from the marketplace." . . .But content discrimination among various instances of a class of proscribable speech often does not pose this threat.

When the basis for the content discrimination consists entirely of the very reason the entire class of speech at issue is proscribable, no significant danger of idea or viewpoint discrimination exists. Such a reason, having been adjudged neutral enough to support exclusion of the entire class of speech from First Amendment protection, is also neutral enough to form the basis of distinction within the class. To illustrate: A State might choose to prohibit only that obscenity which is the most patently offensive *in its prurience*—i.e., that which involves the most lascivious displays of sexual activity. But it may not prohibit, for example, only that obscenity which includes offensive *political* messages. . . . And the federal government can criminalize only those threats of violence that are directed against the president. . . . But the federal government may not criminalize only those threats against the president that mention his policy on aid to inner cities.

Another valid basis for according differential treatment to even a content-defined subclass of proscribable speech is that the subclass happens to be associated with particular "secondary effects" of the speech, so that the regulation is "*justified* without reference to the content of the . . . speech." . . . A State could, for example, permit all obscene live performances except those involving minors. Moreover, since words can in some circumstances violate laws directed not against speech but against conduct (a law against treason, for example, is violated by telling the enemy the nation's defense secrets), a particular content-based subcategory of a proscribable class of speech can be swept up incidentally within the reach of a statute directed at conduct rather than speech. Thus, for example, sexually derogatory "fighting words," among other words, may produce a violation of Title VII's general prohibition against sexual discrimination in employment practices. Where the government does not target conduct on the basis of its expressive content, acts are not shielded from regulation merely because they express a discriminatory idea or philosophy.

These bases for distinction refute the proposition that the selectivity of the restriction is "even arguably 'conditioned upon the sovereign's agreement with what a speaker may intend to say.' " There may be other such bases as well. Indeed, to validate such selectivity (where totally proscribable speech is at issue) it may not even be necessary to identify any particular "neutral" basis, so long as the nature of the content discrimination is such that there is no realistic possibility that official suppression of ideas is afoot.

## II

Applying these principles to the St. Paul ordinance, we conclude that, even as narrowly construed by the Minnesota Supreme Court, the ordinance is facially unconstitutional. Although the phrase in the ordinance, "arouse anger, alarm, or resentment in others," has been limited by the Minnesota Supreme Court's construction to reach only those symbols or displays that amount to "fighting words," the remaining, unmodified terms make clear that the ordinance applies only to "fighting words" that insult, or provoke violence, "on the basis of race, color, creed, religion, or gender." Displays containing abusive invective, no matter how vicious or severe, are permissible unless they are addressed to one of the specified disfavored topics. Those who wish to use "fighting words" in connection with other ideas—to express hostility, for example, on the basis of political affiliation, union membership, or homosexuality—are not covered. The First Amendment does not permit St. Paul to impose special prohibitions on those speakers who express views on disfavored subjects. . . .

In its practical operation, moreover, the ordinance goes even beyond mere content discrimination, to actual viewpoint discrimination. Displays containing some words—odious racial epithets, for example—would be prohibited to proponents of all views. But "fighting words" that do not themselves invoke race, color, creed, religion, or gender—aspersions upon a person's mother, for example—would seemingly be usable *ad libitum* in the placards of those arguing *in favor* of racial, color, etc. tolerance and equality, but could not be used by that speaker's opponents. One could hold up a sign saying, for example, that all "anti-Catholic bigots" are misbegotten; but not that all "papists" are, for that would insult and provoke violence "on the basis of religion." St. Paul has no such authority to license one side of a debate to fight freestyle, while requiring the other to follow Marquis of Queensbury Rules.

What we have here, it must be emphasized, is not a prohibition of fighting words that are directed at certain persons or groups (which would be *facially* valid if it met the requirements of the Equal Protection Clause); but rather, a prohibition of fighting words that contain (as the Minnesota Supreme Court repeatedly emphasized) messages of "bias-motivated" hatred and in particular, as applied to this case, messages "based on virulent notions of racial supremacy." . . . One must wholeheartedly agree with the Minnesota Supreme Court that "[i]t is the responsibility, even the obligation, of diverse communities to confront such notions in whatever form they appear," but the manner of that confrontation cannot consist of selective limitations upon speech. St. Paul's brief asserts that a general "fighting words" law would not meet the city's needs because only a content-specific measure can communicate to minority groups that the "group hatred" aspects of such speech "is not condoned by the majority." . . . The point of the First Amendment is that majority preferences must be expressed in some fashion other than silencing speech on the basis of its content.

. . . St. Paul concedes in its brief that the ordinance applies only to "racial, religious, or gender-specific symbols" such as "a burning cross, Nazi swastika, or other instrumentality of like import." . . . Indeed, St. Paul argued in the Juvenile Court that "[t]he burning of a cross does express a message and it is, in fact, the content of that message which the St. Paul Ordinance attempts to legislate." . . .

The content-based discrimination reflected in the St. Paul ordinance comes within neither any of the specific exceptions to the First Amendment prohibition we discussed earlier, nor within a more general exception for content discrimination that does not threaten censorship of ideas. It assuredly does not fall within the exception for content discrimination based on the very reasons why the particular class of speech at issue (here, fighting words) is proscribable. The reason why fighting words are categorically excluded from the protection of the First Amendment is not that their content communicates any particular idea, but that their content embodies a particularly intolerable (and socially unnecessary) *mode* of expressing *whatever* idea the speaker wishes to convey. St. Paul has not singled out an especially offensive mode of expression—it has not, for example, selected for prohibition only those fighting words that communicate ideas in a threatening (as opposed to a merely obnoxious) manner. Rather, it has proscribed fighting words of whatever manner that communicate messages of racial, gender, or religious intolerance. Selectivity of this sort creates the possibility that the city is seeking to handicap the expressions of particular ideas. That possibility would alone be enough to render the ordinance presumptively invalid, but St. Paul's comments and concessions in this case elevate the possibility to a certainty. . . .

Finally, St. Paul and its *amici* defend the conclusion of the Minnesota Supreme Court that, even if the ordinance regulates expression based on hostility toward its protected ideological content, this discrimination is nonetheless justified because it is narrowly tailored to serve compelling state interests. Specifically, they assert that the ordinance helps to ensure the basic human rights of members of groups that have historically been subjected to discrimination, including the right of such group members to live in peace where they wish. We do not doubt that these interests are compelling, and that the ordinance can be said to promote them. But the "danger of censorship" presented by a facially content-based statute, . . . requires that that weapon be employed only where it is "*necessary* to serve the asserted [compelling] interest." . . . The existence of adequate content-neutral alternatives thus "undercut[s] significantly" any defense of such a statute, . . . casting considerable doubt on the government's protestations that "the asserted justification is in fact an accurate description of the purpose and effect of the law." . . . The dispositive question in this case, therefore, is whether content discrimination is reasonably necessary to achieve St. Paul's compelling interests; it plainly is not. An ordinance not limited to the favored topics, for example, would have precisely the same beneficial effect. In fact the only interest distinctively served by the content limitation is that of displaying the city council's special hostility toward the particular biases thus singled out. That is precisely what the First Amendment forbids. The politicians of St. Paul are entitled to express that hostility—but not through the means of imposing unique limitations upon speakers who (however benightedly) disagree.

Let there be no mistake about our belief that burning a cross in someone's front yard is reprehensible. But St. Paul has sufficient means at its disposal to prevent such behavior without adding the First Amendment to the fire.

The judgment of the Minnesota Supreme Court is reversed. . . .

JUSTICE WHITE, with whom JUSTICE BLACKMUN and JUSTICE O'CONNOR join, and with whom JUSTICE STEVENS joins except as to Part I(A), concurring in the judgment.

I agree with the majority that the judgment of the Minnesota Supreme Court should be reversed. However, our agreement ends there.

This case could easily be decided within the contours of established First Amendment law by holding, as petitioner argues, that the St. Paul ordinance is fatally overbroad because it criminalizes not only unprotected

expression but expression protected by the First Amendment. . . . Instead,
. . . the Court holds the ordinance facially unconstitutional on a ground
that . . . requires serious departures from the teaching of prior cases. . . .

This Court ordinarily is not so eager to abandon its precedents. . . .

But in the present case, the majority casts aside long-established First
Amendment doctrine without the benefit of briefing and adopts an un-
tried theory. This is hardly a judicious way of proceeding, and the Court's
reasoning in reaching its result is transparently wrong.


## IA

This Court's decisions have plainly stated that expression falling within
certain limited categories so lacks the values the First Amendment was
designed to protect that the Constitution affords no protection to that
expression. *Chaplinsky* v. *New Hampshire* . . . made the point in the
clearest possible terms:

> There are certain well-defined and narrowly limited classes of speech, the
> prevention and punishment of which have never been thought to raise any
> Constitutional problem. . . . It has been well observed that such utterances
> are no essential part of any exposition of ideas, and are of such slight social
> value as a step to truth that any benefit that may be derived from them
> is clearly outweighed by the social interest in order and morality.

Thus, as the majority concedes, this Court has long held certain discrete categories of expression to be proscribable on the basis of their content.
For instance, the Court has held that the individual who falsely shouts
"fire" in a crowded theater may not claim the protection of the First Amendment. . . . The Court has concluded that neither child pornography, nor
obscenity, is protected by the First Amendment. . . . And the Court has
observed that, "[l]eaving aside the special considerations when public officials [and public figures] are the target, a libelous publication is not protected by the Constitution." . . .

All of these categories are content based. But the Court has held that
First Amendment does not apply to them because their expressive content is worthless or of *de minimis* value to society. We have not departed
from this principle, emphasizing repeatedly that, "within the confines of
[these] given classification[s], the evil to be restricted so overwhelmingly
outweighs the expressive interests, if any, at stake, that no process of case-
by-case adjudication is required." This categorical approach has provided

a principled and narrowly focused means for distinguishing between expression that the government may regulate freely and that which it may
regulate on the basis of content only upon a showing of compelling need.

Today, however, the Court announces that earlier Courts did not
mean their repeated statement that certain categories of expression are
"not within the area of constitutionally protected speech." The present
Court submits that such clear statements "must be taken in context" and
are not "literally true."

To the contrary, those statements meant precisely what they said: The
categorical approach is a firmly entrenched part of our First Amendment
jurisprudence. Indeed, the Court in *Roth* [v. *United States* (1957)] re-
viewed the guarantees of freedom of expression in effect at the time of
the ratification of the Constitution and concluded, "[i]n light of this history, it is apparent that the unconditional phrasing of the First Amendment was not intended to protect every utterance."

In its decision today, the Court points to "[n]othing . . . in this Court's
precedents warrant[ing] disregard of this longstanding tradition." Nevertheless, the majority holds that the First Amendment protects those narrow categories of expression long held to be undeserving of First Amendment protection—at least to the extent that lawmakers may not regulate
some fighting words more strictly than others because of their content.
The Court announces that such content-based distinctions violate the First
Amendment because "the government may not regulate use based on hostility—or favoritism—toward the underlying message expressed." Should
the government want to criminalize certain fighting words, the Court now
requires it to criminalize all fighting words.

To borrow a phrase, "Such a simplistic, all-or-nothing-at-all approach
to First Amendment protection is at odds with common sense and with
our jurisprudence as well.". . .

The majority's observation that fighting words are "quite expressive
indeed" is no answer. Fighting words are not a means of exchanging views,
rallying supporters, or registering a protest; they are directed against
individuals to provoke violence or to inflict injury. . . . Therefore, a ban
on all fighting words or on a subset of the fighting words category would
restrict only the social evil of hate speech, without creating the danger
of driving viewpoints from the marketplace.

Therefore, the Court's insistence on inventing its brand of First Amendment underinclusiveness puzzles me. The overbreadth doctrine has the re-
deeming virtue of attempting to avoid the chilling of protected expression, . . . but the Court's new "underbreadth" creation serves no desirable function. Instead, it permits, indeed invites, the continuation of

expressive conduct that in this case is evil and worthless in First Amendment terms, until the city of St. Paul cures the underbreadth by adding to its ordinance a catch-all phrase such as "and all other fighting words that may constitutionally be subjected to this ordinance."

Any contribution to this holding to First Amendment jurisprudence is surely a negative one, since it necessarily signals that expressions of violence, such as the message of intimidation and racial hatred conveyed by burning a cross on someone's lawn, are of sufficient value to outweigh the social interest in order and morality that has traditionally placed such fighting words outside the First Amendment. Indeed, by characterizing fighting words as a form of "debate," the majority legitimates hate speech as a form of public discussion.

Furthermore, the Court obscures the line between speech that could be regulated freely on the basis of content (*i.e.,* the narrow categories of expression falling outside the First Amendment) and that which could be regulated on the basis of content only upon a showing of a compelling state interest (*i.e.,* all remaining expression). By placing fighting words, which the Court has long held to be valueless, on at least equal constitutional footing with political discourse and other forms of speech that we have deemed to have the greatest social value, the majority devalues the latter category.

*    *    *

## II

Although I disagree with the Court's analysis, I do agree with its conclusion: The St. Paul ordinance is unconstitutional. However, I would decide the case on overbreadth grounds. . . .

I agree with petitioner that the ordinance is invalid on its face. Although the ordinance as construed reaches categories of speech that are constitutionally unprotected, it also criminalizes a substantial amount of expression that—however repugnant—is shielding by the First Amendment. . . .

In the First Amendment context, "[c]riminal statutes must be scrutinized with particular care; those that make unlawful a substantial amount of constitutionally protected conduct may be held facially invalid even if they also have legitimate application." The St. Paul antibias ordinance is such a law. Although the ordinance reaches conduct that is unprotected, it also makes criminal expressive conduct that causes only hurt feelings, offense, or resentment, and is protected by the First Amendment. The ordinance is therefore fatally overbroad and invalid on its face. . . . I join the judgment, but not the folly of the opinion.

JUSTICE BLACKMUN, concurring in the judgment.

I regret what the Court has done in this case. The majority opinion signals one of two possibilities: it will serve as precedent for future cases, or it will not. Either result is disheartening.

In the first instance, by deciding that a State cannot regulate speech that causes great harm unless it also regulates speech that does not (setting law and logic on their heads), the Court seems to abandon the categorical approach, and inevitably to relax the level of scrutiny applicable to content-based laws. As Justice White points out, this weakens the traditional protections of speech. If all expressive activity must be accorded the same protection, that protection will be scant. The simple reality is that the Court will never provide child pornography or cigarette advertising the level of protection customarily granted political speech. If we are forbidden from categorizing, as the Court has done here, we shall reduce protection across the board. It is said that in its effort to reach a satisfying result in this case, the Court is willing to weaken First Amendment protections.

In the second instance is the possibility that this case will not significantly alter First Amendment jurisprudence, but, instead, will be regarded as an aberration—a case where the Court manipulated doctrine to strike down an ordinance whose premise it opposed, namely, that racial threats and verbal assaults are of greater harm than other fighting words. I fear that the Court has been distracted from its proper mission by the temptation to decide the issue over "politically correct speech" and "cultural diversity," neither of which is presented here. If this is the meaning of today's opinion, it is perhaps even more regrettable.

I see no First Amendment values that are comprised by a law that prohibits hoodlums from driving minorities out of their homes by burning crosses on their lawns, but I see great harm in preventing the people of Saint Paul from specifically punishing the race-based fighting words that so prejudice their community.

I concur in the judgment, however, because I agree with Justice White that this particular ordinance reaches beyond fighting words to speech protected by the First Amendment.

JUSTICE STEVENS, concurring in the judgment.

Conduct that creates special risks or causes special harms may be prohibited by special rules. Lighting a fire near an ammunition dump or a gasoline storage tank is especially dangerous; such behavior may be punished more severely than burning trash in a vacant lot. Threatening someone because of her race or religious beliefs may cause particularly severe trauma or touch off a riot, and threatening a high public official may cause substantial social disruption; such threats may be punished more severely than threats against someone based on, say, his support of a particular athletic team. There are legitimate, reasonable, and neutral justifications for such special rules.

This case involves the constitutionality of one such ordinance. . . .

I

Fifty years ago, the Court articulated a categorical approach to First Amendment jurisprudence.

> There are certain well-defined and narrowly limited classes of speech, the prevention and punishment of which have never been thought to raise any Constitutional problem. . . . It has been well observed that such utterances are no essential part of any exposition of ideas, and are of such slight social value as a step to truth that any benefit that may be derived from them is clearly outweighed by the social interest in order and morality.

We have, as Justice White observes, often described such categories of expression as "not within the area of constitutionally protected speech."

I am, however, . . . troubled by the . . . Court's analysis—namely, its conclusion that the St. Paul ordinance is an unconstitutional content-based regulation of speech. Drawing on broadly worded *dicta,* the Court establishes a near-absolute ban on content-based regulations of expression and holds that the First Amendment prohibits the regulation of fighting words by subject matter. Thus, while the Court rejects the "all-or-nothing-at-all" nature of the categorical approach, it promptly embraces an absolutism of its own: within a particular "proscribable" category of expression, the Court holds, a government must either proscribe *all* speech or no speech at all. This aspect of the Court's ruling fundamentally misunderstands the role and constitutional status of content-based regulations on speech, conflicts with the very nature of First Amendment jurisprudence, and disrupts well-settled principles of First Amendment law. . . .

This is true at every level of First Amendment law. In broadest terms, our entire First Amendment jurisprudence creates a regime based on the content of speech. . . .

Our First Amendment decisions have created a rough hierarchy in the constitutional protection of speech. Core political speech occupies the highest, most protected position; commercial speech and nonobscene, sexually explicit speech are regarded as a sort of second-class expression; obscenity and fighting words receive the least protection of all. Assuming that the Court is correct that this last class of speech is not wholly "unprotected," it certainly does not follow that fighting words and obscenity receive the *same* sort of protection afforded core political speech. Yet in ruling that proscribable speech cannot be regulated based on subject matter, the Court does just that. Perversely, this gives fighting words *greater* protection than is afforded commercial speech. If Congress can prohibit false advertising directed at airline passengers without also prohibiting false advertising directed at bus passengers and if a city can prohibit political advertisements in its buses while allowing other advertisements, it is ironic to hold that a city cannot regulate fighting words based on "race, color, creed, religion, or gender" while leaving unregulated fighting words based on "union membership or homosexuality." The Court today turns First Amendment law on its head: Communication that was once entirely unprotected (and that still can be wholly proscribed) is now entitled to greater protection than commercial speech—and possibly greater protection than core political speech. . . .

Significantly, the St. Paul ordinance regulates speech not on the basis of its subject matter or the viewpoint expressed, but rather on the basis of the *harm* the speech causes. In this regard, the Court fundamentally misreads the St. Paul ordinance. The Court describes the St. Paul ordinance as regulating expression "addressed to one of [several] specified disfavored topics." . . . Contrary to the Court's suggestion, the ordinance regulates only a subcategory of expression that causes *injuries based on* "race, color, creed, religion, or gender," not a subcategory that involves *discussions* that concern those characteristics. The ordinance, as construed by the Court, criminalizes expression that "one knows . . . [by its very utterance inflicts injury on] others on the basis of race, color, creed, religion, or gender." In this regard, the ordinance resembles the child pornography law, . . . which in effect singled out child pornography because those publications caused far greater harms than pornography involving adults.

Moreover, even if the St. Paul ordinance did regulate fighting words based on its subject matter, such a regulation would, in my opinion, be constitutional. As noted above, subject-matter based regulations on commercial speech are widespread and largely unproblematic. As we have long recognized, subject-matter regulations generally do not raise the same concerns of government censorship and the distortion of public discourse presented by viewpoint regulations. Thus, in upholding subject-matter regulations we have carefully noted that viewpoint-based discrimination was not implicated. . . .

Finally, it is noteworthy that the St. Paul ordinance is, as construed by the Court today, quite narrow. The St. Paul ordinance does not ban all "hate speech," nor does it ban, say, all cross-burnings or all swastika displays. Rather it only bans a subcategory of the already narrow category of fighting words. Such a limited ordinance leaves open and protected a vast range of expression on the subjects of racial, religious, and gender equality. As construed by the Court today, the ordinance certainly does not " 'raise the specter that the government may effectively drive certain ideas or viewpoints from the marketplace.' " Petitioner is free to burn a cross to announce a rally or to express his views about racial supremacy, he may do so on private property or public land, at day or at night, so long as the burning is not so threatening and so directed at an individual as to "by its very [execution] inflict injury." Such a limited proscription scarcely offends the First Amendment.

In sum, the St. Paul ordinance (as construed by the Court) regulates expressive activity that is wholly proscribable and does so not on the basis of viewpoint, but rather in recognition of the different harms caused by such activity. Taken together, these several considerations persuade me that the St. Paul ordinance is not an unconstitutional content-based regulation of speech. Thus, were the ordinance not overbroad, I would vote to uphold it.

# 8

# The Hate Debate

## *New Republic* Editorial

The horrific murder of Matthew Shepard, a gay student at the University of
Wyoming who was severely beaten and then lashed to a fence post and literally
left to die, has created a national outcry over bigotry against gays. As this magazine goes to print, gay rights groups are descending upon the Capitol to call for
enactment of more laws against hate crimes on both the state and federal levels.
President Clinton, for his part, has urged Congress to pass the Hate Crimes Pre-
vention Act. That legislation expands the power of federal agencies to investi-
gate crimes motivated by antigay animus (or hostility against someone's gender
or disability), an area currently covered under a patchwork of state laws. The
editorial page of the *New York Times* has also expressed the need for more hate-
crime laws. The death of Matthew Shepard, the *Times* reasoned, demonstrates
"the need for hate-crime laws to protect those who survive and punish those
who attack others, whether fatally or not, just because of who they are."

Clearly, Matthew Shepard's murderers should receive swift and severe punishment. Furthermore, bigotry and violence aimed at gays and lesbians are real
problems in our society. (The FBI estimates that antigay violence comprises
11.6 percent of all hate crimes. We know this thanks to the valuable Hate Crimes
Statistics Act, which requires the federal government to keep reliable data on the
occurrence of hate crimes.) But the proposed new federal statute is not the right
solution.

The law that Clinton has urged Congress to pass would amend an existing federal statute that requires the government to impose stiffer sentences on convicted criminals when animus against certain minorities motivates their acts. In practice, this law has had little impact on the occurrence of hate crimes against the minority groups it seeks to protect, and it would probably have little effect on the occurrence of hate crimes against gays. It's hard to see how Matthew Shepard's killers would have been deterred by the prospect of federally assisted prosecution and a tough federal penalty. Under Wyoming law, and that of most states, murder is already punishable by the ultimate penalty: death.

The basic problem with which all proposed hate-crime laws must contend is that they create a legal distinction between someone who kills a gay man because he hates gays and someone who kills a gas-station attendant in order to steal from his cash register. To create such a distinction in effect penalizes some criminals more harshly, not because of their deeds, but because of their beliefs. This clashes with constitutional principles protecting free thought and equality under the law.

Supporters of hate-crime legislation insist that they aren't engaging in any special pleading. After all, they note, in the 1960s, the federal government enacted civil rights laws that made the murder of African Americans trying to exercise their civil rights (such as voting) a federal offense. The Shepard case, supporters of hate-crime laws say, shows that crimes against gays today are analogous. But the two are hardly the same. In the 1960s, federal intervention was necessary in order to redress Southern states' systematic and calculated indifference to crimes committed against blacks. The federal government had to step in because state courts refused to enforce their own laws and protect the lives and liberty of black citizens.

No such constitutional violations are at issue in the Shepard case. Wyoming's authorities aren't about to set Shepard's alleged killers free. Indeed, they'll probably seek the death penalty. And there is scant evidence that local and state officials generally have deliberately failed to prosecute the murders of gay men or lesbians.

This, then, is an exercise in symbolic politics. For Bill Clinton, endorsement of the federal hate-crime law is of a piece with his mixed record on issues of concern to gay citizens. Organizations like the Human Rights Campaign have rightly hailed Clinton for working harder on behalf of gays and lesbians than any previous president (or any conceivable Republican alternative). And he has taken symbolically important steps, such as appointing a gay man, James Hormel, as ambassador to Luxembourg—whose confirmation is being held up by Republicans because of his homosexuality—and ending the federal policy that made gays and lesbians presumptive security risks. But, when it comes to more substantive change, like a clear-cut policy permitting gays to serve openly in the military, Clinton has fallen short. At times, he has even played into the cultural right's irrational and mean-spirited abhorrence of gays. This is, after all, the president who signed the Defense of Marriage Act denying federal recognition of same-sex marriages and then aired commercials on Christian radio stations bragging about it.

When hate crimes occur, they should be identified and reported, as legislation already on the books requires. The criminals should be dealt with just as harshly as every other kind of criminal. What's needed now is not a knee-jerk reaction by Congress and the states. Fundamentally, bigotry against gays is a cultural issue, to be tackled through the determined pursuit of attitudinal change. What's needed now, then, is loud and principled condemnation of the malicious murder of Matthew Shepard and of the festering bigotry that motivated it. The American public, to its credit, delivered such condemnation swiftly. And it didn't take a hate-crime law to make that happen.

# 9

# Canon to the Ordinary

## Patricia J. Williams

Only hours after Pope John Paul II issued his encyclical on *Fides et Ratio* the body of University of Wyoming student Matthew Shepard was laid to rest in the town of Casper. Outside the funeral a group of protesters, led by a Kansas minister, gathered to shout epithets at the bereaved. Shepard, their signs read, would burn in hell because "God hates fags." At the same time, the Casper City Council declared a one-day ban on protesters—an extreme, unfortunate yet arguably necessary measure under the circumstances—while the Wyoming State legislature could not even agree that there is such a thing as a hate crime. Meanwhile, on the other side of the country, New Yorkers debated whether to cancel the annual Greenwich Village Halloween Parade—a tradition that has evolved into a carnivalesque expression of gay pride—for no reason other than its supposedly having become a "magnet" for gay-bashers.

It has been argued that laws punishing hate crimes punish people for their thoughts. The image evoked is a little like a beaker filled with oil and water. The water is the crime. The hate is the oil. The hate, supposedly floating in the First Amendment realm of protected words and thought, is fully separable from one's criminal conduct. Punish the crime, according to this model, but leave the hate alone. There are many grounds upon which to question such an easy division, but even in those states that have enacted bias-crime statutes, few prosecutors seem ready, willing, or able to wrestle seriously with the admittedly compli-

Patricia J. Williams, "Canon to the Ordinary." Reprinted with permission from the November 9, 1998, issue of *The Nation*.

cated application of those statutes in specific cases. Thus, while public officials fight on about surface tension and emulsion, we are left with the ethical problem of what it means to "leave the hate alone."

I guess I wouldn't worry so much if I thought hate really were left "alone," huddled in a dark alley somewhere, outcast and friendless. But what seems to be happening in this country is more like the active courtship of a venomous yet surprisingly seductive little poltergeist that eternally protests its innocence *sub nomine* The Right to Hate. We acknowledge the manifestation of something called Hate in situation after confrontation after tragic event. With admirable spontaneity we deplore, abhor, and spiritedly denounce the vulgarity of Hate's hateful excesses—for exactly three minutes. Four minutes after the manifestation, and without fail, the poltergeist seizes control and turns the fight from moral reprehensibility or moral stake or what it would take to find our way to moral uplift into a fight about Hate's fight to comfortable haven. After five minutes, the angel of the First Amendment steps in to save Hate, bleating beneath the sheep's clothing of political expression, from its enemies. And here's where, as an ordained lawyer, I must confess a small crisis of faith. I have always revered the Bill of Rights, and I do believe in the greater good of freedom of speech, but my, what big ears, what big eyes, what big teeth has the ordinarily benevolent and time-honored victim. Mere Words.

So for the moment let me put on hold the question of whether there's a right to pure hate; let's just agree that in most instances there's no law against it. Now what?

I was lucky enough to have grown up in an era when the dominant ethic provided an easy answer: Given the lessons of World War II, one should, one must always speak out against prejudice, want, indignity. As a child of the civil rights and antiwar movements, I grew up believing that it is good to witness loudly the things that are wrong in the world. Ever the fresh-faced crusader, I suppose. But when I was a student, college campuses were the sites of "love-ins," those great mosh-pits for the exuberantly idealistic. Today's campuses are not quite so hospitable. In the wake of Shepard's beating, students at Colorado State made fun of him by rigging a scarecrow atop a parade float. I guess we are supposed to celebrate this as just another victory for the First Amendment; certainly no one thought to call for the cancellation of that parade so as to save gay-bashers from themselves.

So here we are, at two minutes after the funeral of Matthew Shepard. The media are awash in earnest condemnation. But mark my words, after three and a half minutes, someone will casually suggest that hatred is just a matter of "ignorance" and "stupidity" and there's no sense in analyzing it too much, because the killers were "just a couple of rednecks." If you're still talking about Matthew Shepard after four minutes, you will be urged to shut up and get on with the healing process. After five minutes, you'll be accused of "magnifying" an isolated misfortune. After six minutes, you will face charges of "exploiting" for personal profit what has already been laid to rest. In thirty minutes, the students at Colorado State will have graduated and gone to Hollywood to write sitcoms about scarecrows, orangutans, and Indian chiefs; if you fail to laugh, you will be dubbed a demagogue. In forty-five minutes, the minister from Kansas will run for governor, and if you protest you will find yourself characterized as a witch-practitioner of the black art of political correctness. After sixty minutes precisely, you will be accused of Stalinist acts of censorship. If you argue that censorship usually refers to acts of state suppression, you will be flogged publicly and without mercy on the Op-Ed page of the *Wall Street Journal*.

When I look at the series of unequivocally biased pronouncements and hateful acts that have dotted our newspapers of late, I wonder at the disconnection we have made between our professions of disdain and our civic refusal to think constructively about the problem. The legal debate is likely to be a long and unsatisfactory one. In the interim, the only proposed solutions depend heavily on the persuasive arts. Yet virtually every recent effort to introduce the challenging histories of race, class, religion, and sexual orientation into the canon of American education or the training sessions of the American workplace have met with irrational accusations of "brainwashing." If we truly believe that the remedy for hate speech is more speech and that the path to civic virtue is in education, then it is high time indeed we got on with it.

# 10

# Civility Without Censorship: The Ethics of the Internet—Cyberhate

## Raymond W. Smith

Thank you, Rabbi Cooper, for the gracious introduction . . . and let me acknowledge the tremendous contributions the Museum and the Center have made toward harmonizing race relations and advancing equality and justice. We're truly honored that you would include us in today's program.

For the past two years, I've been using the "bully pulpit" to alert various civil rights leaders and organizations (like Martin Luther King III and the NAACP) of the dangers posed by cyberhate. If not for the early groundbreaking work by the Simon Wiesenthal Center, I doubt whether I would have even known of this growing threat. Thank you for warning us—and now, for showing us—how extremists are using the Internet for their own purposes.

When thinking about this morning's topic, I can't help but mention a cartoon that recently appeared in the newspapers. Through the doorway, a mother calls out to her teenager—who is surrounded by high-tech equipment—"I hope you're not watching sex stuff on the Internet!" To which her son replies, "Naw, I'm getting it on TV!"

Until recently, the chief concern of parents was pornography—kid's access to it over the Web and the fear of sexual predators cruising cyberspace. Now, we're worried about hatemongers reaching out to our children in digital space.

As we have just seen and heard, Neo-Nazis and extremists of every political stripe who once terrorized people in the dead of night with burning crosses

Address by Raymond W. Smith, Chairman, Bell Atlantic Corporation, delivered at Simon Wiesenthal Center/Museum of Tolerance, Los Angeles, California, on December 1, 1998. First appeared in *Vital Speeches of the Day*, 15 January 1999.

and painted swastikas are now sneaking up on the public—especially our kids—through the World Wide Web.

As cyberhate is nothing less than the attempt to corrupt public discourse on race and ethnicity via the Internet, many people see censorship of websites and Net content as the only viable way to meet this growing threat.

I disagree.

Instead of fearing the Internet's reach, we need to embrace it—to value its ability to connect our children to the wealth of positive human experience and knowledge. While there is, to quote one critic, "every form of diseased intelligence" in digital space, we must remember that it comprises only a small fraction of cyberspace. The Internet provides our children unlimited possibilities for learning and education—the great libraries, cities, and cultures of the world also await them at just the click of a mouse key.

In short, we need to think less about ways to keep cyberhate off the screen, and more about ways to meet it head on: which translates into fighting destructive rhetoric with constructive dialogue—hate speech with truth—restrictions with greater Internet access.

This morning then, I would like to discuss with you the options that are available to combat cyberhate that don't endanger our First Amendment guarantees—and that remain true to our commitment to free speech.

That people and institutions should call for a strict ban on language over the Web that could be considered racist, anti-Semitic, or bigoted is totally understandable. None of us was truly prepared for the emergence of multiple hate-group websites (especially those geared toward children), or the quick adoption of high-technology by skinheads and others to market their digital cargo across state lines and international date lines at the speed of light.

One possible reason some people feel inclined to treat the Internet more severely than other media is that the technology is new and hard to understand. Also, the Internet's global reach and ubiquitous nature makes it appear ominous. As Justice Gabriel Bach, of Israel, noted, this ability makes it especially dangerous. "I'm frightened stiff by the Internet," he said, "billions of people all over the world have access to it."

My industry has seen all this before.

The clash between free speech and information technology is actually quite an old one. Nearly a century ago, telephone companies, courts, and the Congress debated whether "common carriers" (public phone companies) were obligated to carry all talk equally, regardless of content. And in the end—though some believed that the phone would do everything from eliminate Southern accents and increase Northern labor unrest—free speech won out in the courts.

Whatever the technology, be it the radio or the silver screen, history teaches us that white supremacists, anti-Semites, and others will unfortunately come to grasp, relatively early on, a new medium's potential.

We simply can't condemn a whole technology because we fear that a Father Coughlin or a Leni Riefenstahl (early pioneers in the use of radio and film to advance anti-Semitism or Hitler's Reich) is waiting in the wings to use the latest technology to their own advantage. Nor can we expect the Congress, the federal government, or an international regulatory agency to tightly regulate cyberspace content in order to stymie language we find offensive.

The wisdom of further empowering such organizations and agencies like the FCC or the United Nations aside, it is highly doubtful even if they had the authority, that they would have the ability to truly stem the flow of racist and anti-Semitic language on the World Wide Web.

Anybody with a phone line, computer, and Internet connection can set up a website—even broadcast over the Net.

Even if discovered and banned, on-line hate groups can easily jump Internet service providers and national boundaries to avoid accountability. I think cyber guru, Peter Huber, got it right when he said, "To censor Internet filth at its origins, we would have to enlist the Joint Chiefs of Staff, who could start by invading Sweden and Holland."

Then there is the whole matter of disguise. Innocent sounding URLs (handles or website names) can fool even the most traveled or seasoned "cybernaut."

As for efforts on Capitol Hill and elsewhere to legislate all so-called "offensive" language off the Internet, here again, we can expect the courts to knock down any attempts to curtail First Amendment rights on the Internet. As the Supreme Court ruled last year when it struck down legislation restricting the transmission of "indecent" material on-line: (To Quote) "Regardless of the strength of the government's interest, the level of discourse reaching a mailbox simply cannot be limited to what is suitable for a sandbox."

In short, although the temptation is great to look to legislation and regulation as a remedy to cyberhate, our commitment to free speech must always take precedent over our fears.

So, cyberhate will not be defeated by the stroke of a pen.

Now, this is not to say that, because we place such a high value on our First Amendment rights, we can't do anything to combat the proliferation of hate sites on the Internet or protect young minds from such threatening and bigoted language.

Law enforcement agencies and state legislators can use existing laws against stalking and telephone harassment to go after those who abuse e-mail . . . parents can install software filtering programs (such as the Anti-Defamation League's HateFilter, or the one Bell Atlantic uses, CyberPatrol) to block access to questionable Internet sites . . . schools and libraries can protect children by teaching them how to properly use the Internet and challenge cyberhate . . . and Internet Service Providers can voluntarily decline to host hate sites. (Bell Atlantic Internet Services, for instance, reserves the right to decline or terminate service which "espouses, promotes, or incites bigotry, hatred, or racism.")

Given that today's panel has representatives from state government, law enforcement, the courts, and the Internet industry, we can discuss these initiatives later in more detail. The point is, there are other ways besides empowering national or international oversight agencies, or drafting draconian legislation, to lessen the impact of cyberhate.

Freedom, not censorship, is the only way to combat this threat to civility. In short, more speech—not less—is needed on the World Wide Web.

In fact, the best answer to cyberhate lies in the use of information technology itself. As a reporter for the *Boston Globe* recently concluded, (quote) "the same technology that provides a forum for extremists, enables civil rights groups and individuals to mobilize a response in unprecedented ways."

We totally agree.

Our prescription to cyberhate is therefore rather simple, but far reaching in its approach:

The first component is access: if we're to get to a higher level of national understanding on racial and ethnic issues—and strike at the very roots of cyberhate—we must see that no minority group or community is left out of cyberspace for want of a simple Internet connection or basic computer.

At Bell Atlantic, we've been working very hard to provide the minority communities we serve with Internet access. Across our region, thousands of inner-city schools, libraries, colleges, and community groups are now getting connected to cyberspace through a variety of our foundation and state grant programs. Also, our employees have been in the forefront of volunteering their time and energy to wire schools to the Internet during specially designated "Net" days.

Internet access alone, however, won't build bridges of understanding between people—or level the playing field between cyberhaters and the targets of their hate.

The second thing we must do is make sure the Web's content is enriched by minority culture and beliefs, and that there are more websites and home pages dedicated to meeting head-on the racist caricatures and pseudo history often found in cyberspace.

While cyberhate cannot be mandated or censored out of existence, it can be countered by creating hundreds of chatlines, home pages, bulletin boards, and websites dedicated to social justice, tolerance, and equality—for all people regardless of race, nationality, or sexual orientation.

Over the past two years, Bell Atlantic has helped a number of minority and civil rights groups launch and maintain their websites (like the NAACP, the

Leadership Council on Civil Rights, and the National Council of La Raza), and we've done the same for dozens of smaller cultural organizations (like the Harlem Studio Museum and El Museo del Barrio).

We believe that kind of moral leadership can have a tremendous impact. Quite simply, we need more Simon Wiesenthal Centers, Anti-Defamation Leagues, and Southern Poverty Law Centers monitoring and responding to cyberhate.

If we're to bring the struggle for human decency and dignity into cyberspace, we must see that the two most powerful revolutions of the twentieth century—those of civil rights and information technology—are linked even closer together.

Finally, we need to drive real-time, serious dialogue on the religious, ethnic, and cultural concerns that divide us as a nation—a task for which the Internet is particularly suited.

Precisely because it is anonymous, the Internet provides a perfect forum to discuss race, sexual orientation, and other similar issues. On the Internet, said one user, "you can speak freely and not have fears that somebody is going to attack you for what comes out of your heart." It's this kind of open and heartfelt discussion that we need to advance and sponsor on-line.

Already, a number of small groups and lone individuals are meeting the cyberhate challenge through simple dialogue between strangers. I'm talking about websites run by educators to inform parents about on-line hate materials . . . sites operated by "recovering" racists to engage skinheads and other misguided kids in productive debate . . . websites run by concerned citizens to bridge the gap in ignorance between ethnic, racial, and other communities.

The "Y? forum," also known as the National Forum on People's Differences, is a wonderful example of a website where readers can safely ask and follow discussions on sensitive crosscultural topics without having to wade through foul language or "flame wars."

As a columnist from the Miami Herald described the appeal of these kinds of sites: "As long as we are mysteries, one to another, we face a perpetuation of ignorance and a feeding of fear. I'd rather people ask the questions than try to make up the answers. I'd rather, they ask the questions than turn to myth and call it truth."

In closing, my company recognizes that the Internet doesn't operate in a vacuum. We agree that those who profit from information technology have a special responsibility to see that its promise is shared across class, race, and geographic boundaries.

That's why we're working with the public schools and libraries in our region to see that they're all equipped with the pens, pencils, and paper of the twenty-first century . . . why we're helping to further distance learning and telemedicine applications that serve the educational and health needs of the disabled and isolated . . . why we're helping minority groups and civil rights organizations use information technology to spread their vision and their values to the millions of people electronically linked to the global village.

And that's the way it should be.

Let me leave you with a personal story . . .

When growing up, my Jewish friends and I often swapped theology—tales from the Hassidic Masters for stories from the Lives of the Saints. I remember from these discussions that one of the great Rabbis noted that the first word of the Ten Commandments is "I" and the last word is "neighbor." In typical Talmudic fashion, the Rabbi was telling us that if we want to incorporate the Commandments into our lives, we must move from a focus on ourselves to others.

At Bell Atlantic, the more we grow—in both scale and scope—the greater the emphasis we place on being a good corporate citizen, and the more we're driven to see that digital technology is used for purposes of enlightenment and education.

The Internet will fundamentally transform the way we work, learn, do commerce. It will also, if properly used and rightly taught, help bridge the gap in understanding between communities—becoming not a tool of hate, but one of hope.

Thank you again for the invitation to join you this morning.

## Part Four

# What is Hate?

# 11

# Equality

## Abraham Kaplan

The prejudice and discrimination by which both old and young are victimized are special cases of the general problem of *equality,* on which social philosophy has increasingly focused. No known society is without differentiation among its members, especially if the society has easily identifiable minorities. But not all responses to minorities are prejudicial, nor are all treatment of minorities discriminatory. What constitutes prejudice?

In the literal sense, a *prejudice* is a prejudgment, a conviction reached beforehand, shaped by preconceived ideas. The toddler returning from his first day at school is asked, "Are there any colored children in your class?" "No, just black and white." He does not share the prevailing preconceptions which gave the word "colored" a special meaning. Knowledge always builds on what we already know; we have no alternative but to bring to new experience the ideas we have formed from the old. But in sound judgment we move on from what we know rather than digging in where we are, using new experience to test and improve our previous ideas rather than only as an occasion for reaffirming them. Prejudice is locked into its own patterns of thought, generating premises from conclusions already arrived at.

From a logical standpoint prejudice is a tissue of fallacies characteristic of simplistic block thinking, with its hasty generalizations and closed systems of ideas in which negative evidence is explained away. These patterns of illogic may be summed up as the *fallacy of simple predication:* the individual is not responded to as an individual but as a member of the minority group whose stereotyped attributes are then imputed to the individual. Foregone conclusions classify the individual as a member of *that* group rather than the countless others always possible; however a minority be defined, its members always belong as well to majorities in countless other respects. Preconceptions also operate in forming the stereotypes of the group.

Prejudice may be as much at work in a favorable prejudgment as in an unfavorable one; typically, ambivalent attitudes are involved. A prejudice known from many cultures ascribes unusual sexual attractiveness or prowess to the members of the outgroup—perhaps because the outsiders are exempt from the incest taboos which otherwise inhibit sexual impulses. Whatever its causes, the attitude is as much a matter of prejudice as if it ascribed negative attributes; ambivalence is expressed in the common imputation to the outgroup of immortality and perversion. That "they" are "clever" is another frequent prejudice with ambivalence: intelligence and skill are implied, but also sharp practice and unscrupulousness. I was once asked to advise the headmistress of a convent school in Kyoto, where my daughter was then enrolled, and agreed gladly, expecting to be consulted on pedagogical or curricular problems; what was wanted instead was the financial advice usually given by "our friend Mr. Goldberg," who was traveling in Europe at the time. It was taken for granted that I, too, being a Jew, would be something of a financial wizard. I regret to say that I happed to advise a step which turned out to be successful and thereby contributed, I am afraid, to the prejudices of an otherwise delightfully innocent lady.

When prejudice is sufficiently widespread it prevents the formation of community or destroys whatever sense of community already exists. Confusions and misconceptions which might be called *fallacies of community* are at work. The *fallacy of comparison* is that all groups have well-defined characteristics whose worth is always comparable with those of other groups; there is always a comparison to be made, one group being better and the other worse. If my own group is being compared, the outcome is predictable. The *fallacy of incorpation* assumes that "they" are "after all, just like us," a particulary insidious pattern of thought because it purports to be a repudiation of prejudice, while prejudicially denying differences and also denying that community can accommodate differences. The *fallacy of superiority* does not recognize the right to be average, thinking to overcome prejudice by a compensatory attribution. Here the ambivalent core of prejudice is likely to come into play. As applied to one's own group, this is the pattern of thought underlying *chauvinism:* if it's mine, it must be good, indeed, better than anyone else's. Closely related is the *fallacy of uniqueness*—nothing is valuable unless it is distinctive; hence if "we" have it, "they" don't. This gives rise to an *ego-imperialism,* planting the flag on whatever is worth possessing. It is an inverse of chauvinism, holding that if it's good, it must be mine. Russian claims to various inventions, and the cryptic ancestries assigned to the great by minorities wanting to be identified with them, illustrate the pattern.

As a result of the attitudes sustained by these patterns of thought, community is fragmented. "We" belong, but all others are outsiders—what the Greeks called "barbarians," from a root meaning "to stammer, unable to speak properly." "They" not only are perceived as aliens but ultimately as nonpersons, wholly dehumanized. In the years before the French revolution, ladies of the nobility freely undressed in the presence of servants, much as a woman might unthinkingly do before a pet dog. A century later, Huck Finn, reporting an explosion on a steamboat, was asked if anyone was hurt. "No, ma'am," came the reply; "killed a nigger."

The most deeply rooted and most destructive form of prejudice is *reactive prejudice.* It is the self-contempt and self-hatred the victims of prejudice often come to feel. It may be the result of the mechanism psychologists know as "identifying with the aggressor." It is also the result of the values of the prejudiced majority making their claim on the minority. There are therefore Jewish anti-Semites and racist blacks. Those who suffer from prejudice are often prejudiced themselves, not only as a compensation but as a component of their identification with the envied and emulated majority. The victim may be prejudiced against himself and easily join in the prejudice against other groups. The first act of a new nation which has at last achieved some measure of liberation is to declare its enmity to Israel, as though to show that it has "arrived."

Prejudice in thought and feeling eventually finds overt expression in acts of *discrimination.* What constitutes discrimination is not responding differently to different people. Different responses are appropriate to different stimuli; much learning consists in becoming discriminating in this basic sense. The meaning of discrimination as it bears on social equality is that differential responses are made on the basis of differences which are not *relevant* and, indeed, which may not even exist but are projected by prejudice. The College of Cardinals has more members now than ever before in its history; yet there is not a single Jew among them. Here religion is relevant; the absence of Jews among the top executives of the automobile industry or insurance companies is another matter. It is not always easy to say what is relevant.

Prejudice and discrimination are logically independent; empirically, each strengthens the other. We discriminate against those we view prejudicially; we also become prejudiced against the victims of our discrimination. A teacher recently conducted an experiment in which the blue-eyed children of the class were regularly seated in the back of the room, required to eat at a separate table, not to mix with the others at recess, and so on. Though everyone was fully aware that the discrimination was being artificially imposed, the experience became so painful for the victims that strong parental pressures were brought to bear to stop the experiment. Exclusion from community is a punishment which carries with it a burden of "guilt by dissociation." As the Supreme Court made explicit some decades ago, there cannot be "equal but separate" facilities: inequality is intrinsic to separation.

Many causes of discrimination have been identified. There are political factors; the Hindu castes, for instance, may have resulted from successive waves of invasion. There are economic factors, as in the importation of cheap labor or slaves. Several psychological factors have also been noted: scapegoating—the displacement of hostilities produced by frustrations; the enhancement of an impoverished ego, seeking a content for its negative identity; and insecurity, which imagines that "we" will have nothing to fear if "they" are kept in their place. No simplistic explanation is acceptable; all these factors, and others as well, such as religious ones, are at work.

Probably the largest and oldest identifiable group unable to achieve social equality is women. The theme that women are vicious, dangerous, and destructive is common in the world's folklore and literature, from Jezebel, Xantippe, and Medea to Lady Macbeth and Milady de Winter; they lure men to their destruction or lead them into temptation, like Eve, Helen of Troy, Cleopatra (who "lost Mark Antony the world"), the Lorelei, and Thaïs; they are scheming, willful, and manipulating, like Becky Sharp and Scarlett O'Hara; even when they are weak and foolish, more sinned against than sinning (a phrase first applied to a man victimized by women— King Lear), they are still disastrous, like the Duchess of Malfi or Madame Bovary. The Preacher warns, "I find more bitter than death the woman whose heart is snares and nets." Saint Chrysostom notes that though Satan took so many of his loved ones from Job, he spared Job's wife, for she was doing the devil's work. The ancient Chinese collection of poetry, the *Shih Ching,* includes this ode (as translated by Herbert Giles):

A clever man builds a city,
A clever woman lays one low;
With all her qualifications, that clever woman
Is but an ill-omened bird.
A woman with a long tongue
Is a flight of steps leading to calamity;
For disorder does not come from heaven,
But is brought about by women.
Among those who cannot be trained or taught
Are women and eunuchs.

In the seventeenth century, the dramatist Thomas Otway summed up the prejudice: "destructive, damnable, deceitful woman!"

At best, prejudice presents women as decidedly inferior to men. A woman is only "a lesser man," says Plato in his *Republic,* and Aristotle echoes that woman "may be said to be an inferior man." "I have found one virtuous man among a thousand," the Preacher declares, "but not a single woman among all those." The orthodox Jew daily gives thanks that he was not created a woman—because of the privilege of discharging the religious duties devolving upon man alone; yet the privilege suggests that man is innately more deserving of it. (On the other hand, the *Midrash* explicitly comments that God has given more understanding to woman than to man.) Even a philosopher as concerned about the rights of man (!) as Rousseau denies women aesthetic sensibility: "Women have no love for any art; they have no proper knowledge of any; and they have no genius." Schopenhauer denies that they have any aesthetic attractions: "It is only the man whose intellect is clouded by his sexual impulses who could give the name of the fair sex to that undersized, narrow-shouldered, broad-hipped, and short-legged race." Philosophers are no more free of prejudice than are men who do not profess rationality.

The ambivalent attitudes so often characteristic of prejudice are also expressed here. Women are bad, Nietzsche agrees, but not much worse than men: "Woman was God's *second* mistake." Robert Gordis has pointed out that in the passage quoted earlier, the Preacher found virtue among men to be only one-tenth of one percent more common than among women. Throughout myth and folklore woman is also stereotyped as protective, productive, nurturing, a ministering angel "when pain and anguish wring the brow," as Wordsworth has it. She is the Earth Mother, the source of all strength, as of her son, the giant Antaeus, who was invincible so long as he remained in contact with her; Hercules could overcome him only by lifting him off the ground. Woman is man's indispensable helpmate, a circumstance James Matthew Barrie identified as *What Every Woman Knows;* behind every successful man, so runs the cliché, stands a woman who is man's salvation—as were Ariadne, Medea (what ambivalence there is here!), Solveig. It is woman who is man's inspiration—the Muses, Beatrice, Laura, and Marguerite. All our labor is for her.

With so many prejudices shaping men's attitudes toward women, it is to be expected that discrimination will also be marked, as indeed it has been, from Paul's dictum "Man was not created for the woman, but the woman for the man," to the infamous "Küche, Kirche, Kinder" of the Nazi era. "Sexism" does not consist merely in recognizing women as sexual objects but in restricting them to that role and responding differentially to them on that basis in contexts where the difference is irrelevant. In "sexism" even the sexual role is dehumanized. Don Juan's contrast, "Love is of man's life a thing apart, 'tis woman's whole existence," does a serious injustice to both sexes, denying men meaningful relationships with women and denying women productive work. Even in their sexual role, women are discriminated against in assigning them more the status of symbols than of actualities: their packaged glamour is meant to be looked at but not touched. In other roles the discrimination is more flagrant. In the United States the median income of full-time women workers is two-thirds that of men, often for identical work. (A famous university, defending a legal action against such discrimination, pleaded that it was its male employees who were being *over*paid.)

What is to be done about discrimination? First, we must be ready to acknowledge its existence whenever it does exist. Often it is perpetuated by a conspiracy of silence. Not uncommonly we are prepared to recognize prejudice elsewhere but not to acknowledge that it is at work within ourselves. There is a widespread tactic of *prejudice by projection:* I myself, of course, have no objections at all, but my superiors, or my clients, my colleagues, the public . . ." and so on. Another tactic of denial argues that the response is not discriminatory because it is based on real (and admittedly relevant) differences; the argument is viciously fallacious when it purports to justify discrimination by appealing to the effects produced by the discrimination itself—the *circle of discrimination.* "These people wouldn't know what to do with a college education if it were offered to them," a charge which might be true as a result of continued denial of adequate educational opportunities from the primary grades onward.

Second, we must *deny the relevance* of the bases of discrimination, not deny that differences exist. Discrimination is not overcome but fulfilled if we think to avoid it by abandoning our identity. Some women's liberationists make the mistake of demanding that women be treated like men rather than demanding that society change the way it treats women. On the one hand, the move toward unisex impoverishes both sexes; on the other hand, discrimination is strengthened when it becomes reciprocal and man is treated as an enemy for no other reason than that he is a man. In this state of belligerency between the sexes there are guerrillas and even terrorists, and female chauvinists as well as male. Awareness of a woman's sexual attractiveness is not to be condemned as making her a dehumanized sex object; tenderness toward her does not imply that she is weak; protectiveness does not impute helplessness. There is such a thing as love between men and women after all.

Affirmation of identity, although it implies differentiation from others, does not imply hostility or withdrawal. Prizing one's identity is not sexist, racist, or chauvinistic unless the traits involved in the identification are taken to be innately fixed and invoked in every context whether they are relevant or not. Neither prejudice nor discrimination follows from the recognition that men and women have different habits and preferences, that ethnic groups have different values and characteristic responses, and that nations have different traits and culture patterns. Humanity is all the more enriched by such differences; its life is impoverished when prized differences are replaced by stereotyped and preconceived grounds of hostility and contempt.

Denial of identity leaves an emptiness within when it succeeds, and adds despair to self-contempt when it fails. The most assimilated and the least assimilated European Jewish communities in the first third of this century—the German and the Polish—came to the same dismal end. In India a few decades ago hundreds of thousands of Harijans (the caste of untouchables) converted to Buddhism; other Indians continued to mistreat them as before, with the difference only that when the Indian state was established the converts were no longer eligible for the benefits the new laws were conferring upon members of the lowest castes.

Third, to counter discrimination we must abandon the attempts to deal with it by *symbol magic:* sentimental rhetoric, declarations of principles, and even the intellectualization of "facts and figures." (In the conspiracy of silence mentioned above there is also an element of magic—if we speak no evil, then we will hear no evil and see no evil.) Symbols do have importance when they are used to educate and to stimulate and organize appropriate action. The Master said, "The distance between the mouth and the heart is as great as that between heaven and earth—yet the earth is nourished by rain from heaven."

Fourth, discrimination can be ended only by establishing and maintaining *community*. It is not ended by compensatory discrimination, any more than prejudice is overcome when it is given a favorable content. It did no good to blacks to be seen as having "a great sense of rhythm," to Jews as being "smart," to women as being "intuitive." As to the last, in his autobiography, Henry Adams expressed, almost a century ago, a deeply rooted American myth: "Women have, very commonly, a very positive moral sense; that which they will is right; that which they reject is wrong; and their will, in most cases, ends by settling the moral." This prejudice very probably reinforced the discrimination to which women were subjected: it is not easy to relate as equals to those whom we see as moral authorities and disciplinarians. To provide economic or educational opportunities to members of certain groups on the discriminatory basis that they are members of such groups is likely to impose inequalities on other groups and to legitimize discriminatory practices.

Neither does the tactic of toleration establish and maintain community. To "tolerate" another implies something objectionable as well as a passivity on the part of the tolerant rather than an active involvement with the other on a plane of equality. Here pluralism—the recognition that community does not consist in sameness but in acceptance of difference, the faith that in the house of the Lord there are truly many mansions—is fundamental. Tradition has it that there are seventy ways of interpreting the Law, each nation having its own; only such a pluralistic tradition provides a solid foundation for community.

There is no reason why groups of shared identity should not establish their own communities, provided that there are no ghetto walls, whether their gates are locked from within or without, to preclude the acceptance of differences. To denounce as clannishness the warmth of feeling evoked by shared language, customs, and outlook is not to defend and cherish human values but to undermine them. The person who finds it equally easy to be friendly with everyone is no friend of mine. True, he might deserve veneration as a saint; it is more likely that he is controlling, uncaring, and superficial in his relationships.

Finally, discrimination can be overcome only by *social action,* in contrast to individual resolves and societal pronouncements. The law cannot directly deal with prejudice, for thought and feeling are beyond its reach, and prohibiting the expression of prejudice raises other fundamental issues. The law *can* deal with discrimination, and has been doing so throughout history, for some measure of equality is intrinsic to the very conception of law. The law cannot force a man to love his wife and children, but it *can* compel him to provide for their support. In outlawing discrimination we are also combating prejudice. Over eighteen hundred years ago the martyr Akiba ben Joseph interpreted the Law so as to press the interests of the poor and of labor, to raise the status of women, to secure the rights of aliens, and to limit the prerogatives of priests—all in a spirit of universalism.

Such a religious basis for the ideal of equality—*prophetic universalism*—has played an important part in the history of several cultures. Thus Job: "If I despised the cause of my servant when he contended with me, what shall I do when God rises up? When He remembers, what shall I answer Him: Did not He Who made me also make my fellow man? Did not one God fashion us both?" The brotherhood of man on the basis of the common fatherhood of God has a counterpart in the nontheistic Buddhist religion. "Go into all lands and preach this gospel," said the Buddha. "Tell them that the poor and the lowly, and the rich and the high, are all one, and that all castes unite in this religion as do the rivers in the sea." Such equality is a recurrent theme in *midrashic* lore: God created man from one Adam so that no man could boast of a better ancestry than his fellows; if a messiah claims to be better than any other man he is not truly the Messiah; the voice at Sinai spoke in all languages, truth being revealed equally to everyone; and prayers can be recited by anyone, in any language. The question with which the Talmud begins is, at what time of day is it permissible to recite the morning prayers, after sunset on the preceding evening, after midnight, with the first dawn, when it is broad daylight, or when? Among the various answers discussed, the most memorable is, when there is enough light for a man to recognize his brother; until then we are in such darkness that the time for prayer has not yet come.

An important part, historically, has also been played by a philosophical basis for the ideal of equality: *rationalist universalism,* the doctrine that men are equals as sharing in the faculty of reason. Spinoza echoes the rationalist universalism of Maimonides when he says, "Books which teach and speak of whatever is highest and best are equally sacred, whatever be the tongue in which they are written, or the nation to which they belong." Plato's ideal state institutionalizes inequalities, for he supposes philosophers to be more rational than other men, while Aristotle holds that some men are "by nature" born to be masters and others slaves. The Stoics, however, promulgated equality and internationalism on the basis of man's sharing in universal Reason. "Nature has made us relatives," said Seneca, "when it begat us from the same materials and for the same destinies." "My nature is rational and social," Marcus Aurelius declared; "so far as I am Antoninus, my city and my country is Rome; so far as I am a man, it is the world." Epictetus was forthright: "You are a citizen and a part of the world."

The idea of a fundamental equality of all men passed by way of Stoic philosophical theory and Roman legal practice into the tradition of "natural law," significant contributions being made by Thomas Aquinas in the thirteenth century, Hugo Grotius in the seventeenth century, and John Locke, who, in the eighteenth century, markedly influenced Thomas Jefferson and other founders of the American republic. The Declaration of Independence holds it to be a self-evident truth that all men are created equal, the reference to self-evidence harking back to the philosophical basis of equality, while mention of being created invokes the religious basis as well. There was never any question in either tradition of affirming an equality in regard to the actual capacities of men, but only in regard to their rights—especially in regard to their equality before the law. Kant defines civil equality as "the right of the citizen to recognize no one as a superior among the people in relation to himself"—superior, that is, in the juridical attributes belonging to the citizen as such. Here social and political issues intermingle.

The *cha-shitsu,* the teahouse of the Japanese ceremony shaped by Zen, has a low doorway, through which one is obliged to enter almost on all fours. Zen, though appealing especially to the samurai and noblemen of a stratified aristocracy, nevertheless espoused a certain ideal of equality, for all men are as one when they have reduced their lives to the essentials. The door of the teahouse is so low as to require all who would enter to remove their swords and pass through in the posture of humility. The symbolism is political, moral, religious, and aesthetic. . . .

# 12

# The Nature of Hatred

## Gordon W. Allport

Anger is a transitory emotional state, aroused by thwarting some on-going activity. Since it is aroused at a given time by an identifiable stimulus, it leads to impulses to attack the source of the frustration directly and to inflict injury upon this source.

Long ago Aristotle pointed out that anger differed from hatred in that anger is customarily felt toward individuals only, whereas hatred may be felt toward whole classes of people. He observed, too, that a person who gives way to anger is often sorry for his outburst and pities the object of his attack, but in expressing hatred, repentance seldom follows. Hatred is more deep-rooted, and constantly "desires the extinction of the object of hate."[1]

To put the matter another way, we may say that anger is an emotion, whereas hatred must be classified as a sentiment—an enduring organization of aggressive impulses toward a person or toward a class of persons. Since it is composed of habitual bitter feeling and accusatory thought, it constitutes a stubborn structure in the mental-emotional life of the individual. By its very nature hatred is extropunitive, which means that the hater is sure that the fault lies in the object of his hate. So long as he believes this he will not feel guilty for his uncharitable state of mind.

There is a good reason why out-groups are often chosen as the object of hate and aggression rather than individuals. One human being is, after all, pretty much like another—like oneself. One can scarcely help but sympathize with the victim. To attack him would be to arouse some pain in ourselves. Our own "body image" would be involved, for his body is like our own body. But there is no body image of a group. It is more abstract, more impersonal. It is especially so if there is some visibly distinguishing characteristic. A different-colored skin removes the person to some extent from our own circle. We are less likely to consider him an individual, and more likely to think of him only as an out-group member. But even so, he remains at least partially like ourselves.

This sympathizing tendency seems to explain a phenomenon we have frequently noted: people who hate groups in the abstract will, in actual conduct, often act fairly and even kindly toward individual members of the group.

There is another reason why it is easier to hate groups than individuals. We do not need to test our unfavorable stereotype of a group against reality. In fact, we can hold it all the more easily if we make "exceptions" for the individual members we know.

[Eric] Fromm points out that it is essential to distinguish between two kinds of hate: one might be called "rational," the other, "character conditioned."[2] The former kind serves an important biological function. It arises when fundamental natural rights of persons are violated. One hates whatever threatens his own freedom, life, and values. Also, if well socialized, he hates whatever threatens the freedom, lives, and values of other human beings.

Rational hatred does not concern us so much as "character-conditioned" hatred. Here we have, as Fromm points out, a continuing readiness to hate. The sentiment has little relation to reality, although it may be the product of a long series of bitter disappointments in life. These frustrations become fused into a kind of "free-floating hatred"—the subjective counterpart of free-floating aggression. The person carries a vague, temperamental sense of wrong which he wishes to polarize. He must hate *something*. The real roots of the hatred may baffle him, but he thinks up some convenient victim and some good reason. The Jews are conspiring against him, or the politicians are set on making things worse. Thwarted lives have the most character-conditioned hate.

Neither kind of hatred can exist unless something one values has been violated. Love is a precondition of hate. Always some affiliative relationship is interrupted before the agent thought to be responsible for the interruption can be hated.

What governs an individual at the beginning of his life is a dependent, affiliative relationship with the mother. There is little, if any, evidence of destructive instincts. After birth, the affiliative attachment of the child to his environment still remains dominant while nursing, resting, playing. The social smile early symbolizes contentment with people. Toward his entire environment the baby is positive, approaching nearly every type of stimulus, every type of person. His life is marked by eager outgoingness and, normally, by positive social relationships.

The initial affiliative tendencies, when threatened or frustrated, may give way to alarm and defense. Ian Suttie puts the matter picturesquely, "Earth hath no hate but love to hatred turned, and hell no fury but a baby scorned."[3] Thus, the genesis of hatred is secondary, contingent, and relatively late in the development process. It is always a matter of frustrated affiliative desire and the attendant humiliation to one's self-esteem or to one's values.

Perhaps the most perplexing problem in the entire field of human relations is this: why do so relatively few of our contacts with other people fit in with, and satisfy, our predominating affiliative needs, and why do so many find their way into sentiments of hatred and hostility? Why are loyalties and loves so few and restricted, when at bottom human beings feel that they can never love or be loved enough?

The answer to this riddle seems to lie in three directions. One concerns the amount of frustration and the hardness of living that beset people. Because of severe frustration it is easy to fuse one's recurring anger into rationalized hatreds. In order to avoid hurt and achieve at least an island of security it is safer to exclude than to include.

A second explanation has to do with the learning process. We have seen that children brought up in a rejective home, exposed to ready-made prejudices, will scarcely be in a position to develop a trustful or affiliative outlook upon social relationships. Having received little affection, they are not in a position to give it.

Finally, there is a kind of economy in adopting an exclusionist approach to human relations. By taking a negative view of great groups of mankind, we somehow make life simpler. For example, if I reject all foreigners as a category, I don't have to bother with them—except to keep them out of my country. If I can ticket, then, all Negroes as comprising an inferior and objectionable race, I conveniently dispose of a tenth of my fellow citizens. If I can put the Catholics into another category and reject them, my life is still further simplified. I then pare again and slice off the Jews . . . and so it goes.

Thus the prejudiced pattern, involving various degrees and kinds of hatred and aggression, takes its place in the individual's world view. It has an economy about it that we cannot deny. Still it falls considerably short of the dreams men have for themselves. At bottom they still long for affiliation with life and peaceful and friendly relations with their fellow men.

NOTES

1. Aristotle. *Rhetoric*. Book II.
2. E. Fromm. *Man for Himself*. New York: Rinehart, 1947, 214ff.
3. I. D. Suttie. *The Origins of Love and Hate*. London: Kegan Paul, 1935, 23.

# 13

# Portrait of the Anti-Semite

## Jean-Paul Sartre

If a man attributes all or part of his own or the country's misfortunes to the presence of Jewish elements in the . . . community, if he proposes remedying this state of affairs by depriving the Jews of some of their rights or by expelling or exterminating them, he is then said to hold anti-Semitic *opinions*.

This word *opinion* gives us food for thought. It is the word which the mistress of the house uses to end a discussion that is becoming too embittered. It suggests that all judgments are of equal value, thus reassuming and giving an inoffensive cast to thoughts by assimilating them to tastes. There are all kinds of tastes in nature, all opinions are permissible; tastes, ideas, opinions must not be discussed. In the name of democratic institutions, in the name of freedom of opinion, the anti-Semite claims the right to preach his anti-Jewish crusade everywhere. At the same time, used as we are . . . to seeing each object in an analytical spirit, that is, as if it were a whole which can be divided into its component parts, we look at people and characters as if they were mosaics, every stone of which coexists with the others without this coexistence affecting its inherent nature. Thus an anti-Semitic opinion appears like a molecule which can combine with any other set of molecules without changing itself. A man can be a good father and a good husband, a zealous citizen, cultured, philanthropic and an anti-Semite at the same time. He may like to go

First appeared in *Partisan Review* 8, no. 2 (1946). Translated by Mary Guggenheim.

fishing and he may like the pleasures of love, he may be tolerant about religion, full of generous ideas about the condition of the natives of Central Africa—and still despise the Jews. If he does not like them, people say, it is because his experience has taught him that they are bad, because statistics have taught him that they are dangerous, because certain historical factors have influenced his judgment. Thus this opinion seems to be the result of external causes and those who want to study it will neglect the anti-Semite himself and make much of the percentage of Jews mobilized in 1914, of the percentage of Jews who are bankers, industrialists, doctors, lawyers, of the history of the Jews in France. They will succeed in laying before us a strictly objective situation determining a certain current of likewise objective opinion which they will call anti-Semitism, a chart of which they can draw up or the variations of which they can establish from 1870 to 1944. In this way, anti-Semitism seems to be both a subjective taste which combines with other tastes to form the person, and an impersonal and social phenomenon which can be expressed by means of statistics and averages, conditioned by economic, historical, and political constants.

I do not say that these two concepts are necessarily contradictory. I say that they are dangerous and false. I might, strictly speaking, admit that one might have an "opinion" about the government's wine-growing policy, that is, that one might decide for this or that reason to approve or condemn the free importation of wines from Algeria. But I refuse to call an opinion a doctrine which is expressly directed toward particular persons and which tends to suppress their rights or to exterminate them. The Jew whom the anti-Semite wants to reach is not a schematic being defined only by his function as in administrative law, or by his position or his acts as in the legal code. He is a Jew, son of a Jew, recognizable by his physical traits, by the color of his hair, by his clothing perhaps, and they say by his character. Anti-Semitism is not in the category of thoughts protected by the right to freedom of opinion.

Moreover, it is much more than an idea. It is first and foremost a *passion*. Doubtless it can present itself in the form of a theoretical proposition. The "moderate" anti-Semite is a polite person who gently remarks: "I don't detest Jews. I simply prefer for such and such a reason that they play a lesser part in the activity of the nation." But a moment later— if you have won his confidence—he will add the following with more abandon: "You see there must be 'something' about the Jews: physically they are irritating to me." This argument, which I have heard a hundred times, is worth examining. First of all, it is the result of using logic dictated by passion. For can you imagine someone saying seriously: "There must be something about tomatoes because I can't bear them." Moreover it shows that anti-Semitism, even in its most moderate and evolved forms, remains a syncretic totality which is expressed by statements that appear reasonable but which can lead to corporeal modifications. Some men suddenly become impotent if they find out that the woman to whom they are making love is a Jewess. Some people feel disgust for the Jew, just as some others feel disgust for the Chinaman or the Negro. Thus this revulsion is not based on something physical, since you could very well love a Jewess if you didn't know what race she belonged to, but it reaches the body through the mind; it is an involvement of the mind so deep, so complete, that it extends to the physiological as in cases of hysteria.

This involvement is not provoked by experience. I have questioned a hundred people about the reasons for their anti-Semitism. Most of them limit themselves to enumerating the faults which are traditionally attributed to the Jew. "I hate them because they are selfish, intriguing, hard to get rid of, oily, tactless, etc."—"But at least you do go with some Jews?"— "Indeed not!" A painter said to me: "I'm hostile to Jews because, with their critical habit of mind, they encourage our servants to become in-disciplined." Here are some more precise experiences. A young actor with-out talent asserted that the Jews kept him from having a career in the theater by always giving him servile jobs. A young woman said to me: "I've had terrible rows with furriers, they've robbed me, they've burned the furs I entrusted to them. Well, they were all Jews." But why did she choose to hate Jews rather than furriers? Why Jews or furriers rather than such and such a Jew or such and such a furrier? Because she had a predisposition to anti-Semitism. A classmate of mine at the lycee told me that Jews "irritated" him because of the thousand injustices which "bejewed" social organizations committed in their favor. "A Jew got a scholarship the year I missed it and you're not going to try to make me believe that that fellow whose father came from Krakow or Lemberg understood one of Ronsard's poems or one of Virgil's eclogues better than I." But he admitted the next moment that he disdained the scholarship, that it was all a muddle and that he hadn't prepared for the competition. Thus he had two systems of interpretation to explain his failure, like an insane man who in his delirium pretends to be the King of Hungary but when suddenly put to the test admits that he is a shoemaker. His thinking moves on two planes without the least difficulty. Better still, he will succeed in justifying his past laziness by saying that it would have been too silly to prepare for an examination in which Jews are passed in preference to good Frenchmen. Moreover he was 27th on the final list. There were 26 before him, 12 of whom were accepted and 14 were not. Would he have gotten any further if Jews had been excluded altogether? And even if he had been the first of those who were not accepted, even if by eliminating one of the successful candidates he could have had his chance to be accepted, my classmate had to adopt in advance a certain idea of the Jew, of his nature, of his social role. And in order to be able to decide that among 26 more fortunate contestants it was the Jew who stole his place, he would apriori have to be the kind of person who runs his life on the basis of emotional reasoning.

It becomes obvious that no external factor can induce anti-Semitism in the anti-Semite. It is an attitude totally and freely self-chosen, a global attitude which is adopted not only in regard to Jews but in regard to men in general, to history and society; it is a passion and at the same time a concept of the world. No doubt certain characteristics are more pronounced in such and such an anti-Semite than in another. But they are always present together and they govern one another. It is this syncretic totality which we must now try to describe.

I stated a few minutes ago that anti-Semitism presents itself as a passion. Everyone has understood that it is a question of hate or anger. But ordinarily hate and anger are provoked: I hate the person who has made me suffer, the person who scorns or insults me. We have just seen that the anti-Semitic passion is not of such a nature: it precedes the facts which should arouse it, it seeks them out to feed upon, it must even interpret them in its own way in order to render them really offensive. And yet if you speak of the Jew to an anti-Semite, he evinces signs of lively irritation. If we remember, moreover, that we must *consent* to anger before it can manifest itself, and that we *grow* angry, to use the correct expression, we must admit that anti-Semitism has chosen to exist on the passionate level. It is not unusual to choose an emotional way of life rather than a reasonable one. But ordinarily one loves the *objects* of passion: women, glory, power, money. Since the anti-Semite has chosen hatred, we are forced to conclude that it is the emotional state that he loves. Ordinarily this kind of feeling is not pleasing: he who passionately desires a woman is passionate because of the woman and in spite of passion: one distrusts emotional reasoning which by every means aims at pointing out opinions dictated by love or jealousy or hate; one mistrusts passionate aberrations and that which has been termed monoideism. And this is what the anti-Semite chooses first of all. But how can one choose to reason falsely? Because one feels the nostalgia of impermeability. The rational man seeks the truth gropingly, he knows that his reasoning is only probable, that other considerations will arise to make it doubtful; he never knows too well where he's going, he is "open," he may even appear hesitant. But there are people who are attracted by the durability of stone. They want to be massive and impenetrable, they do not want to change: where would change lead them? This is an original fear of oneself and a fear of truth. And what frightens them is not the content of truth which they do not even suspect, but the very form of the true—that thing of indefinite approximation. It is as if their very existence were perpetually in suspension. They want to exist all at once and right away. They do not want acquired opinions, they want them to be innate; since they are afraid of reasoning, they want to adopt a mode of life in which reasoning and research play but a subordinate role, in which one never seeks but that which one has already found, in which one never becomes other than what one already was. Only passion can produce this. Nothing but a strong emotional bias can give instant certitude, it alone can hold reasoning within limits, it alone can remain impervious to experience and last an entire lifetime. The anti-Semite has chosen hate because hate is a religion: he has originally chosen to devaluate words and reasons. Since he then feels at ease, since discussions about the right of the Jew appear futile and empty to him, he has at the outset placed himself on another level. If out of courtesy he consents momentarily to defend his point of view, he lends himself without giving himself; he simply tries to project his intuitive certainty onto the field of speech.

A few moments ago I quoted some statements made by anti-Semites, all of them absurd: "I hate Jews because they teach indiscipline to servants, because a Jewish furrier robbed me, etc." Do not think that anti-Semites are completely unaware of the absurdity of these answers. They know that their statements are empty and contestable; but it amuses them to make such statements: it is their adversary whose duty it is to choose his words seriously because he believes in words. They have a *right* to play. They even like to play with speech because by putting forth ridiculous reasons, they discredit the seriousness of their interlocutor; they are enchanted with their unfairness because for them it is not a question of persuading by good argument but of intimidating or disorienting. If you insist too much they close up, they point out with one superb word that the time to argue has passed. Not that they are afraid of being convinced: their only fear is that they will look ridiculous or that their embarrassment will make a bad impression on a third party whom they want to get on their side. Thus if the anti-Semite is impervious, as everyone has been able to observe, to reason and experience, it is not because his conviction is so strong, but rather his conviction is strong because he has chosen to be impervious. . . .

But, you will say, what if he were only that way in regard to Jews? If he conducted himself sensibly in regard to all other matters? I answer that this is impossible: here is a fishmonger who, in 1942, irritated by the competition of two Jewish fishmongers who made a secret of their race, picked up a pen one day and denounced them. I was assured that in other respects he was kind and jovial, the best son in the world. But I don't believe it: a man who finds it natural to denounce men cannot have our concept of the humane; he does not even see those whom he aids in the same light as we do; his generosity, his kindness are not like our kindness, our generosity; one cannot localize passion.

The anti-Semite willingly admits that the Jew is intelligent and hard-working. He will even admit that he is inferior to him in this respect. This concession costs him little. He has put these qualities, as it were, in parentheses. Or rather, they draw their merit from the man who possesses them: the more virtues a Jew has, the more dangerous he is. As for the anti-Semite, he has no illusions about what he is. He considers himself an average man, modestly average, and in the last analysis a mediocre person. There is no example of an anti-Semite claiming individual superiority over the Jews. But do not believe for a second that this mediocrity is cause for shame. On the contrary, he is well satisfied with it, I might even say he has chosen it. This man is afraid of any kind of solitude, that of the genius as well as that of the murderer: he is the man of the mob; no matter how short he is, he still takes the precaution of stooping for fear of standing out from the herd and of finding himself face to face with himself. If he has become an anti-Semite, it is because one cannot be anti-Semitic alone. This sentence: "I hate the Jews," is a sentence which is said in chorus; by saying it one connects oneself with a tradition and a community: that of the mediocre man. It is also well to recall that by consenting to mediocrity one is not necessarily humble, nor even modest. It is just the opposite: there is a passionate pride in being mediocre and anti-Semitism is an attempt to make mediocrity as such a virtue, to create an elite of the mediocre. For the anti-Semite, intelligence is Jewish, he can therefore disdain it in all tranquility, like all other Jewish virtues: these are all ersatz qualities which the Jews use to replace the well-balanced mediocrity which they will always lack. . . .

We begin to understand that anti-Semitism is not simply an "opinion" about the Jews and that it involves the entire personality of the anti-Semite. We are not done with him yet: for he does not limit himself to furnishing moral and political directives. He is a process of thought and a worldview all in himself. One would in fact be unable to affirm what he affirms without implicitly referring to certain intellectual principles. The Jew, he says, is entirely bad and entirely Jewish; his virtues, if any, become vices simply because they are *his* virtues, the work that comes from his hands necessarily bears his stigma: and if he builds a bridge, this bridge is bad because it is Jewish from the first span to the last. The same act committed by a Jew and by a Christian is by no means identical in the two cases. The Jew renders execrable everything he touches. The first thing the Germans did was to forbid Jews the use of swimming pools: it seemed to them that if the body of a Jew plunged into this water, it would be utterly tainted. The Jew literally sullies even the air he breathes. . . .

Everything becomes clear if we give up expecting the Jew to behave reasonably in conformity with his interests, if we discern in him, on the contrary, a metaphysical principle which forces him *to do evil* under all circumstances, though in so doing he destroys himself. . . . [T]he Jew is free *to do evil*, not good. He has only as much free will as is necessary to bear the full responsibility of the crimes he commits, but not enough to be able to reform. Strange freedom which instead of preceding and constituting the essence, remains entirely subordinate to it, and which is but an irrational quality of it and yet remains freedom!

There is but one creature to my knowledge, as totally free and wedded to evil and that is the Spirit of Evil, Satan himself. Thus the Jew is assimilable to the spirit of evil. His will, contrary to the Kantian will, is one which desires to be purely, gratuitously, and universally evil, it is *the will to evil*. Evil comes to the world through him; all that is bad in society (crises, wars, famines, upheavals, and revolts) is directly or indirectly imputable to the Jew. The anti-Semite is afraid of discovering that the world is badly made: for then things would have to be invented, modified, and man would find himself once more master of his fate, filled with agonizing and infinite responsibility. He localizes all the evil of the universe in the Jew. If nations wage war, it is not due to the fact that the idea of nationalism in its present form involves imperialism and conflict of interests. No, the Jew is there breathing discord—somewhere behind all governments. If there is class struggle, it is not caused by an economic organization which leaves something to be desired: it is because Jewish ringleaders, hook-nosed agitators, have seduced the workers. Thus anti-Semitism is primarily Manicheanism; it explains the course of the world by the struggle between the principles of Good and Evil. There is no conceivable truce between these two principles: one of them must of necessity triumph and the other be destroyed. . . .

The anti-Semitic Manichean['s] emphasis is on destruction. It is not a question of a conflict of interests but of the damage that an evil power causes to society. Behind the bitterness of the anti-Semite is concealed the belief that harmony will be reestablished of itself once evil has been ejected. His task therefore is purely negative: there is no question of building a society but only of purifying the one that exists. Like the Good Knight, the anti-Semite is sacred; but the Jew is also sacred in his own way: sacred like the untouchables, like taboo natives. Thus the battle is waged on a religious level and the end of the struggle can only be an act of sacred destruction. The advantages of this position are multiple: first of all it favors sluggishness of mind. We have seen that the anti-Semite understands nothing concerning modern society, and he would be incapable of inventing a constructive plan; his action cannot be put on the technical level, it remains basically emotional. He prefers an explosion of rage. . . . His intellectual activity limits itself to *interpretation;* in historical events he seeks the sign of the presence of an evil power. Whence these puerile and complicated inventions which render him comparable to the real paranoiac. The anti-Semite, moreover, canalizes revolutionary thrusts toward the destruction of certain men, not institutions; an anti-Semitic mob would consider that it had done enough if it had massacred a few Jews and burned a few synagogues. It therefore represents a safety valve for the ruling classes which encourage it. . . . But, above all, this naive dualism is eminently reassuring to the anti-Semite himself: if it is only a matter of getting rid of Evil, it means that Good is already *assumed.* There is no reason to seek it in anguish, to invent it, to debate it patiently when one has found it, to prove it in action, to verify its consequences and finally to saddle oneself with the reponsibilities of the moral choice thus made. It is not by chance that the great anti-Semitic uprisings hide a kind of optimism: the anti-Semite has decided about evil so as not to have to decide about the good. The more absorbed I become in combatting Evil, the less I am tempted to question the Good. . . . When he has fulfilled his mission as the sacred destroyer, the Lost Paradise will rebuild itself. For the time being the anti-Semite is absorbed by so many duties that he has no time to think about it: he is forever on the verge, he fights and each of his outbursts of indignation is a pretext which distracts him from the anguished search for the good.

But there is more to it and at this point we approach the domain of psychoanalysis. Manicheanism masks a profound attraction to evil. For the anti-Semite, evil is his lot, his "job." Others will come later who will be concerned with good, if need be. He is at the outpost of society, he turns his back on the pure virtues which he defends; he deals only with evil, his duty is to unmask it, to denounce it, to establish its dimensions.

Thus we see that he is solely worried about amassing anecdotes which reveal the lewdness of the Jew, his cupidity, his ruses, and his betrayals. He washes his hands in filth. One should reread Drumont's *La France Juive:* this book "characterized by high French morality" is a collection of ignoble and obscene stories. Nothing better reflects the complex nature of the anti-Semite: since he did not want to *choose* his own good and, for fear of being different, allowed everyone else's concept of the good to be imposed upon him, his ethics are never based on the intuition of values or on what Plato calls Love; it manifests itself only by the strictest taboos, by the severest and most gratuitous imperatives. But the thing he contemplates constantly, the thing he understands intuitively and has a taste for is evil. He can thus minutely examine to the point of obsession the description of obscene or criminal acts which trouble him and which satisfy his perverse leanings; but since, at the same time, he attributes them to these infamous Jews whom he treats with disdain he can seek gratification without compromising himself. In Berlin I knew a Protestant whose sexual desire took the form of indignation. The sight of women in bathing suits infuriated him; he welcomed this rage, spending his time in swimming pools. The anti-Semite does the same thing.

One of the components of his hatred is a deep sexual attraction to Jews. First of all it is curiosity fascinated by evil. But above all, I believe, it is connected with sadism. We understand nothing about anti-Semitism if we do not recall that the Jew, the object of such loathing, is perfectly innocent, I might even say inoffensive. The anti-Semite is also careful to tell us about secret Jewish organizations, of terrifying clandestine free-masonry. But if he meets a Jew face to face he is most of the time a weak individual who, ill prepared for violence, does not even succeed in defending himself. The anti-Semite is not unaware of this individual weak-ness of the Jew which makes him the helpless victim of pogroms. In fact, this situation delights him. Hatred of the Jew is not comparable to the hatred which the Italians felt for the Austrians in 1830 or to that which the French felt for the Germans in 1942. In the last two cases it was a question of oppressors, of hard, cruel, and strong men who possessed arms, money, power, and who could do more harm to rebels than the latter could have dreamt of doing to them. The sadistic tendency was not an element of this hatred. But since evil for the anti-Semite is incarnate in these unarmed and harmless men, he never finds himself in the painful necessity of being heroic: it is *amusing* to be anti-Semitic. One can beat and torture the Jews without fear: the most they can do is to appeal to the laws of the Republic; but the laws are not hard. The sadistic attraction to the Jew which the anti-Semite feels is so strong that it is not unusual to see one of these sworn enemies of Israel surround himself with Jewish friends. Of course he calls them "exceptional Jews," he says: "They aren't like the others." In a prominent place in the studio of the painter whom I mentioned a little while ago and who in no way reproached the butchers of Lublin, there was a portrait of a Jew who was a dear friend of his and whom the Gestapo had executed. But such protestations of friendship are not sincere, for there is no idea in their conversation of sparing the "good Jews"; and while recognizing some virtues in those they know, they do not admit the fact that their interlocutors might also have met some who were equally good. In fact, it pleases them to protect these few people by a kind of inversion of their sadism; they like to keep before their eyes the living picture of these people whom they despise. Anti-Semitic women often feel a mixture of repugnance and sexual attraction for Jews. One whom I knew had intimate relations with a Polish Jew. She sometimes got into bed with him and let him caress her breasts and shoulders, but nothing more. She got enormous pleasure from the fact that he was respectful and submissive and also from the fact that she divined his violently frustrated and humiliated desire. She afterwards had normal sexual relations with other men. In the words "a beautiful Jewess" there is a specific sexual connotation, very different from that which is understood in the words "a beautiful Romanian," "a beautiful Greek woman," or "a beautiful American." The phrase "a beautiful Jewess" has a kind of flavor of rape and massacre. The beautiful Jewess is the woman whom the Czar's cossacks drag by the hair through the streets of a flaming village; and the special works devoted to descriptions of flagellation give Jewesses a place of honor. But we do not have to search through esoteric literature. From Rebecca in *Ivanhoe* down to the Jewess in "Gilles," not to leave out those of *Ponson du Terrail,* Jewesses have a well-defined function in the most serious novels. Frequently raped or beaten, they sometimes succeed in escaping dishonor by death, but that is as it should be; those who keep their virtue are docile servants or humiliated women in love with indifferent Christians who marry Aryans. No more is needed to show the sexually symbolic importance of the Jewess in folklore.

With destruction his function, the anti-Semite—a sadist pure of heart—is in the depths of his soul a criminal. What he desires and prepares is the *death* of the Jew. Of course all the enemies of the Jew do not overtly demand his death, but the measures which they propose and which are all aimed at his debasement, his humiliation, his banishment, are the prerequisites of this murder which they are contemplating: they are symbolic murders. Only the anti-Semite has a clear conscience: he is a criminal with a worthy motive. It is not his fault after all if his mission is to destroy evil with evil. . . . Of course he does not have occasion to use them everyday, but make no mistake: these sudden outbreaks of anger, these thunderous reproaches which he hurls against "kikes," are so many death sentences. Popular awareness divined this and invented the expression "Jew baiting." Thus the anti-Semite has chosen to be a criminal—a *pure* criminal: here again he evades responsibilities, he has censured his instinct for murder but he has found a way of satisfying it without admitting it to himself. He knows he is bad but since he is doing evil *for the sake of good;* since a whole people is awaiting deliverance at his hands, he considers himself a sort of bad sacred bull. By a kind of inversion of all values, examples of which we find in certain religions and, for instance, in India, where there is sacred prostitution, it is to anger, pillage, murder, and all forms of violence that the anti-Semite accords respect and enthusiasm; and at the very moment he is drunk with evil, he feels the lightness of heart and the peace afforded by a clear conscience and the satisfaction of duty well done. . . .

We can now understand him. He is a man who is afraid. Not of the Jews of course, but of himself, of his conscience, of his freedom, of his instincts, of his responsibilities, of solitude, of change, of society and the world; of everything except the Jews. He is a coward who does not want to admit his cowardice to himself; a murderer who represses and censures his penchant for murder without being able to restrain it and who nevertheless does not dare to kill except in effigy or in the anonymity of a mob; a malcontent who dares not revolt for fear of the consequences of his rebellion. By adhering to anti-Semitism, he is not only adopting an opinion, he is choosing himself as a person. He is choosing the permanence and the impenetrability of rock, the total irresponsibility of the warrior who obeys his leaders—and he has no leader. He chooses to acquire nothing, to deserve nothing but that everything be given him as his birthright— and he is not noble. He chooses finally, that good be ready made, not in question, out of reach; he dare not look at it for fear of being forced to contest it and seek another form of it. The Jew is only a pretext: elsewhere it will be the Negro, the yellow race. The Jew's existence simply allows the anti-Semite to nip his anxieties in the bud by persuading himself that his place has always been cut out in the world, that it was waiting for him and that by virtue of tradition he has the right to occupy it. Anti-Semitism, in a word, is fear of man's fate. The anti-Semite is the man who wants to be pitiless stone, furious torrent, devastating lightning: in short, everything but a man.

# 14

# The Construction, Deconstruction, and Reconstruction of Difference

## Paula Rothenberg

The construction of difference is central to racism, sexism, and other forms of oppressive ideologies. Few theorists have better understood the importance of constructing difference and the centrality of that construction to racism (and by extension, other forms of oppression) than Albert Memmi (1971, 186–95). At a time when liberal theoreticians still grounded their political philosophy on a metaphysic that accepted "natural" differences between women and men and then set out to win certain rights for women by arguing over which differences provided a legitimate basis for limiting women's rights and which did not, Memmi had already recognized that difference was created not discovered. "Making use of the difference is an essential step in the racist process," he wrote, "but it is not the difference which always entails racism; it is racism which makes use of the difference" (1971, 187). This insight prompted Memmi to define racism as

. . . the generalized and final assigning of value to real or imaginary difference, to the accuser's benefit and at his victim's expense, in order to justify the former's privileges or aggression. (1971, 185)

From *Hypatia* 5. no. 1 (Spring 1990): 42-57. Copyright © 1990 by Paula Rothenberg. Reprinted by permission of the author.

Note that it is the process of assigning value to difference, not whether the difference is real or imagined, that is the key to the process by which "the racist aims to intensify or cause the *exclusion,* the *separation* by which the victim is placed outside the community or even outside humanity" (Memmi 1971, 187). Placing the victim outside humanity is of course essential if one is to justify the inhumanity of slavery and colonialism. Placing the victim outside the community (of equals, or adults, or decent women) is essential if one is to rationalize the violence and the denial of personhood that lies at the heart of sexism.

What Memmi failed to notice, however, is the two-sided or dialectical nature of the process wherein difference is defined. For it is not only the racist or sexist who constructs difference but the victim of each or both who seeks to create difference as well. At times the "victim" has done so in response to the racism and/or sexism of the society in order to survive, but at other times movements made up of these "victims" have sought to redefine difference as part of a struggle for power and personhood.[1] At least in part this is because the particular paradigm for expressing race or gender difference that holds sway in society at any given moment carries with it both implicit and explicit prescriptions for social policy. At certain moments in history, oppressed people have been able to exert control over the process of defining difference with a view to reconstructing difference in what they perceive to be their own interest. Social, political, and intellectual disagreements or struggles over both the appropriate social construction of race and gender and disagreements about the appropriateness of particular paradigms of race and gender can best be understood as disputes over the nature of difference that the society is prepared to establish and by implication the nature of the social policies it is prepared to entertain.

## THE CONSTRUCTION OF DIFFERENCE

If we undertake a historical survey of the construction of difference in the United States, we find that difference claims have been expressed in the vocabulary of numerous different ideologies. In spite of the historical specificity which determines the form and content of each particular claim, we can distinguish three fundamental categories according to which race and gender difference has been alleged: difference in nature, difference in moral sensibilities, and difference in culture and/or values (Whitbeck 1975). Claims about difference in nature have been the most numerous and have assumed the most diverse forms. At times they have been attributed to biology, to physiognomy, to genetic makeup, and so forth. Difference in moral sensibilities has alternately been treated as either innate or acquired, and the cultural/value differences have received similar treatment. It is not uncommon for one or more of these categories of difference to be used in combination.

Claims about difference are often difficult to deal with precisely because they are offered under the guise of value-free descriptions yet smuggle in normative considerations that carry with them the stigma of inferiority. Where white, male, middle-class, European heterosexuality provides the standard of and the criteria for rationality and morality, difference is always perceived as deviant and deficient.[2] In addition, though difference claims are usually couched in the language of the academy, most often bearing the trappings of the natural or social sciences, difference claims are essentially metaphysical. Even though they often point to or allege some readily observable difference, such as skull size, brain weight, or family structure, a reasoned refutation of the empirical claim rarely results in a change in attitude on the part of those who allege difference. They merely seek some other vocabulary or conceptual framework in which to reformulate their charge. This has led some thinkers to suggest that racism (and, by extension, sexism) have the belief status of delusions which by definition are impervious to contrary evidence (Pierce 1974, 513).

## THE NATURE/BIOLOGY PARADIGM

Underlying all racism and sexism is the notion of a natural or biological difference alleged to separate the groups in question in a fundamental, inevitable, and irreversible way. This natural difference is then called upon to explain any and all observable differences in opportunity or achievement between white people and people of color or men and all women. Science, medicine, religion, and the law have all made important contributions to the force and longevity of this theory providing "evidence" to ground this basic claim of natural inferiority. The strength of the paradigm lies in its ability to translate readily observable physical differences in appearance into qualitative and even "moral" differences.

While the idea of natural difference is central to both racism and sexism, it functions somewhat differently in each. In the case of race, the nature/biology paradigm is used to portray a difference in nature between whites and blacks so fundamental and so enormous as to exclude black people from the human community and thus make it possible for otherwise kind and decent people to carry out the unspeakable acts of inhumanity and violation that constitute the history of slavery and its aftermath.

Sexism works differently. Since men have mothers and often have wives, daughters, and sisters as well, the nature/biology paradigm expresses a weaker form of difference with respect to gender. Women are not portrayed as excluded from humanity but as separated from the relevant community, be it the community of men or adults. While racist ideology has entertained the question as to whether or not black people were part of the human species and has, at times, answered in the negative, sexist ideology has simply sought to exclude women by virtue of their nature from membership in the community that enjoyed or had a proper claim to certain privileges or rights.

The weak version of this same paradigm, which evolves after the Civil War and is bound up with the Industrial Revolution, offers white women a "separate sphere." Here difference is seen as endowing white women with certain noble or positive attributes which fit them for certain important roles that men are unable to fulfill. This complementary paradigm of gender difference replaces natural inferiority with "different and better if not equal." In doing so, it manages to preserve the sense of difference which excludes all women from certain areas and functions (and rights and privileges) but sugarcoats this exclusion with the assurance that that sphere isn't worthy of women anyway.

No comparable weak version of the paradigm exists for race nor does the weak version itself apply to black women. Beginning with slavery, black women are excluded from the community of women who need and deserve "special protection" and who inhabit a "separate sphere." Historically, white people have denied the existence of gender difference within the black community at the very same time that "separate sphere" sex roles functioned as part of male identity and privilege in the white world. This denial of gender difference became part of the construction of difference that is racism. To put it another way, the difference in appropriate social roles for women and men that was the mark of "civilized" society was denied to black community whose members, not coincidentally, were consistently portrayed as having a bestial or animal nature. This difference in the social construction of gender within each race must be understood as part of the construction of difference that is central to racism.

In the case of both race and gender, the way difference is defined by the nature/biology paradigm performs certain critical functions. First, it implicitly and explicitly defines or establishes hierarchy as natural, that is present in the natural order of things. Second, it absolves those in power from any responsibility for the condition of the inferior group and thus blames the victim for its victimization. Third, it undercuts all efforts to alter relations between the races or the sexes since it portrays the difference as one of kind not degree. Social policy and practice must be predicated on difference and ought not seek to mitigate suffering caused by it.

While the nature/biology paradigm is often portrayed (and even dismissed) as crude and unsophisticated it has never been entirely replaced or supplanted. In fact, additional paradigms have been generated at different historical moments to meet the changing economic, social, and political conditions and their attendant needs, but these new paradigms always function within the context of the nature/biology paradigm; they never replace it. The relation between old and new paradigms is very much like that among the contents of "Grandmother's trunk" in the children's memory game where, though new items are added with each turn, the old items persist and remain an integral part of each recitation.

## CHALLENGES TO THE NATURE/BIOLOGY PARADIGM

Challenges to the nature/biology paradigm take many forms but all have in common the desire to portray difference as a matter of degree, not kind. While they need not be committed to the idea that there are no differences between people, and even entertain the idea that there can be differences of race and/or gender, they emphasize the social nature of the categories "race" and "gender" and try to move from a normative to a descriptive use of the concept of difference.

The "separate but equal" approach to race relations and the "different but equal" or liberal model for gender roles are early examples of attempts to modify the nature/biology model by beginning to incorporate the idea of difference as degree while still retaining a strong hold on the difference in kind paradigm. For example, the justices in *Plessy* v. *Ferguson* (1896), which effectively establishes "separate but equal" as the nation's policy of race relations for almost sixty years, go to great pains to maintain that separating the races in public education, transportation, and other areas is simply a way of recognizing difference but involves no normative judgment. In fact, they specifically assert that such segregation does not "necessarily imply the inferiority of either race to the other. . . ." Portraying the other as "equal" though different paves the way for future accommodation. After all, negotiations or accommodations are only possible between equals.

## THE ETHNICITY PARADIGM

During the latter portion of the nineteenth century and the first half of the twentieth, the biologistic/social Darwinist paradigm of race still predominates but the legal doctrine of separate but equal helps undermine its force, and gradually race difference comes to be redefined using the ethnicity paradigm. This paradigm functions both descriptively and prescriptively bringing with it its celebration of cultural pluralism (Wolff 1965). Now race difference is no longer irrevocably "other" and no longer places people of color, in Memmi's words, "outside of humanity." The ethnicity paradigm goes beyond "separate but equal" to offer a picture of society where race is simply one more difference on the all-American continuum of ethnic diversity.[3]

The implications and consequences of this portrayal of difference are enormous. Because the adoption of ethnicity as the dominant paradigm for race transforms race from a biological to a social category, it presents a progressive alternative to the crude and unyielding nature/biology paradigm it attempts to replace or supplement. At the same time, by denying both the centrality and uniqueness of race as a principle of socioeconomic organization, it redefines difference in a way that denies the history of racism in the United States and thus denies white responsibility for the present and past oppression and exploitation of people of color. Further, while one version of the paradigm celebrates diversity in the form of cultural pluralism, another version regards difference as a problem and offers as its solution "assimilation." The emergence of black nationalism during the sixties, as well as Garvey's Pan Africanism of the 1920s, can be understood as a direct response to the inadequacies of this paradigm and an attempt on the part of black Americans to redefine difference in what they perceived to be their interests.

By focusing on the dynamics of colonialism, the nation-based paradigm for race reasserts the unique history of people of color in the United States and points to the inadequacy of the ethnicity paradigm. The popular movement to replace "Negro" and "colored" with "black" and "Afro-American" represented a dramatic attempt on the part of black Americans to reassert race as the primary social-political-economic category and principle of social organization and to reject outright all solutions to "the negro problem" that proselytized assimilation.[4] The cultural nationalism of the period which was perhaps most visible to white Americans in the form of *dashikis* and *afros* was part of the group's attempt to assert its own power to define and create difference. Looked at in this way, the nation-based paradigm and its attendant linguistic and lifestyle recommendations represented an attempt on the part of black Americans to assert their right to define difference specifically by rearticulating the meaning of "separate but equal."

## EMBRACING GENDER DIFFERENCE

During the latter portion of the nineteenth century, the "separate sphere" gender paradigm is modified and ultimately replaced by a picture of gender which portrays women as "different but equal."[5] Predicated on the notion of difference, the liberal paradigm for gender raises the possibility that at least some gender difference may be social rather than natural or biological. Part of the justification, offered by Mill and others, for introducing a principle of "perfect equality" between the sexes is that such a principle will not suppress whatever natural differences exist. The "different but equal" model for gender relations prevails for a considerable period of time. Its essential ambiguity about the nature and origins of difference between the sexes guarantees that the "nature/biology" paradigm it seeks to replace will continue to exert considerable control at both the psychological and social level. In a context where wealthy, white males set the standard, race and gender paradigms that assert either "separate" or "different" but "equal" will always perform the dual function of implicitly evaluating as "inferior" what they purport to be describing as "different."

During the sixties and seventies we find attempts by significant sectors of the white women's movement to redefine difference in ways which parallel struggles carried out by the black community. Just as the nation-based paradigm challenges ethnicity by heightening race difference instead of trying to deny or de-emphasize it, the radical feminism typified and precipitated by Shulamith Firestone's *The Dialectics of Sex* (1971) and the more recent feminist essentialism which portrays feminine nature as different than and preferable to "maleness" represent attempts by women to identify and embrace sex difference rather than apologize for it. At certain points, Firestone's argument bears remarkable similarity to Mill's insofar as both argue that traditional ways of formulating social policy about gender converts a physical fact to a legal right, subsuming the history of gender relations under the principle of "might makes right." Early radical feminism quite dramatically embraces the nature/biology paradigm for gender only to stand it on its head. The thrust of the paradigm as it expresses and perpetuates male-domination is that nature/biology can't be changed; it is immutable. Firestone and others (following Rousseau of *The Social Contract* and John Stuart Mill) suggest that the proper way to deal with natural inequality is to overcome it, not institutionalize it. What we have here is an attempt on the part of the women's movement to assert its right to redefine difference.

Other segments of the women's movement entered the political struggle over definition by offering androgyny as the proper paradigm for gender.[6] The androgyny paradigm, now very much out of favor, shares many similarities with the ethnicity paradigm for race. Now gender difference is clearly portrayed as a matter of degree not kind. In place of a model which assumes two sexes, the androgyny paradigm portrays gender difference as points on the continuum of gender. Difference now reflects, not two separate and different sexes, but a whole range of human possibilities.

The androgyny paradigm has been criticized in much the same way as the ethnicity/cultural pluralism model for race. Both have been charged with building in an essentially conservative picture of the (static) components (i.e., "qualities" and "groups") that constitute the reality they seek to describe. Further, by prematurely seeking to replace male and female with "human," the androgyny paradigm is guilty of rendering both race and gender difference invisible at a time when differences based on gender as they impact on people's lives need to be uncovered and dismantled, not covered over. This parallels the charge that the ethnicity paradigm denies race its unique history of slavery and colonization, rendering the very factors that create its virulence invisible.

Finally, at those times when racial oppression has been regarded as the most serious kind of injustice in the society, white women have attempted to employ race as the paradigm for gender in order to appeal to those male social reformers who failed to acknowledge the extent and severity of women's oppression as women. During the 1850s and 1860s feminists drew parallels between the situation of white women and the situation of blacks, arguing that in the eyes of custom and the law, white women's status was equivalent to that of Negro slaves. In her famous speech before the New York State Legislature in 1854, Elizabeth Cady Stanton spends considerable time drawing this parallel. And, more than a hundred years later, during the 1960s and 1970s, feminists once again attempted to draw this analogy as part of their effort to redefine gender difference in a way that would capture the attention of white, male activists who considered racism a serious evil but tended to trivialize charges of sexism. Such attempts have often rightfully angered black Americans who have argued that they improperly equated the situation of middle-class white women with the brutalization suffered by black people under slavery. It must also be noted that the very same white women who drew this analogy participated in fostering the invisibility of black women both by drawing the analogy in the first place and by failing to speak out about the double burden of black women's exploitation in the second.

## CONTEMPORARY PARADIGMS AND THEIR CRITICS

In the contemporary period we find considerable confusion over what explicit paradigms are to be adopted for race and gender. Literature in philosophy as well as the social sciences reflects a concern on the part of some to identify "the new racism," alternately referred to as "symbolic racism," "modern racism" or even (with a touch of irony) "civilized racism."[8] While analysts disagree over some of the specific features and implications of these "new" racisms, all are concerned with distinguishing their more subtle contemporary manifestation from so-called "old-fashioned" racism which is seen as crude and explicit. The new racism expresses itself by using "code words" in place of explicitly racist language and arguments.

In *Racial Formations in the U.S.*, Omi and Winant define code words as "phrases and symbols which refer indirectly to racial themes but do not directly challenge popular democratic or egalitarian ideals . . ." (1986, 120). As an example of this approach, they point to the way in which the earlier explicit attack on school integration has been replaced by an attack on busing which is rejected on the grounds that it interferes with "the family's" or "the parent's" right to decide where their children will attend school or with "the community's" right to decide upon appropriate housing patterns and school districts. Having made similar observations, Donald Kinder, who has written extensively on "symbolic racism," sets out to explain why so many white Americans express a commitment to "equality of opportunity" while opposing concrete efforts to bring about racial equality (Kinder and Sears 1981, Kinder 1986). Rejecting both the earlier prejudice model and the later self-interest account, Kinder formulates the concept of symbolic racism to account for the new phenomenon he observes. He points to

> . . . a blend of anti-black affect and the kind of traditional American values embodied in the Protestant Ethic. Symbolic racism represents a form of resistance to change in the racial status quo based on moral feelings that blacks violate such traditional American Values as individualism and self-reliance, the work ethic and discipline. (Kinder and Sears 1981, 416)

Kinder and others who offer this account of the new racism have been taken to task by others who argue that it underestimates the continued virulence of old-fashioned racism with its explicit assumption of black inferiority and its straightforward commitment to segregationist sentiments (Weigel and Howes 1985; Sniderman and Tetlock 1986). And Kinder himself has recently responded to his critics by acknowledging that he and others "claimed too much when we declared that white America had become, even in principle, racially egalitarian and that traditional forms of racial prejudice had been replaced by symbolic racism. Old-fashioned racism remains alive and all too well" (1986, 161).

What are we to make of the current debate about the nature and extent of racism in contemporary American society? Returning to the perspective of this paper, we can understand competing theories as reflecting a struggle over how difference is to be constructed in the present period and over who is to have the power to define difference.

Politicians and intellectuals have joined forces, intentionally or unintentionally, to make race invisible. It is this invisibility which is both highlighted and reinforced by accounts of the New Racism, accounts which on the one hand seem appealing to many of us because they capture something of what we sense to be the flavor of "a new racism" and disturbing on the other because we fear they contribute to the mythology that "*real racism*" is a thing of the past.

Understanding contemporary racist ideology requires that we recognize that the "old-fashioned" notion of racial difference as natural and fundamental persists alongside contemporary formulations of that doctrine which now point to difference as moral deficiency. By correlating physical moral deficiencies with observable differences in physical appearance, the nature/biology paradigm obtains a virtual stranglehold on thought processes that continues to this day, making it very difficult to persuade the uninitiated that this paradigm is really already part of the social construction of race and gender and not a reflection of natural difference at all. The nature/biology paradigm has not been replaced, it has simply been supplemented by additional and more sophisticated expressions of racism and sexism that have the effect of continuing to reinforce the so-called "crude" paradigm while at the same time allowing people to avoid confronting that crude model or taking responsibility for it.

According to the new racism, the problem with people of color in general and blacks in particular is that they are not willing to work hard and defer gratification.[9] Their failure to attain economic self-sufficiency and social recognition lies in an essential difference in their nature. This difference legitimately excludes them from the community of citizens who deserve either or both support and sympathy from the government or "the American People." Note here that people of color, according to this ideology, are already excluded from the community that is intended by the phrase "The American People," which is then understood to be circumscribed by a certain set of values "we" (as opposed to "they") all share.[10]

What we are witnessing in the contemporary period is the resurrection of the nature/biology paradigm now in a more dangerous and more ideologically loaded form.[11] The political ideology of the day is Conservative with a capital "C" and Conservatism always relies upon some theory of natural and fundamental difference to explain and justify the inequality of opportunity and conditions which it fails to find problematic. In its older, crude version, the nature/biology paradigm is quite straightforward about the fundamental difference between the races that separates them irrevocably. In its new sophisticated version, the blatant racism is muted and its assertion of fundamental difference between the races appears to be its unavoidable (perhaps even regrettable) conclusion not its premise.

According to the new ideology, we are enjoined from ever seeing race difference. The differences we notice are differences in moral character. Since race has been obliterated as a category, the only way to explain differences in achievement is by pointing to individual difference. If blacks as a group fail to achieve, the implication is that there is something in their nature that prevents them from achieving. To say that they lack a commitment to the Protestant work ethic and a willingness to delay gratification is simply a polite way of restating the old litany that "Blacks are shiftless and lazy," but in this more sophisticated form we are left with pointing out a moral deficiency or a deficiency of character which can claim to be colorblind.

The work of two contemporary black social scientists, Thomas Sowell (1981) and William J. Wilson (1978) have helped to gain credibility for the neoconservative approach by de-emphasizing the significance of race as a factor in contemporary American society. In particular, Sowell's discussion of the relative economic success or lack of success enjoyed by members of various ethic and racial groups in the country, can easily be interpreted as supporting the implicit ascription of moral deficiency.

The current refusal to acknowledge the existence of race difference leads to a redefinition of race as once again a biological or natural category and actually brings us much closer to a return to the biologistic/social Darwinist paradigm. Now there are no races, just human beings. Some of those human beings are morally deficient (or, grow up in deviant families, which amounts to shorthand for the same claim) and hence don't/won't/can't achieve. Many of these morally deficient human beings are blacks, so there must be something in the nature of black people that explains this failure. Success proves that you have worked hard and delayed gratification and deserve to succeed. "Failure" simply indicates that you were deficient in those moral qualities or character attributes that guarantee success. At the heart of the "new racism" is a reconstruction of difference which returns to a paradigm which both explains and justifies why certain individuals are excluded from the community of those whose efforts government is there to support. Government is to create and enforce conditions which guarantee equality of opportunity so that all those who work hard can succeed. Addicts and criminals (and, by implicit equation, "lazy blacks"), have excluded themselves from that community. Their failure to achieve is simply proof that they were never members of it and didn't deserve to be. We return to the earliest formulation of classical liberal ideology with its emphasis on individualism, and its insistence that hierarchy is part of nature, now fused with a revitalized social Darwinism.

The only alternative paradigm that has been proposed for race in the most recent period comes from Jesse Jackson's Rainbow Coalition. Jackson's rainbow is of course awash with the color that was left out of the ethnicity paradigm, color that is totally absent from the new right's return to a modified social Darwinism, but it is an analogy that thus far has had limited usefulness for formulating social policy. The thing about rainbows is that as soon as you begin to get close to them, they fade and ultimately disappear, an account that some would argue provides a disturbingly accurate account of the Rainbow Coalition's role in both the 1988 Democratic campaign and its aftermath. While Omi and Winant and others like the Rainbow analogy because it moves beyond a purely racially based agenda (1986, 142–43), in the current climate it's not clear whether this will prove to be a viable political strategy for coalition building or a (perhaps unavoidable) move in the direction of a paradigm that plays right into the contemporary preoccupation with denying the existence of race. Viewed in this light, Jackson's announcement in December of 1988 that henceforth black Americans were to be called "African Americans" suggests an attempt on his part to revitalize the ethnicity paradigm as a way to reassert the existence of black Americans as a group. If we are, in fact, experiencing a resurrection of the biology/nature paradigm combined with emphasis on a rabid individualism, redefining difference by adopting the term "African American" may be the best chance black people have to reassert their common history at a time when the new right seeks to focus on individual opportunity and merit.

If we turn our attention to the construction of gender during the contemporary period we find a similar return to a nostalgic past where gender difference and female biology or sexuality lies at the heart of social organization. Far from wishing to obliterate gender as it has done with race, the new right sees gender difference everywhere and is prepared to use it to justify differences in opportunity or achievement where appropriate. Where the ideal woman of the late 1970s was portrayed as a kind of a superwoman who could and *should* be able to combine successfully her multiple roles of corporate attorney, girl scout leader, femme fatale, super mom, loving wife, PTA volunteer, gourmet cook, little league coach, bonsai gardener, and fashion model, the ideal woman a decade or so later is encouraged to self-define as a wife and mother with an emphasis on the latter. Unable to actually turn back the clock on some of the concrete gains that white, middle-class women have made in the labor force, the new right is prepared to close its eyes to that participation as long as women with careers embrace the ideology that defines their primary role is as wife and mother. The media is filled with stories about high power professional women who put their careers on hold or find a way to convert full-time careers to part-time, home-based work, in order to stay home and raise their kids. Politicians and media portrayals made it clear that these women are allowed to build a work life into their home life as long as they assure us that their primary source of satisfaction and fulfillment lies in motherhood not work. Highly visible women in society from Supreme Court justices to law school deans to best-selling authors are presented to us as women who stayed home and took their motherhood role seriously thus earning the right to pursue their careers later.

While social pressure to return to the home during childrearing years has increased on middle- and upper-class, white women, cuts in food stamps and Medicaid along with a new emphasis on "workfare" seems determined to insure that poor women and women of color are out of the home and in the labor force filling the jobs that no one else wants at wages no one else will accept. This continues the phenomenon we noticed earlier of using the construction of gender difference between women of different races as another way of constructing race (and, one might add, class) difference.

Where early stages in the contemporary women's movement focused on analyzing "sex-role socialization," the later stages have been concerned with understanding the construction of gender. This move reflects a new and more profound understanding of the way the constitution of difference lies at the heart of sexism, an understanding which parallels Memmi's insights about racism. In the mid-seventies Gayle Rubin (1975) wondered about the claim that men and women are polar opposites, different as night and day. Stepping back to reflect on what many took to be obvious, Rubin pointed out a very different reality:

In fact, from the standpoint of nature, men and women are closer to each other than either is to anything else—forests, mountains, kangaroos, or coconut palms. The idea that men and women are more different from one another than either is from anything else must come from somewhere other than nature. . . . The idea that men and women are two mutually exclusive categories must arise out of something other than a nonexistent "natural" opposition. (1975, 179)

More recently, Catharine MacKinnon has argued that "gender is not difference, gender is hierarchy . . . the idea of gender difference helps keep male dominance in place" (1987, 3). Writing from a similar perspective, Zillah Eisenstein has suggested that "equality of opportunity is simply a form of male privilege" (1984, 67) and Carol Gilligan has urged us to listen to "a different voice" (1982).

In both its theory and its practice, the contemporary women's movement has demonstrated a determination to deconstruct gender combined with a strong commitment to redefining difference. In an important essay Andre Lorde has asked us to recognize that "It is not our differences which separate women, but our reluctance to recognize those differences and to deal effectively with the distortions which have resulted from ignoring and misnaming those differences" (1984, 115). She concludes, "Now we must recognize differences among women who are equals, neither inferior nor superior, and devise ways to use each others' difference to enrich our visions and our joint struggles" (1984, 122).

Responding to Lorde's challenge, the Women's Movement has begun to search for a metaphor that will facilitate the project Lorde envisions. A popular poster celebrating international women's solidarity adopts the slogan "One Ocean, Many Waves," while the 1987 National Women's Studies Association Conference used the theme of "Weaving Women's Colors," and the 1989 New Jersey Research Conference on Women, *Celebration of Our Work,* at Douglass College bears the title "Mosaics of Inclusion." Each of these represents an attempt to find a metaphor for difference that reflects both diversity and unity. Each is an attempt to move beyond a portrayal of women which is narrowly white, professional, and Western in nature to one which recognizes and celebrates difference.


THE CHALLENGE OF THE 1990S

The challenge that faces progressive movements . . . is enormous. In the face of a return to an implicit dependence on the nature/biology paradigm for expressing both race and gender difference, how can we reinstate the "deconstruction" projects of the seventies and create the basis for forging broad-based political coalitions that can transform the political-social-economic agenda and priorities of the nation? While attempts to recognize and analyze the social construction of gender and race were important intellectual projects a decade or two ago, this relatively sophisticated conceptual project has been made even more difficult by the conservative ideological bias that permeates much of popular culture and communication during the current period. At a "commonsense" level, the natural difference paradigm is reinforced constantly in the most casual interaction between people: dark skin is not light skin; women's bodies are not male bodies. In the presence of such obvious physical differences, most people find it difficult even to entertain the notion of race and gender as social and political categories. What can it mean to claim that difference is created by racism and sexism not simply and (appropriately) reflected by them?

Those of us committed to social change must look for the answer by focusing on the essential contradictions that lie at the heart of the new Conservatism—Conservatism that is committed simultaneously to asserting fundamental natural differences between races while seeking to make race invisible—a Conservatism that, in addition, is committed to asserting fundamental natural differences based upon gender, yet is unable to institutionalize this difference as the basis for social policy with the force and comprehensiveness it once could. Once again, our project is to turn the natural difference paradigm on its head. We must simultaneously deconstruct the social construction of difference that constitutes racism and sexism while we reconstruct difference as unlimited human and humane possibilities. This means that we must use every opportunity to show the way in which race and gender difference has been constructed in order to justify racism and sexism at the same time that we teach ourselves and others to name and value the differences that help to define each of us but which are the very strengths of the community we seek to create. We must do this at every opportunity by focusing on the contradictions between Conservative rhetoric and the reality of the lives of women and men who live and work in a multiracial, multicultural, class society. Local, regional, and national organizing around issues that expose the contradictions inherent in the prevailing paradigms provide the best long-term hope for redirecting economic and social policy toward human interests.

NOTES

1. The former occurs when oppressed people participate in the creation of difference in order to protect themselves from violating or seeming to violate the norms of behavior established by those in power.

2. Audre Lorde has described what she calls this "mythical norm" as "white, thin, young, heterosexual, christian and financially secure" (1984, 116).

3. My discussion of the ethnicity paradigm and challenges to it is based upon the analysis offered by Michael Omi and Howard Winant in their important book *Racial Formation in the United States* (1986). Even at those points where I disagree with their analysis, I am indebted to it.

4. Commenting on the impetus for replacing "colored" and "Negro" with "black," Robert Baker writes: "All of these movements and their partisans wished to stress that Afro-Americans were different from other Americans and could not be merged with them because the difference between the two was as great as that between black and white" (1981, 163).

5. In their fascinating account of a hundred and fifty years of the experts' advice to women, *For Her Own Good,* Barbara Ehrenreich and Deirdre English refer to these views respectively as "sexual romanticism" and "sexual rationalism" (1979, 21).

6. For some accounts of the androgyny paradigm and its critics, see, for example, Caroline Bird (1968), Ann Ferguson's "Androgyny as an Ideal for Human Development" (1977), and Betty Roszak's "The Human Continuum" (1971, 297ff.) as well as Mary Daly's (1975) "The Qualitative Leap Beyond Patriarchal Religion," and Janice Raymond's "The Illusion of Androgyny" (1975).

7. See Gail Rubin's "Woman as Nigger" (1971, 230ff.).

8. Omi and Winant quote political scientist Merle Blacks as pointing out that "Reagan's kind of civilized the racial issue" (1986, 135).

9. This stereotypical portrayal is not applied to Asian Americans or to Cuban Americans at the present time.

10. This trick of exclusion has a long history. Portraying civil rights for blacks and women as a special interest, for example, sets things up so that extending civil rights to these groups appears to take something away from everybody else instead of enhancing democracy for all.

11. This in contrast to Omi and Winant who argue that "we are witnessing the resurrection of the ethnicity paradigm in a new form" (1986, 141).

12. See, for example, Jeffrey Prager's discussion of Ronald Reagan's portrayal of black Americans during his 1985 State of the Union Address. Prager points out that Reagan subtly attempted to divide black Americans into two groups, those who were "virtuous black workers" and those who were "menacing addicts, criminals, etc." (1987, 70).

## REFERENCES

Baker, Robert. 1981. " 'Pricks' and 'Chicks': A Plea for 'Persons.' " In *Sexist Language.* M. Vetterling-Bragin, ed. Totowa, N.J.: Littlefield Adams.

Bird, Caroline. 1968. *Born Female: The High Cost of Keeping Women Down.* New York: McKay.

Daly, Mary. 1975. "The Qualitative Leap beyond Patriarchal Religion." *Feminist Quarterly* 1(4): 29ff.

Ehrenreich, Barbara, and Deirdre English. 1979. *For Her Own Good: 150 Years of the Experts' Advice to Women.* Garden City, N.Y.: Anchor Press/Doubleday.

Eisenstein, Zillah R. 1984. *Feminism and Sexual Equality.* New York: Monthly Review Press.

Ferguson, Ann. 1977. "Androgyny as an Ideal for Human Development." In *Feminism and Philosophy.* See Vetterling-Braggin (1977).

Firestone, Shulamith. 1971. *The Dialectic of Sex.* New York: Bantam Books.

Gilligan, Carol. 1982. *In a Different Voice.* Cambridge, Mass.: Harvard University Press.

Kinder, Donald R. 1986. "The Continuing American Dilemma: White Resistance to Racial Change 40 Years after Myrdal." *Journal of Social Issues* 42(2): 151–71.

Kinder, Donald R., and D. O. Sears. 1981. "Prejudice and Politics: Symbolic Racism versus Racial Threats to the Good Life." *Journal of Personality and Social Psychology* 40: 414–43.

Lorde, Audre. 1984. "Age, Race, Class and Sex: Women Redefining Difference." In *Sister Outsider.* Trumansburg, N.Y.: The Crossing Press.

MacKinnon, Catharine A. 1987. *Feminism Unmodified.* Cambridge, Mass.: Harvard University Press.

Memmi, Albert. 1971. *Dominated Man.* Boston: Beacon Press.

Omi, Michael, and Howard Winant. 1986. *Racial Formation in the United States.* New York: Routledge and Kegan Paul.

Pierce, Chester M. 1974. "Psychiatric Problems of the Black Minority." In *American Handbook of Psychiatry.* New York: Basic Books.

Prager, Jeffrey. 1987. "American Political Culture and the Shifting Meaning of Race." *Ethnic and Racial Studies* 10(1): 62–81.

Raymond, Janice. 1975. "The Illusion of Androgyny." *Quest* 2(1).

Roszak, Betty. 1971. "The Human Continuum." In *Masculine/Feminine.* See Roszak, Betty, and T. Roszak (1971).

Roszak, Betty, and T. Roszak, eds. 1971. *Masculine/Feminine.* New York: Harper Colophon Books.

Rubin, Gail. 1971. "Woman as Nigger." In *Masculine/Feminine.* See Roszak (1971).

———. 1975. "The Traffic in Women: Notes on the 'Political Economy' of Sex." In *Toward an Anthropology of Women.* Rayna R. Reiter, ed. New York: Monthly Review Press.

Sniderman, Paul M., and Philip E. Tetlock. 1986. "Symbolic Racism: Problems of Motive Attribution in Political Analysis." *Journal of Social Issues* 42: 129–50.

Sowell, Thomas. 1981. *Ethnic America.* New York: Basic Books.

Vetterling-Braggin, Mary, and Frederick A. Elliston et al. 1977. *Feminism and Philosophy.* Totowa, N.J.: Littlefield Adams.

Weigel, Russel H., and Paul W. Howes. 1985. "Conceptions of Racial Prejudice: Symbolic Racism Reconsidered." *Journal of Social Issues* 41(3): 117–38.

Whitbeck, Caroline. 1975. "Theories of Sex Difference." *The Philosophical Forum* 5(1–2): 54–80.

Wilson, William Julius. 1978. *The Declining Significance of Race.* 2nd ed. Chicago: University of Chicago Press.

Wolff, Robert Paul. 1965. "Beyond Tolerance." In *A Critique of Pure Tolerance.* Boston: Beacon Press.

# Part Five
# Explanations of Hate

# 15

# Causes of Prejudice

## Elliot Aronson

As we have seen, one determinant of prejudice in a person is a need for self-justification. . . . we have seen that, if we have done something cruel to a person or a group of people, we derogate that person or group in order to justify our cruelty. If we can convince ourselves that a group is unworthy, subhuman, stupid, or immoral, it helps *us* to keep from feeling immoral if we enslave members of that group, deprive them of a decent education, or murder them. We can then continue to go to church and to feel like good Christians, because it isn't a fellow human we've hurt. Indeed, if we're skillful enough, we can even convince ourselves that the barbaric slaying of old men, women, and children is a Christian virtue— as the crusaders did when, on the way to the holy land, they butchered European Jews in the name of the Prince of Peace. Again, as we have seen, this form of self-justification serves to intensify subsequent brutality.

Of course, there are other human needs in addition to self-justification. For example, there are status and power needs. Thus, an individual who is low on the socioeconomic hierarchy may need the presence of a down-trodden minority group in order to be able to feel superior to somebody. Several studies have shown that a good predictor of prejudice is whether or not a person's social status is low or declining. Regardless of whether it is prejudiced against blacks[1] or against Jews,[2] if a person's social status

is low or declining, that individual is apt to be more prejudiced than someone whose social status is high or rising. It has been found that people
who are at or near the bottom in terms of education, income, and occupa-
tion not only are the highest in their dislike of blacks but also are the
ones most likely to resort to violence in order to prevent the desegregation of schools.[3]

These findings raise some interesting questions. Are people of low
socioeconomic and educational status more prejudiced because (1) they
need someone to feel superior to, (2) they most keenly feel competition
for jobs from minority-group members, (3) they are more frustrated than
most people and therefore more aggressive, or (4) their lack of education
increases the probability of their taking a simplistic stereotypical view of
the world? It is difficult to disentangle these variables, but it appears that
each of these phenomena contributes to prejudice. Indeed, there is no single cause of prejudice. Prejudice is determined by a great many factors.
Let's look at some of these major determinants.

. . . We will look at four basic causes of prejudice: (1) economic and
political competition or conflict, (2) displaced aggression, (3) personality
needs, and (4) conformity to existing social norms. These four causes
are not mutually exclusive—indeed, they may all operate at once—but
it would be helpful to determine how important each cause is, because
any action we are apt to recommend in an attempt to reduce prejudice
will depend on what we believe to be the major cause of prejudice. Thus,
for example, if I believe bigotry is deeply ingrained in the human personality, I might throw my hands up in despair and conclude that, in
the absence of deep psychotherapy, the majority of prejudiced people
will always be prejudiced. This would lead me to scoff at attempts to
reduce prejudice by reducing competitiveness or by attempting to coun-
teract the pressures of conformity.

## ECONOMIC AND POLITICAL COMPETITION

Prejudice can be considered to be the result of economic and political
forces. According to this view, given that resources are limited, the dominant group might attempt to exploit or derogate a minority group in
order to gain some material advantage. Prejudiced attitudes tend to increase when times are tense and there is conflict over mutually exclusive
goals. This is true whether the goals are economic, political, or ideological. Thus, prejudice has existed between Anglo and Mexican-American
migrant workers as a function of a limited number of jobs, between Arabs

and Israelis over disputed territory, and between Northerners and Southerners over the abolition of slavery. The economic advantages of discrimination are all too clear when one looks at the success certain craft unions have had, over the years, in denying membership to women and members of ethnic minorities, thus keeping them out of the relatively high-paying occupations the unions control. For example, the decade between the mid-1950s and the mid-1960s was one of great political and legal advancement for the civil rights movement. Yet in 1966 only 2.7 percent of union-controlled apprenticeships were filled with black workers—an increase of only 1 percent over the preceding ten years. Moreover, in the mid-1960s, the U.S. Department of Labor surveyed four major cities in search of minority-group members serving as apprentices among union plumbers, steamfitters, sheetmetal workers, stone masons, lathers, painters, glaziers, and operating engineers. In the four cities, they failed to find a single black person thus employed. Clearly, prejudice pays off for some people.[4] While the 1970s and 1980s have produced significant changes in many of these statistics, they also show that the situation remains far from equitable for minority groups.

Discrimination, prejudice, and negative stereotyping increase sharply as competition for scarce jobs increases. In one of his classic early studies of prejudice in a small industrial town, John Dollard documented the fact that, although there was initially no discernible prejudice against Germans in the town, it came about as jobs became scarce:

> Local whites largely drawn from the surrounding farms manifested considerable direct aggression toward the newcomers. Scornful and derogatory opinions were expressed about these Germans, and the native whites had a satisfying sense of superiority toward them. . . . The chief element in the permission to be aggressive against the Germans was rivalry for jobs and status in the local woodenware plants. The native whites felt definitely crowded for their jobs by the entering German groups and in case of bad times had a chance to blame the Germans who by their presence provided more competitors for the scarcer jobs. There seemed to be no traditional pattern of prejudice against Germans unless the skeletal suspicion against all outgroupers (always present) can be invoked in its place.[5]

Similarly, the prejudice, violence, and negative stereotyping directed against Chinese immigrants in the United States fluctuated wildly throughout the nineteenth century—spurred largely by changes in economic competition. For example, when the Chinese were attempting to mine gold in California, they were described as "depraved and vicious . . . gross gluttons . . . bloodthirsty and inhuman."[6] However, just a decade later, when they were willing to accept dangerous and arduous work building the transcontinental railroad—work that Caucasian Americans were unwilling to undertake—they were generally regarded as sober, industrious, and law-abiding. Indeed, Charles Crocker, one of the western railroad tycoons, wrote: "They are equal to the best white men. . . . They are very trusty, very intelligent and they live up to their contracts."[7] After the completion of the railroad, however, jobs became more scarce; moreover, when the Civil War ended, there was an influx of former soldiers into an already tight job market. This was immediately followed by a dramatic increase in negative attitudes toward the Chinese: The stereotype changed to "criminal," "conniving," "crafty," and "stupid."

These data suggest that competition and conflict breed prejudice. Moreover, this phenomenon transcends mere historical significance—it seems to have enduring psychological effects as well. In a survey conducted in the 1970s, most anti-black prejudice was found in groups that were just one rung above the blacks socioeconomically. And, as we might expect, this tendency was most pronounced in situations in which whites and blacks were in close competition for jobs.[8] At the same time, there is some ambiguity in interpreting the data, because in some instances the variables of competition are intertwined with such variables as educational level and family background.

In order to determine whether competition causes prejudice in and of itself, an experiment is needed. But how can we proceed? Well, if conflict and competition lead to prejudice, it should be possible to produce prejudice in the laboratory. This can be done by the simple device of (1) randomly assigning people of differing backgrounds to one of two groups, (2) making those two groups distinguishable in some arbitrary way, (3) putting those groups into a situation in which they are in competition with each other, and (4) looking for evidence of prejudice. Such an experiment was conducted by Muzafer Sherif and his colleagues[9] in the natural environment of a Boy Scout camp. The subjects were normal, well-adjusted, twelve-year-old boys who were randomly assigned to one of two groups, the *Eagles* and the *Rattlers*. Within each group, the youngsters were taught to cooperate. This was largely done through arranging activities that made each group highly interdependent. For example, within each group, individuals cooperated in building a diving board for the swimming facility, preparing group meals, building a rope bridge, and so on.

After a strong feeling of cohesiveness developed within each group, the stage was set for conflict. The researchers arranged this by setting up a series of competitive activities in which the two groups were pitted against each other in such games as football, baseball, and tug-of-war. In order to increase the tension, prizes were awarded to the winning team. This resulted in some hostility and ill will during the games. In addition, the investigators devised rather diabolical devices for putting the groups into situations specifically designed to promote conflict. In one such situation, a camp party was arranged. The investigators set it up so that the *Eagles* were allowed to arrive a good deal earlier than the *Rattlers*. In addition, the refreshments consisted of two vastly different kinds of food: About half the food was fresh, appealing, and appetizing; the other half was squashed, ugly, and unappetizing. Perhaps because of the general competitiveness that already existed, the early arrivers confiscated most of the appealing refreshments, leaving only the less interesting, less appetizing, squashed, and damaged food for their adversaries. When the *Rattlers* finally arrived and saw how they had been taken advantage of, they were understandably annoyed—so annoyed they began to call the exploitive group rather uncomplimentary names. Because the *Eagles* believed they deserved what they got (first come, first served), they resented this treatment and responded in kind. Name calling escalated into food throwing, and within a very short time a full-scale riot was in progress.

Following this incident, competitive games were eliminated and a great deal of social contact was initiated. Once hostility had been aroused, however, simply eliminating the competition did not eliminate the hostility. Indeed, hostility continued to escalate, even when the two groups were engaged in such benign activities as sitting around watching movies. Eventually, the investigators succeeded in reducing the hostility. Exactly how this was accomplished will be discussed later. . . .

## THE "SCAPEGOAT" THEORY OF PREJUDICE

In [an earlier discussion] . . . I made the point that aggression is caused, in part, by frustration and such other unpleasant or aversive situations as pain or boredom. . . . We saw [that] there is a strong tendency for a frustrated individual to lash out at the cause of his or her frustration. Frequently, however, the cause of a person's frustration is either too big or too vague for direct retaliation. For example, if a six-year-old boy is humiliated by his teacher, how can he fight back? The teacher has too much power. But this frustration may increase the probability of his aggressing against a less powerful bystander—even if the bystander has nothing to do with his pain. By the same token, if there is mass unemployment, who is the frustrated, unemployed worker going to strike out against—the economic system? The system is much too big and much too vague. It would be more convenient if the unemployed worker could find something or someone less vague and more concrete to blame. The president? He's concrete, all right, but also much too powerful to strike at with impunity.

The ancient Hebrews had a custom that is noteworthy in this context. During the days of atonement, a priest placed his hands on the head of a goat while reciting the sins of the people. This symbolically transferred the sin and evil from the people to the goat. The goat was then allowed to escape into the wilderness, thus cleansing the community of sin. The animal was called a scapegoat. In modern times the term *scapegoat* has been used to describe a relatively powerless innocent who is made to take the blame for something that is not his or her fault. Unfortunately, the individual is not allowed to escape into the wilderness but is usually subjected to cruelty or even death. Thus, if people are unemployed, or if inflation has depleted their savings, they can't very easily beat up on the economic system—but they can find a scapegoat. In Nazi Germany, it was the Jews; in nineteenth-century California, it was Chinese immigrants; in the rural South, it was black people. Some years ago, Carl Hovland and Robert Sears[10] found that, in the period between 1882 and 1930, they could predict the number of lynchings in the South in a given year from a knowledge of the price of cotton during that year. As the price of cotton dropped, the number of lynchings increased. In short, as people experienced an economic depression, they probably experienced a great many frustrations. The frustrations apparently resulted in an increase in lynchings and other crimes of violence.

Otto Klineberg,[11] a social psychologist with a special interest in the cross-cultural aspects of prejudice, describes a unique scapegoating situation in Japan. The Eta or Burakumin are a group of two million outcasts, scattered throughout Japan. They are considered unclean and fit only for certain undesirable occupations. As you might imagine, the Eta usually live in poor, slum areas. Their IQ scores are, on average, sixteen points lower than that of other Japanese. Eta children are absent from school more often and their delinquency rate is three times higher than other Japanese children. For a non-Eta to marry an Eta is taboo, although there is some "passing." For an Eta to "pass" is relatively easy because there are *no inherited racial or physical differences* between the Eta and other Japanese. The Eta are an invisible race—an outgroup defined more by social class than physical characteristics. They can only be identified because of their distinctive speech pattern (which has developed from years of nonassociation with other Japanese) and their identity papers. Although the historical origins of the Eta are unclear, they probably occupied the lower rungs of the socioeconomic ladder until an economic depression led to their complete expulsion from Japanese society. Now the Japanese consider the Eta to be "innately inferior," thus justifying further scapegoating and discrimination.

It is difficult to understand how the lynching of blacks or the mistreatment of the Eta could be due only to economic competition. There is a great deal of emotion in these actions that suggests the presence of deeper psychological factors in addition to economics. Similarly, the zeal with which Nazis carried out their attempt to erase all members of the Jewish ethnic group (regardless of economic status) strongly suggests that the phenomenon was not exclusively economic or political, but was (at least in part) psychological.[12] Firmer evidence for the existence of psychological processes comes from a well-controlled experiment by Neal Miller and Richard Bugelski.[13] Individuals were asked to state their feelings about various minority groups. Some of the subjects were then frustrated by being deprived of an opportunity to attend a film and were given an arduous and difficult series of tests instead. They were then asked to restate their feelings about the minority groups. These subjects showed some evidence of increased prejudicial responses following the frustrating experience. A control group that did not go through the frustrating experience did not undergo any change in prejudice.

Additional research has helped to pin down the phenomenon even more precisely. In one experiment,[14] white students were instructed to administer a series of electric shocks to another student as part of a learning experiment. The subjects had the prerogative to adjust the intensity of the shocks. In actuality, the learner was an accomplice of the experimenter who (of course) was not really connected to the apparatus. There were four conditions: The accomplice was either black or white; he was trained to be either friendly or insulting to the subject. When he was friendly, the subjects administered slightly *less* intense shocks to the black student; when he insulted them, they administered far more intense shocks to the black student than to the white student. In another experiment,[15] college students were subjected to a great deal of frustration. Some of these students were highly anti-Semitic; others were not. The subjects were then asked to write stories based on pictures they were shown. For some subjects, the characters in these pictures were assigned Jewish names; for others, they were not. There were two major findings: (1) After being frustrated, anti-Semitic subjects wrote stories that directed more aggression toward the Jewish characters than did people who were not anti-Semitic; and

(2) there was no difference between the anti-Semitic students and the others when the characters they were writing about were not identified as Jewish. In short, frustration or anger leads to a specific aggression—aggression against an outgroup member.

The laboratory experiments help to clarify factors that seem to exist in the real world. The general picture of scapegoating that emerges is that individuals tend to displace aggression onto groups that are disliked, that are visible, and that are relatively powerless. Moreover, the form the aggression takes depends on what is allowed or approved by the ingroup in question: In society, lynchings of blacks and pogroms against Jews are not frequent occurrences, unless they are deemed appropriate by the dominant culture or subculture.

## THE PREJUDICED PERSONALITY

As we have seen, the displacement of aggression onto scapegoats may be a human tendency, but not all people do it to a like degree. We have already identified socioeconomic status as a cause of prejudice. Also, we have seen that people who dislike members of a particular outgroup are more apt to displace aggression onto them than are people who do not dislike members of that outgroup. We can now carry this one step further. There is some evidence to support the notion of individual differences in a general tendency to hate. In other words, there are people who are predisposed toward being prejudiced, not solely because of immediate external influences, but because of the kind of people they are. Theodor Adorno and his associates[16] refer to these individuals as "authoritarian personalities." Basically, authoritarian personalities have the following characteristics: They tend to be rigid in their beliefs; they tend to possess "conventional" values; they are intolerant of weakness (in themselves as well as in others); they tend to be highly punitive; they are suspicious; and they are respectful of authority to an unusual degree. The instrument developed to determine authoritarianism (called the $F$ scale) measures the extent to which each person agrees or disagrees with such items as these:

1. Sex crimes such as rape and attacks on children deserve more than mere imprisonment; such criminals ought to be publicly whipped, or worse.

2. Most people don't realize how much our lives are controlled by plots hatched in secret places.

3. Obedience and respect for authority are the most important virtues children should learn.

A high degree of agreement with such items indicates authoritarianism. The major finding is that people who are high on authoritarianism do not simply dislike Jews or dislike blacks, but, rather, they show a consistently high degree of prejudice against *all* minority groups.

Through an intense clinical interview of people high and low on the *F* scale, Adorno and his colleagues have traced the development of this cluster of attitudes and values to early childhood experiences in families characterized by harsh and threatening parental discipline. Moreover, people high on the *F* scale tend to have parents who use love and its withdrawal as their major way of producing obedience. In general, authoritarian personalities, as children, tend to be very insecure and highly dependent on their parents; they fear their parents and feel unconscious hostility against them. This combination sets the stage for the emergence of an adult with a high degree of anger, which, because of fear and insecurity, takes the form of displaced aggression against powerless groups, while the individual maintains an outward respect for authority.

Although research on the authoritarian personality has added to our understanding of the possible dynamics of prejudice, it should be noted that the bulk of the data are correlational. That is, we know only that two variables are related—we cannot be certain what causes what. Consider, for example, the correlation between a person's score on the *F* scale and the specific socialization practices he or she was subjected to as a child. Although it is true that adults who are authoritarian and highly prejudiced had parents who tended to be harsh and to use "conditional love" as a socialization technique, it is not necessarily true that this is what *caused* them to develop into prejudiced people. It turns out that the parents of these people tend, themselves, to be highly prejudiced against minority groups. Accordingly, it may be that the development of prejudice in some people is due to conformity through the process of *identification*. . . . That is, a child might consciously pick up beliefs about minorities from his or her parents because the child identifies with them. This is quite different from, and much simpler than, the explanation offered by Adorno and his colleagues, which is based on the child's unconscious hostility and repressed fear of his or her parents.

This is not to imply that, for some people, prejudice is not rooted in unconscious childhood conflicts. Rather, it is to suggest that many people may have learned a wide array of prejudices on Mommy's or Daddy's knee. Moreover, some people may conform to prejudices that are limited and highly specific, depending upon the norms of their sub-culture. Let's take a closer look at the phenomenon of prejudice as an act of conformity.

## PREJUDICE THROUGH CONFORMITY

It is frequently observed that there is more prejudice against blacks in the South than in the North. This often manifests itself in stronger atti-tudes against racial integration. For example, in 1942, only 4 percent of all southerners were in favor of the desegregation of transportation facili-ties, while 56 percent of all northerners were in favor of it.[17] Why? Was it because of economic competition? Probably not; there is more prejudice against blacks in those southern communities in which economic com-petition is low than in those northern communities in which economic competition is great. Are there relatively more authoritarian personalities in the South than in the North? No. Thomas Pettigrew[18] administered the $F$ scale widely in the North and in the South and found the scores about equal for northerners and southerners. In addition, although there is more prejudice against blacks in the South, there is *less* prejudice against Jews in the South than there is in the nation as a whole; the prejudiced personality should be prejudiced against everybody—the southerner isn't.

How then do we account for the animosity toward blacks that exists in the South? It could be due to historical causes: the blacks were slaves, the Civil War was fought over the issue of slavery, and so on. This could have created the climate for greater prejudice. But what sustains this cli-mate? One possible clue comes from the observation of some rather strange patterns of racial segregation in the South. One example, a group of coal miners in a small mining town in West Virginia, should suffice. The black miners and the white miners developed a pattern of living that consisted of total and complete integration while they were under the ground, and total and complete segregation while they were above the ground. How can we account for this inconsistency? If you truly hate someone, you want to keep away from him—why associate with him below the ground and not above the ground?

Pettigrew has suggested that the explanation for these phenomena is *conformity*. In this case, people are simply conforming to the norms that exist in their society (above the ground!). The historical events of the South set the stage for greater prejudice against blacks, but it is conformity that keeps it going. Indeed, Pettigrew believes that, although economic competition, frustration, and personality needs account for some prejudice, the greatest proportion of prejudiced behavior is a function of slavish conformity to social norms.

How can we be certain conformity is responsible? One way is to determine the relation between a person's prejudice and that person's general pattern of conformity. For example, a study of interracial tension in South Africa[19] showed that those individuals who were most likely to conform to a great variety of social norms also showed a higher degree of prejudice against blacks. In other words, if conformists are more prejudiced, the suggestion is that prejudice may be just another thing to conform to. Another way to determine the role of conformity is to see what happens to people's prejudice when they move to a different area of the country. If conformity is a factor in prejudice, we would expect individuals to show dramatic increases in their prejudice when they move into areas in which the norm is more prejudicial, and to show dramatic decreases when they are affected by a less prejudicial norm. And that is what happens. In one study, Jeanne Watson[20] found that people who had recently moved to New York City and had come into direct contact with anti-Semitic people became more anti-Semitic themselves. In another study, Pettigrew found that, as southerners entered the army and came into contact with a less discriminatory set of social norms, they became less prejudiced against blacks.

The pressure to conform can be relatively overt, as in the Asch experiment. On the other hand, conformity to a prejudicial norm might simply be due to the unavailability of accurate evidence and a preponderance of misleading information. This can lead people to adopt negative attitudes on the basis of hearsay. Examples of this kind of stereotyping behavior abound in the literature. For example, consider Christopher Marlowe's *The Jew of Malta* or William Shakespeare's *The Merchant of Venice*. Both of these works depict the Jew as a conniving, money-hungry, cringing coward. We might be tempted to conclude that Marlowe and Shakespeare had had some unfortunate experiences with unsavory Jews, which resulted in these bitter and unflattering portraits—except for one thing: The Jews had been expelled from England some three hundred years before these works were written. Thus, it would seem that the only thing with which Marlowe and Shakespeare came into contact was a lingering stereotype. Tragically, their works not only reflected the stereotype but undoubtedly contributed to it as well.

Even casual exposure to bigotry can affect our attitudes and behavior toward a group that is the victim of prejudice. For example, research has demonstrated that merely overhearing someone use a derogatory label— such as a racial or ethnic epithet—toward a given group can increase our likelihood of viewing someone from that group—or someone merely *associated* with that group—in a negative light. In one experiment,[21] Shari Kirkland and her co-researchers asked subjects to read a transcript of a criminal trial in which a white defendant was represented by a black attorney, whose picture was attached to the trial transcript. While reading the transcript, the subject "overhears" a brief exchange between two experimental confederates, who are posing as subjects. Some subjects hear the first confederate call the black lawyer a "nigger," while other subjects hear the confederate call him a "shyster." In both conditions, the second confederate expresses agreement with the first confederate's derogatory opinion of the black lawyer. With this conformity dynamic in place, the experimenters then asked the subject to evaluate the attorney and the defendant. An analysis of these ratings revealed that subjects who overheard the racial slur rated the black lawyer more negatively than those who overheard a derisive comment that was not related to the lawyer's race. Moreover, the white defendant received particularly harsh verdicts and highly negative evaluations from subjects who heard the racial slur against the black attorney. This latter finding indicates that conformity to the prejudiced norms can have damaging effects that extend beyond the initial target of racism.

Bigoted attitudes can also be fostered intentionally by a bigoted society that institutionally supports these attitudes. For example, a society that supports the notion of segregation through law and custom is supporting the notion that one group is inferior to another. A more direct example: One investigator[22] interviewed white South Africans in an attempt to find reasons for their negative attitudes toward blacks. He found that the typical white South African was convinced that the great majority of crimes were committed by blacks. This was erroneous. How did such a misconception develop? The individuals reported they saw a great many black convicts working in public places—they never saw any white convicts. Doesn't this prove blacks are convicted of more crimes than whites? No. In fact, the rules forbade white convicts from working in public places! In short, a society can *create* prejudiced beliefs by its very institutions. In our own society, forcing blacks to ride in the back of the bus, keeping women out of certain clubs, preventing Jews from staying at exclusive hotels are all part of our recent history—and create the illusion of inferiority or unacceptability.

## NOTES

1. J. Dollard. *Class and Caste in a Southern Town* (New Haven: Yale University Press, 1987).

2. B. Bettelheim and M. Janowitz. *Social Change and Prejudice, Including Dynamics of Prejudice* (New York: Free Press, 1964).

3. M. Tumin, P. Barton, and B. Burrus. "Education, Prejudice, and Discrimination: A Study in Readiness for Desegregation," *American Sociological Review* 23 (1958): 41–49.

4. M. Levitas. *America in Crisis* (New York: Holt, Rinehart and Winston, 1969).

5. J. Dollard. "Hostility and Fear in Social Life," *Social Forces* 17 (1938): 15–26.

6. E. Roberts, quoted by P. Jacobs and S. Landau. *To Serve the Devil* Vol. 2 (New York: Vintage Books, 1971), p. 71.

7. C. Crocker, quoted by P. Jacobs and S. Landau. *To Serve the Devil* Vol. 2 (New York: Vintage Books, 1971), p. 81.

8. A. Greeley and P. Sheatsley. "The Acceptance of Desegreation Continues to Advance," *Scientific America* 225, no. 6 (1971): 13–19; see also R. D. Vanneman and T. F. Pettigrew, "Race and Relative Deprivation in the Urban United States," *Race* 13 (1972): 461–86.

9. M Sherif, O. J. Harvey, B. J. White, W. Hood, and C. Sherif. *Intergroup Conflict and Cooperation: The Robbers Cave Experiment* (Norman: University of Oklahoma Institute of Intergroup Relations, 1961).

10. C. Hovland and R. Sears. "Minor Studies of Aggression: Correlation of Lynchings with Economic Indices," *Journal of Psychology* (1940): 301–210.

11. O. Klineberg. "Black and White in International Perspective," *American Psychologist* 26 (1971): 119–28.

12. A Speer, *Inside the Third Reich: Memoirs,* R. Winston and C. Winston, trans. (New York: Macmillan, 1970).

13. N. Miller and R. Bugelski. "Minor Studies in Aggression: The Influence of Frustraions Imposed by the In-group on Attitudes Expressed by the Out-group," *Journal of Psychology* 25 (1948): 437–42.

14. R. Rogers and S. Prentice-Dunn. "Deindividuation and Anger-mediated Interracial Aggression: Unmasking Regressive Racism," *Journal of Personality and Social Psychology* 41 (1981): 63–73.

15. D. Weatherly. "Anti-Semitism and the Expression of Fantasy Aggression, *Journal of Abnormal and Social Psychology* 62 (1961): 454–57.

16. T. Adorno, E. Frenkel-Brunswick, D. Levinson, and R. N. Sanford. *The Authoritarian Personality* (New York: Harper, 1950).

17. Greeley and Sheatsley, "Acceptance of Desegregation."

18. T. F. Pettigrew. "Regional Differences in Anti-Negro Prejudice," *Journal of Abnormal and Social Psychology* 59 (1959): 28–36.

19. T. F. Pettigrew. "Personality and Sociocultural Factors and Interroup Attitudes: A Cross-national Comparison," *Journal of Conflict Resolution* 2 (1958): 29–42.

20. J. Watson. "Some Social and Psychological Situations Related to Change in Attitude," *Human Relations* 3 (1950): 15–56.

21. S. L. Kirkland, J. Greenberg, and T. Pyszczynski. "Further Evidence of the Deleterious Effects of Overheard Derogatory Ethnic Labels: Derogation Beyond the Target," *Personality and Social Psychology Bulletin* 13 (1987): 216–27.

22. I. MacCrone. *Race Attitudes in South Africa* (London: Oxford University Press, 1937).

# 16

# The Biology of Nepotism

## Pierre L. van den Berghe

. . . I suggest that there now exists a theoretical paradigm of great scope and explanatory power—evolutionary biology—that sheds a new light on phenomena of ethnocentrism and racism. In so doing, I am fully cognizant of the protest that such an endeavor will elicit.

My basic argument is quite simple: ethnic and racial sentiments are extensions of kinship sentiments. Ethnocentrism and racism are thus extended forms of nepotism—the propensity to favor kin over nonkin. There exists a general behavioral predisposition, in our species as in many others, to react favorably toward other organisms to the extent that these organisms are biologically related to the actor. The closer the relationship is, the stronger the preferential behavior.

Why should parents sacrifice themselves for their children? Why do uncles employ nephews rather than strangers in their business? Why do inheritance laws provide for passing property on along lines of kinship? Why, in short, do people, and indeed other animals as well, behave nepotistically. To many, these questions appear so intuitively obvious as to require no explanation. We favor kin because they *are* kin. This is no answer, of course, but a mere restatement of the problem. Besides, we do not *always* favor kin. Profligate sons are sometimes disinherited, incompetent nephews not hired, and so on. Yet, on the whole we are nepotists, and when we are not, it is for some good reason. Nepotism, we intuitively feel, is the natural order of things. Where we feel nepotism would interfere with efficiency, equity, or some other goals, we institute explicit safeguards against it and, even then, we expect it to creep in again surrepticiously.

But why? . . . The theorem of "altruism," "kin selection," or "inclusive fitness," as biologists often refer to nepotism, was increasingly discovered to be the keystone of animal sociality. Soon, a theoretical synthesis of population genetics, ecosystem theory, and ethology gave birth to the new discipline of "sociobiology" as E. O. Wilson labeled it.[1] . . .

The problem that posed itself to biologists was the seemingly self-sacrificial behavior of some animals under some conditions, e.g., the emission of alarm calls to warn conspecifics, the mimicking of injuries to distract predators, or seeming restraints on reproduction under adverse ecological conditions. . . . Seeming altruism is, in fact, the ultimate in genetic selfishness. Beneficent behavior is the product of a simple fitness calculus (presumably an unconscious one in most animals, though often a partially conscious one in humans) that takes two factors into account: the cost-benefit ratio of the transaction between altruist and recipient, and the coefficient of relatedness $r$ between altruist and recipient. Simply put, an altruistic transaction can be expected if, and only if, the cost-benefit ratio of the transaction is smaller than the coefficient of relatedness between the two actors.

The coefficient of relatedness between any two organisms is the proportion of genes they share through common descent. It can range from a value of one (for organisms that reproduce asexually, e.g., through cell division) to zero (between unrelated organisms). In sexually reproducing organisms, parents and offspring and full siblings share one-half of their genes; half-siblings, grandparents and grandchildren, uncles-aunts and nephews-nieces share one-fourth; first cousins, one-eighth, and so on.

Reproduction, in the last analysis, is passing on one's genes. This can be done directly through one's own reproduction or indirectly through the reproduction of related organisms. The fitness of an organism is, by definition, its reproductive success. The *inclusive* fitness of an organism is the sum of its own reproductive success plus that of related organisms discounted for their coefficient of relatedness. Thus, it takes two children to reproduce the genetic equivalent of ego; but the same effect can be achieved through four nephews or eight first cousins.

As brilliantly argued by Richard Dawkins,[2] the ultimate unit of replication is the gene, not the organism. Bodies are, in Dawkins's words, mere mortal and expendable "survival machines" for potentially immortal genes. Such genes, therefore, as predispose their carrying organisms to behave nepotistically will be selected for, because, by favoring nepotism, they enhance their own replication. Nepotistic organisms foster the fitness of relatives who have a high probability of carrying the same gene or genes for nepotism. Nepotism genes, therefore, will spread faster than genes that program their carriers to care only for their own direct survival and reproduction—genes, for instance, that would program organisms to eat their siblings when hungry. This phenomenon of fostering inclusive fitness through *kin selection* or nepotism has been conclusively shown (mostly by studies of social insects, but also, increasingly, of vertebrates) to be the basis of much animal sociality.[3] . . .

Animal societies, from social insects to higher vertebrates, are held together primarily by cooperating kin who thereby enhance each other's fitness. This seeming "altruism" is thus the ultimate genic selfishness of maximizing one's *inclusive* fitness. An individual will only behave "altruistically" (i.e., in such a way as to reduce its own direct fitness) if, by doing so, the increment of fitness of a relative more than makes up for the loss to ego. For instance, my full sister shares half of her genes with me; she must, therefore, get more than twice as much out of my beneficent act to her than what that act costs me. For a half-sister or a niece, who only shares one-fourth of her genes with me, the benefit-cost ratio of the transaction would have to be better than four to one— and so on, according to the coefficient of relatedness between giver and receiver. The biological golden rule is "give unto others as they are related unto you."

. . . Relatedness is a relative matter. Kinship might be schematized as a series of concentric circles around ego, each circle representing a degree of relatedness. . . . In the smallest circles are small numbers of highly related (r = ½ or ¼) individuals. As the circles become larger, so does the number of persons involved, but r becomes smaller (⅛, ¹⁄₁₆, ¹⁄₃₂, and so on), and therefore the intensity of kin selection rapidly declines.

In theory, we could have a wide-open network of such overlapping ego-centered kinship circles, with no particular clustering. At the limit, all of humanity would consist of one vast undifferentiated surface of overlapping concentric circles with no cluster or boundaries between them. This condition would be produced by what population biologists call *panmixia*—that is, random mating. Panmixia never happens in humans, nor in other animals, for a very simple reason: if nothing else, space exerts a passive restraint on who mates with whom. Sheer physical propinquity determines who has sexual access to whom. Geographical barriers, such as mountain ranges, bodies of water, deserts, and the like, isolate animal populations from each other, and create breeding boundaries between them, that can and often do lead to speciation and subspeciation.

In humans, however, the story does not stop there. In addition to the purely physical impediments of distance, topography, and so on, human groups create cultural prescriptions and proscriptions concerning their mating systems. There is not a single known human group that lacks them and that even approximates panmixia. Rules specify whom one may, may not, should, or must marry. These rules and practices are almost invariably of a twofold nature. Certain individuals or members of some kin groups (such as lineages and class) *cannot* intermarry, while a wider group constitutes the people who are normally *expected* to mate and marry.

Indeed, nearly all of the small-scale, stateless, human societies are groups ranging from a couple of hundred to a few thousand people, defined almost entirely by ties of descent and marriage. These breeding populations are internally divided into smaller kin groups that swap daughters and sisters for spouses between the men.[4] . . . The relevance of all this to ethnicity is that the primeval model of the human ethnic group is, in fact, the breeding population of a few hundred individuals, the structure of which we have just sketched. This is what the anthropologists used to call the "tribe" —a group characterized by internal peace, preferential endogamy, and common ancestry (real or putative).

At this point, I would like to introduce the neologism *ethny* for "ethnic group." "Ethnic group" is clumsy and "tribe" has many different connotations—several pejorative. The French and Spanish cognates *ethnie* and *etnia* are already in common usage, and it is time to start using such a convenient term in English as well. The ideology usually referred to as "ethnocentrism" might then be more parsimoniously called *ethnism*.

. . . Ethnicity is thus defined in the last analysis by *common descent*. Descent by itself, however, would leave the ethny unbounded, for, by going back enough, all living things are related to each other. *Ethnic boundaries* are created *socially* by *preferential endogamy* and physically by *territoriality*. Territoriality and endogamy are, of course, mutually reinforcing for without physical propinquity people can hardly meet and mate and, conversely, successful reproduction, with all the lavish parental investment it requires for humans, favors territorialized kin groups. The prototypical ethny is thus a descent group bounded socially by inbreeding and spatially by territory.

Until the last few thousand years, such groups were of limited size as witnessed by many surviving "primitive" societies. The natural ethny in which hominids evolved for several thousand millennia probably did not exceed a couple of hundred individuals at the most. Evidence for this is the great mental and emotional strain on the human brain to "know" more than a few hundred individuals. We can recognize by sight many thousands, but our ability to associate complex personalities with faces and to make reliable enough predictions about people's behavior to render interaction sufficiently unstrained is quite limited. Urban life constantly strains these physiological limits, and when we must constantly interact with a larger and rapidly changing cast of characters the very nature of the interaction changes drastically, as has been repeatedly noted by social scientists and others. There are many fundamental differences between what the German sociologists called *Gemeinschaft* (the small-scale, intimate, face-to-face group of a few hundred people or the prototypical ethny in my terms) and *Gesellschaft* (the large, anomic, impersonal society characteristic of the industrial age).

We have evolved, I am arguing, the kind of brain to deal with small-scale, *Gemeinschaft*-type groups, the prototype of which is the ethny, the "we-group," the "in-group" of intimates who think of each other as an *extended family*. Beyond that kind and size of group, the strain of having to deal with people we do not know well enough, and therefore cannot trust, is of such a nature as to alter radically the very nature of the interaction. In the larger world, we expect ruthless self-interest and cheating to be rampant and to be constrained principally by the coercive power of the state. Furthermore, our brain, which in other respects is a stupefying complex instrument, rebels at "knowing" intimately more than a few hundred people at the limit. If we try to exceed an upper limit of, say, 500, we either have to slough off old acquaintances to allow new ones, or we simply fake familiarity and conviviality beyond our emotional and intellectual capabilities.

The primordial ethny is thus an extended family; indeed, the ethny represents the outer limits of that inbred group of near or distant kinsmen whom one knows as intimates and whom therefore one can trust. One intuitively expects fellow ethnics to behave at least somewhat benevolently toward one because of kin selection, reinforced by reciprocity. The shared genes predispose toward beneficence; the daily interdependence reinforces that kin selection. Fellow ethnics are, in the deepest sense, "our people."

This prototype of the small, endogamous, kin-related ethny is, of course, importantly modified in practice, especially in the larger societies that have arisen since the development of agriculture some 10,000 years ago, of large states some 5,000 years ago, and most recently of the industrial revolution 200 years ago. So far, we have merely sketched the revolutionary scenario of the ethny. Now we must fill in the picture by introducing the qualifications.

Ethnic endogamy is seldom strict and prescriptive. Generally, it is merely preferential, and, most importantly, asymmetrical by sex. The double standard of sexual morality that is so apparent in many aspects of our behavior and so readily understandable in terms of the biology of asymmetrical parental investment[5] . . . is also glaringly present in the application of ethnic endogamy. Much of the abundant literature on ethnicity and sex has been psychoanalytically oriented, invoking elaborate theories of frustration-aggression, sadomasochism, repression of libidinal urges, and attaction of forbidden fruits.[6] . . . The sociobiological paradigm provides a much simpler explanation. In nearly all species, the female is the scarce reproductive resource for the male rather than vice versa. There are fewer females available for insemination than males ready to inseminate. Eggs are big, few, and therefore costly; sperms are small, abundant, and therefore cheap. Since females invest much more in the reproductive process than males, they maximize their fitness by being choosy about their mating partners. They seek to pick the best possible mates in terms of genetic qualities and resources they have to offer. The male, on the other hand, maximizes his fitness by being promiscuous and by outcompeting his rivals in access to reproductive females.

Seen in that light, the ethny is a corporation of related men seeking to enhance each others' fitness by retaining a monopoly of sexual access to the women of their own group. This, however, does not preclude men from further enhancing their reproductive success by making the most of every opportunity to inseminate women from other groups. In fact, the whole history of ethnic relations powerfully confirms this interpretation. Men jealously "protect" "their" women from men of other groups, deeply resenting ethnic exogamy on the part of women, while at the same time seeking access to women from other groups. In ethnically stratified societies, this double standard takes the form of polygamy of the dominant-group men, with subordinate-group women becoming secondary wives and concubines. Where several ethnies live side by side in an unstratified system, the groups constantly raid each other for women.

This sexual asymmetry of endogamy has, of course, one important consequence—namely that no ethny is a completely closed breeding system. The circulation of women between ethnies continuously brings in fresh blood. One may then look at ethnic relations from the point of view of the circulation of women, and arrive at the following formulation. *Within the ethny,* a group of related men peaceably exchange kinswomen for wives among themselves. After the system has been in operation for several generations, the wives are also related to their husbands; frequently, they are preferentially cousins, in fact. This leads to a certain degree of inbreeding that is all the greater as the ethny is small.

*Between ethnies,* men use power and violence to secure access to women from other groups, and this reduces the level of inbreeding. When the ethnies in presence are equally matched, male competition for foreign women takes the form of interethnic raids. After an ethnic hierarchy has been established, subordinate-group men lose all or part of their control of "their" women and their reproductive success is curtailed, while upper-group men are polygynous and incorporate subordinate-group women. An ethnic hierarchy, therefore, generally results in a reduced fitness for subordinate-group males. The classical scenario for conquest is to rape the women and kill, castrate, or enslave the men.

Asymmetry of reproductive strategies for males and females has another important corollary for ethnic relations. In a situation of ethnic hierarchy, ethnic solidarity between men and women is undermined. The men of the subordinate group are always the losers and therefore have a reproductive interest in overthrowing the system. The women of the subordinate group, however, frequently have the option of being reproductively successful with dominant-group males. Indeed, even where forced into relationships with dominant males, they must cooperate in the interest of their children. . . .

Descent, I asserted, is the central feature of ethnicity. Yet, it is clear that, in many cases, the common descent ascribed to an ethny is fictive. In fact, in most cases, it is at least *partly* fictive. If such is the case, does not the fictive or putative character of kinship invalidate the sociobiological argument presented here? I think not. Ethnicity, I suggested, is extended kinship. Even in restricted kinship, descent is sometimes a fiction. In most societies, some children are adopted or are not the offspring of their supposed fathers. Nevertheless, these exceptions do not invalidate the general proposition that human kinship systems reflect biological relatedness. . . .

If kinship in the most restricted circle of the nuclear family is sometimes a biological fiction, it is little wonder that the greatly extended kind of kinship implicit in ethnicity should often be putative. The larger the ethny, the more likely this is. Clearly, for 50 million Frenchmen or 100 million Japanese, any common kinship that they may share is highly diluted, and known to be so. Similarly, when 25 million Afro-Americans call each other "brothers" and "sisters," they know that they are greatly extending the meaning of these terms. The enormous ethnies, running into millions of members, that characterize industrial societies are limiting cases, far removed from the evolutionary prototype of a few hundred people that we have been talking about.

Yet—and this is what begs explanation—the fiction of kinship, even in modern industrial societies, has to be sufficiently credible for ethnic solidarity to be effective. One cannot create an instant ethny by creating a myth. The myth has to be rooted in historical reality to be accepted. Ethnicity can be *manipulated* but not *manufactured*. Unless ethnicity is rooted in generations of shared historical experience, it cannot be created *ex nihilo*. . . .

If myths of ethnicity must be credible, what tests of ethnicity are used to decide on their credibility? What criteria do people use to decide whether an individual is a fellow ethnic or not? In the small-scale societies typical of our species until a few thousand years ago, the simple test of acquaintance based on previous association sufficed in most circumstances. We share with other higher vertebrates, such as dogs and monkeys, the ability to recognize individuals and to carry faces in our memories for long periods of time. Occasionally a person kidnapped by another group early in life might face the problem of establishing his filiation with his group of origin, but, in most cases, in societies of a few hundred people the test of membership is straightforward enough: the person belongs if he is known to belong; he does not belong either if he is known not to belong or if he is not known to belong.

Obviously, the larger the society gets, the more difficult the problem of ascertaining membership becomes. Already in "primitive" societies that run into tens of thousands, membership is no longer always established *prima facie*; it must be proven. At that level the test is generally genealogical: the unknown individual claims membership through filiation with known members. Kinship, that is, is explicitly used to establish ethnicity. Australian aborigines are said to have been able to do so across the face of the continent, but this is an extreme case. Usually, tracing filiation only works in groups of moderate size (a few thousand) and spatial dispersal (a few hundred square kilometers).

Where societies run into hundreds of thousands or even millions of members, and cover vast stretches of territory, the situation becomes complicated. Ethnicity can no longer be so easily ascertained and, therefore, it can be faked. If ethnism is a way of maximizing fitness through extended nepotism, then a clever animal like man can be expected to fake common ethnicity for gain. Con games in which individuals gain "undeserved" advantage by exaggerating or counterfeiting a relationship to their victims thrive in large-scale societies that lack the easy controls of recognition and intimacy found in small societies. Ethnicity is one of these manipulable relationships. At the same time, there are occasions where ethnicity has to be established quickly, where one literally shoots first and asks questions later. How, then, can one establish ethnicity quickly and reliably and also keep cheats under control? What features will be chosen as *ethnic markers*?

There are many possibilities, tending to fall into three main categories of traits. The three are not mutually exclusive, and their respective effectiveness varies greatly according to circumstances.

*First*, one can pick a genetically transmitted phenotype, such as skin pigmentation, stature (as with the Tuzi of Rwanda and Burundi), hair texture, facial features, or some such "racial" characteristic. Groups that are socially defined by genetic phenotypes are called "races," and societies that put emphasis on biological traits to differentiate groups within it can be called "racist."

*Second*, one can rely on a man-made ethnic uniform. Members of one's group are identified by bodily mutilations and/or adornments carried as visible badges of group belonging. These markers range from clothing and headgear to body painting; tatooing; circumcision; tooth filing; and sundry mutilations of the lips, nose, and earlobes.

*Third*, the test can be behavioral. Ethnicity is determined by speech, demeanor, manners, esoteric lore, or some other proof of competence in a behavioral repertoire characteristic of the group.

A brief review of the three classes of ethnic markers is useful at this point, for each has a different set of properties and of structural consequences. Race would seem the most obvious solution to the problem of ethnic recognition, especially if there is a biological basis for the extended nepotism that we are discussing. Does it not stand to reason that genetically inheritable phenotypes are the most reliable markers of ethnicity, if by ethnicity one means, in the last analysis, genetic relatedness? Would not one, therefore, expect racism to be universal? The answer to the first question, a theoretical one, is "yes," and to the second, an empirical question, "no." . . .

It is also important to stress that phenotypes chosen for social relevance, while often clearly visible markers of genetic origin, are typically biologically trivial in terms of fitness, abilities, aptitudes, and temperament —indeed, anything of social consequence. To suggest that the sociobiological theory presented here is racist . . . is nonsensical. Our theory says nothing about racial differences between human groups—much less about any invidious ranking between them. On the contrary, it stresses a common biological propensity, not only of all humans, but also of all social animals, to favor kin over nonkin, a propensity that gets translated into ethnism and sometimes (but only sometimes) into racism. . . .

Now, let us return to the problem of the presence or absence of racism in human societies. With our contemporary knowledge of human genetics, we categorically exclude parenthood on the basis of a single non-matching allele and, conversely, we can establish kinship beyond reasonable doubt by matching individuals on a multiplicity of alleles of known frequency distribution in certain populations. In practice, however, most people are not geneticists and, indeed, until less than a century ago, people had only the vaguest notions of how characteristics were inherited. The outcome is that while in many, perhaps most, human societies, tests of physical resemblance are used to assess probability of kinship and, by extension, ethnicity, these tests are seldom the only ones or even the main ones that are relied upon, at least as far as establishing ethnic membership is concerned.

The reason for this seeming paradox is apparent enough. At the rudimentary level of folk genetics, racial phenotypes are often very poor indicators of group membership because neighboring populations typically maintain a sufficient rate of migration to create genetic gradients such as that *intragroup* variation on specific loci is much greater than *intergroup* variation. In short, neighboring populations—the very ones that are concerned about maintaining and defending ethnic boundaries—typically look very much like each other. Phenotype is useful to distinguish individuals within groups but not to distinguish between groups. Let us take the example of eye and hair color in Europe. There is a gradient from south to north of increasing frequency of the recessive alleles for blue eyes and blond hair. A Greek army fighting in Finland might make reasonably effective use of these genetic traits as markers of ethnicity—but not in the far more likely circumstance of having to fight Albanians or Turks. Similarly, skin color might be used by a Moroccan army crossing the Sahara, but not between Moroccans and Algerians, or Ghaneans and Togolese. The most crucial ethnic boundaries most of the time are those between groups competing for scarce resources in the same general vicinity. Those are precisely the circumstances under which racial distinctions are most useless.

One can therefore expect racism to appear only where long-distance immigration has suddenly put in presence substantial numbers of people whose physical appearance is different enough as to make genetic phenotype a reliable basis for distinguishing between groups. People must migrate across genetic gradients before their physical appearance can be used as a reliable basis of inferring group membership. . . .

For these reasons, racism, as the primary basis for group distinctions, has been the exception rather than the rule. Racism is not a Western, much less a capitalist, monopoly. For example, when the tall Hamitic Tuzi conquered shorter Bantu speakers to the South, they invented their own brand of racism (more specifically, "heightism") to buttress their domination of the Rwanda and Burundi kingdoms.[7] . . . But there, too, the reason was the same as for the development of Western racism in the wake of European colonial expansion: long-distance migration across a wide genetic gradient—in this case, in body stature. In short, racism can be expected to develop and thrive where genetically inherited phenotypes are the easiest, most visible, and most reliable predictors of group membership. When phenotypes lose these properties through intermixture of groups, cultural criteria typically supplant racial criteria of group membership. . . .

The theory presented here accounts better for the appearance and disappearance of racism in various times and places than competing theories that attribute racism either to ideological factors . . . or to the capitalist mode of production. . . . More than anything else, it is long-distance migration over genetic gradients that creates racism: conversely, miscegenation attenuates it. And miscegenation almost invariably occurs because racism as such does little to inhibit it. Dominant-group men, whether racist or not, are seldom reluctant to maximize their fitness with subordinate-group women. It takes extraordinary measures of physical segregation, such as long existed in South Africa and the United States, to preserve a racial caste system. Racism is the exception rather than the rule in intergroup relations, and racially based systems are peculiarly conflict-ridden and unstable. Attempts at maintaining them often result in cataclysmic bloodshed. . . .

Both the second and the third categories of cultural markers are manmade and cultural, but the second is visual and artifactual, while the third is behavioral. The two types of marker are often used conjointly, as multiple tests of ethnicity. If we turn first to what I have called the "ethnic uniform" type of marker, it has the advantage of providing a visible and therefore rapid clue of group membership. This is quite useful in combat or contest situations, for example, as witnessed by the widespread use of uniforms by armies, sport teams, and the like. Then the premium is on easy, quick detection at a distance. A drawback of many of these easily visible clues provided by headgear, clothing, plumage, body paint, and the like, is that they can be faked. A system of ethnic recognition based solely on these would be widely open to cheating, and indeed cheating does occur as when opposing armies try to infiltrate each other by donning their opponents' uniforms. The sanctions against such cheating, incidentally, are often exceptionally severe, such as immediate execution when, normally, simple capture would be expected.

Ethnic markers based on bodily mutilations, such as facial tattoos; tooth filing; circumcision; nose, lip, and ear piercing; and the like, are not easily reversible, but they are often not so striking and can only be identified at close quarters.

Finally, there are behavioral ethnic markers, which are among the most reliable and hence commonly used. They have the advantage of being difficult to fake, because the performance criteria are often of considerable subtlety and intricacy, but they require skill and time in being applied and hence do not satisfy the criteria of ease and immediacy. Behavioral criteria may include styles of body movement, gesturing, eating, or greeting etiquette, and the like, but language holds pride of place among them. The way people speak places them more accurately and reliably than almost any other behavioral trait. Language and dialect can be learned, of course, but the ability to learn a foreign tongue without a detectable accent drops sharply around puberty. Therefore, speech quality is a reliable (and difficult to fake) test of what group an individual has been raised in. Moreover, acquisition of foreign speech is extremely difficult except through prolonged contact with native speakers, another safety feature of the linguistic test.

. . . Fellow ethnics are those whose speech is sufficiently like one's own to allow for the unhindered communication of the entire range of human emotions and messages. Other languages are learned for the sake of instrumental convenience; the mother tongue is spoken for the sheer joy of it. It is probably this fundamental difference in the speaking of first versus second languages that, more than any single factor, makes for the profound qualitative difference between intraethnic and interethnic relations. The mother tongue is the language of kinship. Every other tongue is a mere convenience between strangers.

Let us summarize the argument so far. Humans, like other social animals, are biologically selected to be nepotistic because, by favoring kin, they maximize their inclusive fitness. Until the last few thousand years, hominids interacted in relatively small groups of a few score to a couple of hundred individuals who tended to mate with each other and, therefore, to form rather tightly knit groups of close and distant kinsmen. Physical boundaries of territory and social boundaries of inbreeding separated these small human societies from each other. Within the group, there was a large measure of peace and cooperation between kinsman and in-laws (frequently both kinds of relationship overlapped). Relations between groups were characterized at best by mistrust and avoidance—but frequently by open conflict over scarce resources. These solidary groups were, in fact, primordial ethnies.

Such was the evolutionary origin of ethnicity: an extended kin group. With the progressive growth in the size of human societies, the boundaries of the ethny became wider; the bonds of kinship were correspondingly diluted, and indeed sometimes became fictive, and ethnicity became increasingly manipulated and perverted to other ends, including domination and exploitation. The urge, however, to continue to define a collectivity larger than the immediate circle of kinsmen on the basis of biological descent continues to be present even in the most industrialized mass societies of today. A wide variety of ethnic markers are used to define such collectivities of descent, but their choice is not capricious. Those markers will be stressed that are, in fact, objectively reliable predictors of common descent, given the environment in which the discriminating group finds itself. Sometimes, but rather rarely, race is the paramount criterion; more commonly, cultural characteristics, especially language, do a much better job of defining ethnic boundaries.

So far, we have suggested the *raison d'être* of ethnicity—the reason for its persistence and for its seeming imperviousness to rationality. Ethnic (and racial) sentiments often seem irrational because they have an underlying driving force of their own, which is ultimately the blunt, purposeless natural selection of genes that are reproductively successful. Genes favoring nepotistic behavior have a selective advantage. It does not matter whether their carrying organisms are aware of being nepotistic or even that they consciously know their relatives. Organisms must only behave *as if they knew*. It happens that, in humans, they often know in a conscious way, though they are sometimes mistaken.

The phenomenon of ethnicity in humans, however, is not in principle different from the phenomenon of boundary maintenance between animal societies. Other animals maintain clear boundaries between themselves and other species, most importantly barriers to matings between closely related species that are the very mechanism making for speciation in the first instance.[8] . . . But humans are not even unique in maintaining societal boundaries *within* the species. Thousands of species of eusocial insects keep different colonies of the same species quite distinct from each other, often using pheromones (smell signals) to recognize each other.[9] . . . Among mammals, man included, the boundaries between societies are, on the whole, much *less* rigid than among the eusocial insects but nevertheless, societal boundaries between groups of conspecifics are clearly marked and defended.

We conventionally restrict the meaning of ethnicity to humans, but we would not be unduly extending the meaning of the term by applying it to troops of macaques, prides of lions, or packs of wolves. These other animal societies, too, are held together by kin selection and must compete with other societies of conspecifics for scarce resources.[10] . . . In principle, the problems of boundary maintenance are the same for humans and other animals, despite the vastly greater order of complexity of human societies. . . .

NOTES

1. Edward O. Wilson, *Sociobiology: The New Synthesis* (Cambridge, Mass.: Harvard University Press, 1975).

2. Richard Dawkins, *The Selfish Gene* (London: Oxford University Press, 1976).

3. Edward O. Wilson, *Sociobiology: The New Synthesis;* Martin Daly and Margo Wilson, *Sex, Evolution and Behavior* (North Scituate, Mass.: Duxbury Press, 1978).

4. Claude Lévi-Strauss, *The Elementary Structures of Kinship* (Boston: Beacon Press, 1969). Originally published in French in 1949.

5. Daly and Wilson, *Sex, Evolution and Behavior;* Robert L. Trivers, "Parental Investment and Sexual Selection," in B. Campbell (ed.), *Sexual Selection and the Descent of Man* (Chicago: Aldine, 1972).

6. T. W. Adorno et al., *The Authoritarian Personality* (New York: Harper, 1950); Roger Bastide, *Sociologie et Psychanalyse* (Paris: Presses Universitaires de France, 1950); Gilbert Freyre, 1964. *The Masters and the Slaves* (New York: Knopf, 1964); O. Mannoni, *Prospero and Caliban* (New York: Praeger, 1964); Lilian Smith, *Killers of the Dream* (New York: Anchor, 1963); Charles Herbert Stember, *Sexual Racism* (New York: Elsevier, 1976).

7. Jacques J. Maquet, *The Premise of Inequality in Ruanda* (London: Oxford University Press, 1961).

8. Ernst Mayr, *Animal Species and Evolution* (Cambridge, Mass.: Harvard University Press, 1963).

9. Edward O. Wilson, *The Insect Societies* (Cambridge, Mass.: Harvard University Press, 1971).

10. Edward O. Wilson, *Sociobiology: The New Synthesis.*

# 17

# Prejudice and Reason

## Brice R. Wachterhauser

I

Perhaps no other aspect of Hans-Georg Gadamer's *Wahrheit und Methode* [*Truth and Method*] has generated more controversy and caustic criticism than his attempt to defend the role of "prejudice" (*Vorurteil*) in human understanding. Gadamer's goal in challenging what he calls "the Enlightenment's prejudice against prejudice"[1] is not to defend irresponsible, idiosyncratic, parochial, or otherwise self-willed understanding in the human sciences, but to argue that all human cognition is "finite" and "limited" in the sense that it always involves, to borrow Polanyi's phrase, a "tacit dimension" of implicit judgments, concerns, or commitments which shape definitively our grasp of the subject matter in ways we cannot anticipate or control. . . . Gadamer is suggesting that the human intellect is always, at least in part, conditioned and determined in important ways by historical factors outside its control. Hence a human intellect can never become fully autonomous; it remains forever and always "finite." But the presence of a tacit determining factor also suggests another sense in which the human intellect can be called "finite." Such prejudices preclude the possibility of either viewing the subject matter as such, from a perspective-

Originally published as "Prejudice, Reason, and Force," *Philosophy* 63, no. 244 (April 1988): 231–53. Copyright © 1988 by Cambridge University Press. Reprinted in edited form by permission of the publisher and the author.

free viewpoint, or of so mastering all possible prejudices that one could go freely from one set of prejudices to another until one had exhausted all the possible perspectives from which the subject matter could show itself. The fact that these perspectives are relative to a historical context and the fact that there are an infinite number of potential perspectives from which we might see an issue or subject matter in a significantly different light makes the anticipation of future prejudices impossible to anticipate. Hence we can never grasp the subject matter as such or all at once. This leads Gadamer to deny, for example, that phenomenology's goal of a pre-suppositionless seeing is possible to achieve. In fact, Gadamer would deny that human reason has any such capacity to see "from nowhere,"[2] or from any perspective outside a specific historic context which might justify the presumption to understand, as it were, *sub specie aeternitatis*. Such locutions harbor views of human rationality that ignore the fact that human rationality is always limited and "situated," and it is this context-bound nature of reason that Gadamer wishes to emphasize and explore. . . .

According to Gadamer, . . . seminal prejudices have two intimately related sources. They arise, first of all, from the intellectual traditions in which our intellects and sensibilities have been formed and they arise, secondly, from the exigencies of our current historical situation which impinge on our inquiries in equally powerful but scarcely noticed ways. . . . [T]his two-sided involvement in history provides the basis for Gadamer's claim that we never understand anything "as such," i.e., as a fully discrete, fully determined, and intelligible entity in its own right (as Plato, for example, may have claimed for the philosopher's grasp of the Ideas). Rather we always understand a text or an issue both as "situated" in a tradition in which the text or issue is rooted in a history of interpretation *and* vis-à-vis our own historically mediated needs. In this sense, Gadamer argues that no text or subject matter exists in an historical vacuum or in a pure logical space. Rather every subject matter we can understand exists in a . . . "history of effects" which makes our grasp of it part of an ongoing process of "interpretation" and "dialogue" between our past and present.

## II

This emphasis on the role of historically informed prejudices in understanding is also essential to Gadamer's critique of "method" in the human sciences. Gadamer's rejection of "method" is not a rejection of the need for rigor, discipline, or painstaking care in our intellectual endeavors. Rather it is a rejection of the Cartesian ideal, which our culture has been pursuing for over 300 years now, that there is some *explicit* and *universal* procedure which will enable us to settle all of our significant disputes and disagreements once and for all. Because prejudice points to an indispensable but tacit and changing element in human cognition, such a method seems impossible in principle to achieve. All prejudices are rooted in our past, our historicity, which is covered over and occluded by the many events and layers of meaning that have shaped that past. Hence, Gadamer argues that the conditions that give rise to prejudices can never be objectified completely and critically evaluated. The role of prejudice in cognition seems to render the ideal of a fully *explicit* procedure impossible to achieve. Insofar as any procedure would develop from historical roots and these roots themselves are, in large part, irretrievably lost, an *implicit* element is always involved inexorably in any method. But in addition to the fact that all our present activities are grounded in a past we can never again make completely present, it is also the case, according to Gadamer, that the prejudices which determine any one intellectual community change from community to community and from age to age. Hence if such prejudices always play a role in influencing the outcome of our intellectual deliberations, then there is no way that we could ever escape their ever-changing influence and put in their place a truly universal method for settling our disputes. Instead all our attempts to understand are relative to historically situated prejudgments we bring to our inquiries.

Gadamer's challenge to the Cartesian ideal of an explicit and universal "method" for adjudicating disputes is, I think, a serious one. It becomes even more telling, however, when we consider that Gadamer seems to be arguing that prejudices often have a mode of existence which is categorically different than that of a theory, a belief, or a fully developed concept. The main point to be grasped here is that prejudices, as they actually operate in our historically situated lives, are often nonpropositional in nature.[3] This is an important point because if it is ignored one could plausibly argue that we can at least approach the Cartesian goal by making as many of our prejudices thematic as is humanly possible in order to evaluate them critically one by one. This is not possible according to Gadamer because many, although not all, of our prejudices simply cannot be made thematic. Prejudices can be placed on a continuum which ranges from the propositional belief or preference to an inchoate, vague, but effective nonpropositional intuition, "bent of mind," or "intellectual sensibility." More often than not, prejudices are *not* fully determinate, objectifiable standards, beliefs, propositions, etc., which are simply applied unconsciously in cases where judgment is called for. Rather, they are more likely to be inchoate intuitions or predispositions of mind which both help, in an essential way, to determine the subject matter they interact with *and* are simultaneously determined by them. This means, strictly speaking, that prejudices are often not fixed, objective realities which can be studied reflexively on their own terms. Prejudices are, more often than not, inherently elusive. This is so because prejudices change over time in the course of their interactions with the subject matter of understanding as much as the meanings of these same subject matters change over time in the course of their interactions with prejudices. Thus, if Gadamer is right, we are never in a position to make them fully explicit and asymptotically approach their objective justification; they are inherently elusive and nonobjectifiable in principle.

This understanding of the role of inchoate but powerful prejudgments in cognition is not as foreign to our experience as it might first appear. For example, it is often held that moral intuitions play an indispensable role in our ethical judgments. It is precisely the elusive and inscrutable nature of such intuitions which often limits our ability to reach consensus on controversial ethical problems. We often find it impossible to make such intuitions fully thematic in order to evaluate them rationally. And yet such intuitions, however limiting and seemingly inscrutable and intractable they are, do change over time through rational argumentation. They are not immune from criticism and development. Although we may never transcend our original moral intuitions entirely, they do adjust themselves (at least to some exent) to relevant facts and compelling logic. In short, although they may continue to influence our moral grasp of things, such moral intuitions can reach a kind of *quid pro quo* arrangement with critical rationality which avoids both wholesale domination of our moral reason and subsumption under its supposed autonomy. As Rawls has phrased it, moral inquiry tends toward a kind of "reflective equilibrium" between intuition and theoretical argument.

Gadamer's point seems to be that something like a process of reflective equilibrium can be seen in all of our experience. We are always moving back and forth between prejudice (or historical shaped intuitions) and explicit reasoning without being exactly sure where we stand at any one time. The human condition is such that although we can with some confidence claim to be rational, we can never divorce that reason from all historically mediated intuitions and interests. Of course, as experience grows we become more aware of past prejudices but this does not mean that we are approaching a point without prejudice; it implies simply that some of our prejudices have shifted sufficiently to cast light on some of our former prejudices. Consider Gadamer's claim that:

One of the fundamental structures of all speaking is that we are guided by preconceptions and anticipations in our talking in such a way that these continually remain hidden and that it takes a disruption in oneself of the intended meaning of what one is saying to become conscious of these prejudices as such. In general the disruption comes about through some new experience in which a previous opinion reveals itself to be untenable. But the basic prejudices are not easily dislodged and protect themselves by claiming self-evident certainty for themselves. . . .[4]

This dialectic of shifting prejudices, some concealed and some revealed, is . . . a potentially infinite dialectic between prejudice and critical reflection. . . . The human mind never quite, as it were, catches up with itself. Our roots in history go deeper than the eye of reflective consciousness can see. This is why we can criticize and reject some of our prejudices without approaching a prejudice-free or presuppositionless state. As our historical experience expands we are constantly forming new prejudices and transforming old ones. As "finite" beings we are never completely aware of everything that goes into this process but the fact that Gadamer is stressing is that historical beings do not stagnate; they are made and remade in the course of time. Hence we are always occupying new points of view and abandoning old ones. . . . This implies that self-knowledge of our prejudices is never complete and where it is had it always contains an element of alienation, i.e., of separation of ourselves from a past way of being and experiencing the world. Such an "alienated" knowledge of prejudices is not an immediate knowing of them as they operate; it is a knowing in retrospect after they had been shaped and transcended by the historical process of which they are a part. Moreover, some prejudices always remain hidden. In this sense, prejudices are not like the Kantian categories which are explicit, knowable as such, fixed, and unchanging and also invaringly able to impose their meaningful structures on the manifold of sense. Instead the prejudices of Gadamerian consciousness are fluid with respect to each other and the world; they affect the meaning of our world; but they are equally affected by it.

This fact that we "suffer" our prejudices, the fact that we passively experience our prejudices as conditions of our lives over which we have limited control (despite the fact that they are continually revised), leads Gadamer to make the deep claim that our prejudices always constitute, at least in part, who we *are*. This is a claim about the ontological status of human being. To be human is to find oneself in a historical context that always does more to us than determine, say, the particular style of clothes we wear or the particular grammar and syntax of the language we speak. History goes deeper in that it determines the possibilities of our lives; in short, it influences our ability to experience ourselves and the world in the particular way we do. . . .


NOTES

1. Hans-Georg Gadamer, *Wahrheit und Methode* (Tübingen: J. C. B. Mohr [Paul Siebeck], 1960), pp. 254, 255. English translation, *Truth and Method* (New York: Seabury Press, 1975), pp. 239–40.

2. Thomas Nagel, *The View from Nowhere* (Oxford University Press, 1985).

3. This is, admittedly, an interpretative attempt on my part to understand what Gadamer seems to be saying. It seems to be consistent with the elusive and changing nature of prejudices as Gadamer understands them. More explicitly, I think, it explains why Gadamer feels we cannot asymptotically approach an objective justification of our prejudices. For a critique of Gadamer that takes him to task for overlooking such a pursuit of objectivity see Charles Larmore, "Tradition, Objectivity, and Hermeneutics," in Brice Wachterhauser, ed., *Hermeneutics and Modern Philosophy* (Albany, N.Y.: SUNY Press, 1986).

4. Hans-Georg Gadamer, "Semantics and Hermeneutics," in David E. Linge, ed., *Philosophical Hermeneutics* (Berkeley: University of California Press, 1976), p. 92.

# 18

# Evolutionary Morality and Xenophopia

## Edward O. Wilson

The empiricist view concedes that moral codes are devised to conform to some drives of human nature and to suppress others. *Ought* is not the translation of human nature but of the public will, which can be made increasingly wise and stable through the understanding of the needs and pitfalls of human nature. It recognizes that the strength of commitment can wane as a result of new knowledge and experience, with the result that certain rules may be desacralized, old laws rescinded, and behavior that was once prohibited freed. It also recognizes that for the same reason new moral codes may need to be devised, with the potential in time of being made sacred.

If the empiricist worldview is correct, *ought* is just shorthand for one kind of factual statement, a word that denotes what society first chose (or was coerced) to do, and then codified. The naturalistic fallacy is thereby reduced to the naturalistic dilemma. The solution of the dilemma is not difficult. It is this: *Ought* is the product of a material process. The solution points the way to an objective grasp of the origin of ethics.

A few investigators are now embarked on just such a foundational inquiry. Most agree that ethical codes have arisen by evolution through the interplay of biology and culture. In a sense they are reviving the idea of moral sentiments developed in the eighteenth century by the British empiricists Francis Hutcheson, David Hume, and Adam Smith.

By moral sentiments is now meant moral instincts as defined by the modern behavioral sciences, subject to judgment according to their consequences. The sentiments are thus derived from epigenetic rules, hereditary biases in mental development, usually conditioned by emotion, that influence concepts and decisions made from them. The primary origin of the moral instincts is the dynamic relation between cooperation and defection. The essential ingredient for the molding of the instincts during genetic evolution in any species is intelligence high enough to judge and manipulate the tension generated by the dynamism. That level of intelligence allows the building of complex mental scenarios well into the future, as I described in the earlier chapter on the mind. It occurs, so far as known, only in human beings and perhaps their closest relatives among the higher apes.

A way of envisioning the hypothetical earliest stages of moral evolution is provided by game theory, particularly the solutions to the famous Prisoner's Dilemma. Consider the following typical scenario of the Dilemma. Two gang members have been arrested for murder and are being questioned separately. The evidence against them is strong but not compelling. The first gang member believes that if he turns state's witness, he will be granted immunity and his partner will be sentenced to life in prison. But he is also aware that his partner has the same option. That is the dilemma. Will the two gang members independently defect so that both take the hard fall? They will not, because they agreed in advance to remain silent if caught. By doing so, both hope to be convicted on a lesser charge or escape punishment altogether. Criminal gangs have turned this principle of calculation into an ethical precept: Never rat on another member; always be a stand-up guy. Honor does exist among thieves. If we view the gang as a society of sorts, the code is the same as that of a captive soldier in wartime obliged to give only name, rank, and serial number.

In one form or another, comparable dilemmas that are solvable by cooperation occur constantly and everywhere in daily life. The payoff is variously money, status, power, sex, access, comfort, and health. Most of these proximate rewards are converted into the universal bottom line of Darwinian genetic fitness: greater longevity and a secure, growing family.

And so it has likely always been. Imagine a Paleolithic hunter band, say composed of five men. One hunter considers breaking away from the others to look for an antelope on his own. If successful he will gain a large quantity of meat and hide, five times greater than if he stays with the band and they are successful. But he knows from experience that his chances of success alone are very low, much less than the chances of a band of five working together. In addition, whether successful alone or not, he will suffer animosity from the others for lessening their own prospects. By custom the band members remain together and share the animals they kill equitably. So the hunter stays. He also observes good manners while doing so, especially if he is the one who makes the kill. Boastful pride is condemned because it rips the delicate web of reciprocity.

Now suppose that human propensities to cooperate or defect are heritable: Some members are innately more cooperative, others less so. In this respect moral aptitude would simply be like almost all other mental traits studied to date. Among traits with documented heritability, those closest to moral aptitude are empathy to the distress of others and certain processes of attachment between infants and their caregivers. To the heritability of moral aptitude add the abundant evidence of history that cooperative individuals generally survive longer and leave more offspring. It is to be expected that in the course of evolutionary history, genes predisposing people toward cooperative behavior would have come to predominate in the human population as a whole.

Such a process repeated through thousands of generations inevitably gave birth to the moral sentiments. With the exception of stone psychopaths (if any truly exist), these instincts are vividly experienced by every person variously as conscience, self-respect, remorse, empathy, shame, humility, and moral outrage. They bias cultural evolution toward the conventions that express the universal moral codes of honor, patriotism, altruism, justice, compassion, mercy, and redemption.

The dark side to the inborn propensity to moral behavior is xenophobia. Because personal familiarity and common interest are vital in social transactions, moral sentiments evolved to be selective. And so it has ever been, and so it will ever be. People give trust to strangers with effort, and true compassion is a commodity in chronically short supply. Tribes cooperate only through carefully defined treaties and other conventions. They are quick to imagine themselves victims of conspiracies by competing groups, and they are prone to dehumanize and murder their rivals during periods of severe conflict. They cement their own group loyalties by means of sacred symbols and ceremonies. Their mythologies are filled with epic victories over menacing enemies.

The complementary instincts of morality and tribalism are easily manipulated. Civilization has made them more so. Only ten thousand years ago, a tick in geological time, when the agricultural revolution began in the Middle East, in China, and in Mesoamerica, populations increased in density tenfold over those of hunter-gatherer societies. Families settled on small plots of land, villages proliferated, and labor was finely divided as a growing minority of the populace specialized as craftsmen, traders, and soldiers. The rising agricultural societies, egalitarian at first, became hierarchical. As chiefdoms and then states thrived on agricultural surpluses, hereditary rulers and priestly castes took power. The old ethical codes were transformed into coercive regulations, always to the advantage of the ruling classes. About this time the idea of law-giving gods originated. Their commands lent the ethical codes overpowering authority, once again—no surprise—to the favor of the rulers.

Because of the technical difficulty of analyzing such phenomena in an objective manner, and because people resist biological explanations of their higher cortical functions in the first place, very little progress has been made in the biological exploration of the moral sentiments. Even so, it is an astonishing circumstance that the study of ethics has advanced so little since the nineteenth century. As a result the most distinguishing and vital qualities of the human species remain a blank space on the scientific map. I think it an error to pivot discussions of ethics upon the free-standing assumptions of contemporary philosophers who have evidently never given thought to the evolutionary origin and material functioning of the human brain. In no other domain of the humanities is a union with the natural sciences more urgently needed.

When the ethical dimension of human nature is at last fully opened to such exploration, the innate epigenetic rules of moral reasoning will probably not prove to be aggregated into simple instincts such as bonding, cooperativeness, or altruism. Instead, the rules most probably will turn out to be an ensemble of many algorithms whose interlocking activities guide the mind across a landscape of nuanced moods and choices.

Such a prestructured mental world may at first seem too complicated to have been created by autonomous genetic evolution alone. But all the evidence of biology suggests that just this process was enough to spawn the millions of species of life surrounding us. Each kind of animal is furthermore guided through its life cycle by unique and often elaborate sets of instinctual algorithms, many of which are beginning to yield to genetic and neurobiological analyses. With all these examples before us, it is not unreasonable to conclude that human behavior originated the same way.

Meanwhile, the mélanges of moral reasoning employed by modern societies are, to put the matter simply, a mess. They are chimeras, composed of odd parts stuck together. Paleolithic egalitarian and tribalistic instincts are still firmly installed. As part of the genetic foundation of human nature, they cannot be replaced. In some cases, such as quick hostility to strangers and competing groups, they have become generally ill-adapted and persistently dangerous. Above the fundamental instincts rise superstructures of arguments and rules that accommodate the novel institutions created by cultural evolution. These accommodations, which reflect the attempt to maintain order and further tribal interests, have been too volatile to track by genetic evolution; they are not yet in the genes.

Little wonder, then, that ethics is the most publicly contested of all philosophical enterprises. Or that political science, which at foundation is primarily the study of applied ethics, is so frequently problematic. Neither is informed by anything that would be recognizable as authentic theory in the natural sciences. Both ethics and political science lack a foundation of verifiable knowledge of human nature sufficient to produce cause-and-effect predictions and sound judgments based on them. Surely it will be prudent to pay closer attention to the deep springs of ethical behavior. The greatest void in knowledge in such a venture is the biology of the moral sentiments. In time this subject can be understood, I believe, by paying attention to the following topics.

- *The definition of the moral sentiments*: first by precise descriptions from experimental psychology, then by analysis of the underlying neural and endocrine responses.

- *The genetics of the moral sentiments*: most easily approached through measurements of the heritability of the psychological and physiological processes of ethical behavior, and eventually, with difficulty, by identification of the prescribing genes.

- *The development of the moral sentiments as products of the interactions of genes and environment*. The research is most effective when conducted at two levels: the histories of ethical systems as part of the emergence of different cultures, and the cognitive development of individuals living in a variety of cultures. Such investigations are already well along in anthropology and psychology. In the future they will be augmented by contributions from biology.

- *The deep history of the moral sentiments*: why they exist in the first place, presumably by their contributions to survival and reproductive success during the long periods of prehistoric time in which they genetically evolved.

From a convergence of these several approaches, the true origin and meaning of ethical behavior may come into focus. If so, a more certain measure can then be taken of the strengths and flexibility of the epigenetic rules composing the various moral sentiments. From that knowledge, it should be possible to adapt the ancient moral sentiments more wisely to the swiftly changing conditions of modern life into which, willy-nilly and largely in ignorance, we have plunged ourselves.

Then new answers might be found for the truly important questions of moral reasoning. How can the moral instincts be ranked? Which are best subdued and to what degree, which validated by law and symbol? How can precepts be left open to appeal under extraordinary circumstances? In the new understanding can be located the most effective means for reaching consensus. No one can guess the form the agreements will take. The process, however, can be predicted with assurance. It will be democratic, weakening the clash of rival religions and ideologies. History is moving decisively in that direction, and people are by nature too bright and too contentious to abide anything else. And the pace can be confidently predicted: Change will come slowly, across generations, because old beliefs die hard even when demonstrably false.

# 19

# The Hate That Makes Men Straight: Psychoanalysts Probe the Roots of Homophobia

## Richard Goldstein

If the murder of Matthew Shepard accomplishes nothing else, it will have focused attention on a bias so pervasive that it hardly seems like bias at all. This is homophobia, the last acceptable form of bigotry; the prejudice that enshrines itself in sermons and Senate speeches; the hate that does not hesitate to speak its name. Yet precisely because it is so embedded in the culture, homophobia doesn't register as anything more than an appropriate response, albeit one that sometimes gets out of hand. It takes a horrendous image—like the body of a waiflike young man strung up on a fence, his face so bloody from pistol-whipping that his flesh shows only through the streaks of his tears—to penetrate America's indifference to this systematic loathing.

On Friday the American Psychoanalytic Association will host its first public forum on homophobia at the Waldorf Astoria. The roster of presenters ranges from Democratic bulldog Barney Frank to Harvard pastor Peter Gomes to Berkeley psychoanalyst Nancy Chodorow. That night, *Out* magazine and the New School will sponsor a discussion featuring Arthur Dong, whose documentary *License to Kill* graphically demonstrates that gay-bashers are, at heart, regular guys. These two events are part of a growing recognition that something irrational but nevertheless central to the sexual order is involved in the hatred for gay people.

Murder is only the most extreme expression of this fury. According to a comprehensive recent study, nearly half of all lesbians and gay men have been threatened with violence, 33 percent have been chased or followed, 25 percent have had objects thrown at them, 13 percent have been spat upon, 9 percent have been assaulted with a weapon, and 80 percent have been verbally harassed. The homophobic-crime rate may actually be rising as the religious right steps up its antigay organizing, and as homosexuals achieve greater visibility. Despite police denials, activists maintain that the incidence of antigay attacks in New York City has increased dramatically over the past year, especially in neighborhoods like Chelsea, the Village, and Park Slope, where bashers can count on finding queer prey.

These crimes follow a pattern so predictable that one can virtually read the structure of homophobia on its victims' bodies. All too typically, there is gruesome violence—"overkill," in the activists' words—as well as an unusual preference for weapons like clubs and knives, and rituals of sexual degradation or mutilation. Allen Schindler, the gay sailor murdered in a men's room by his shipmates, suffered severe lacerations of his penis. Matthew Shepard's groin was black and blue from repeated kicking. Brandon Teena, whose offense was passing so successfully as a man, was raped as well as murdered. This pattern attests to the psychic venom that underlies antigay violence, but ultimately, like other hate crimes, gay bashing is a social act.

The perpetrators are usually young men, often operating in a pack, with such a profound sense of righteousness that they take little trouble to hide their crimes. As in a lynching, Shepard's body was strung up as if the killers intended it to be displayed (strange fruit, indeed). And just as the rationale for lynching is typically some sexual transgression on the victim's part, Shepard's accused killers gave police the classic justification for antigay violence: they said he had come on to them. This is the homophobic version of the rapist's cry: she asked for it. "It's the excuse that usually comes up in trials," says Carl Locke, director of client services at New York's Anti-Violence Project. "If straight women were allowed to plead 'He hit on me,' there would be no straight men left in the world."

Like lynching and rape, gay bashing is merely the most violent practice of a theory that also shows itself in ordinary male banter; in the laff-riot produced by the mere flick of a limp wrist; in the endless array of pejoratives for butch women and femmy men; and ultimately in the laws that sanction this hate, from sodomy statutes to prohibitions on gay soldiering and parenting to the insistence that it should be legal to fire homosexuals and deny them a home. "It's too easy to blame the kids who throw the punches, as if they are doing something aberrant," says Kevin Cathcart, executive director of Lambda Legal Defense, which will be represented at the APA event. "But in fact, homophobia is background noise in our society, and our basic rights are still a matter of political debate."

There is no consensus about homophobia like the one that condemns racism and sexism in all its forms. Nearly thirty years after Stonewall, the combined effect of discrimination and denial still profoundly shapes the homosexual, sentencing most gay people to a civil version of Franz Kafka's *In the Penal Colony*, in which punishment is meted out by a machine that slowly carves the nature of the crime into an offender's back. That machine is masculinity.

Ever since Sigmund Freud posited that all paranoia stems from the repression of homosexual desire, there has been a vague awareness that some pathology is behind the fear and loathing of gay people. But only in 1972 did a sociologist coin the term *homophobia*, giving this syndrome a name. Within a year (and only after being zapped repeatedly by gay activists), the APA dropped its diagnosis of homosexuality as an illness, finally catching up with Freud, who had written in a 1935 letter to a worried American mother that, though homosexuality was "assuredly no advantage," neither was it an illness or "anything to be ashamed of."

It has taken the APA twenty-five years to address homophobia in a public forum, and it has yet to label this hate an illness, if only because, as Cathcart quips, "you can't call half the U.S. Senate pathological." Leon Hoffman, who chairs the APA's committee on public information, puts it more gingerly: "The nonanalytic attitude toward homosexuality has prevented analysts from studying this question."

Until now. Psychoanalysts are finally beginning to focus on homophobia, adding their perspective to the work social scientists have already done. The result is a new theory that regards homophobia as a key component of male dominance. As the critic Eve Kosofsky Sedgwick writes in her landmark study *Epistemology of the Closet*, "male homosexual panic [is] the normal condition of male heterosexual entitlement."

Gratifying as it might be to see this syndrome diagnosed as a pathology, many students of homophobia would disagree. Antigay bias is "not a phobia in the clinical sense," researcher Gregory M. Herek insists. For one thing, it's too functional; for another, it doesn't necessarily spring from a secret desire. True, there is some clinical evidence that homophobes are more likely to be aroused by gay pornography than are other men, but according to Hoffman, that could be the result of an erection caused by anxiety. Yes, some guys go hard from fear.

The idea that all phobes are closet cases has an appealing symmetry, but it doesn't begin to describe the web of impulses and beliefs that supports homophobia. NYU Medical Center's Donald Moss offers a more inclusive definition: "Homophobia will refer to the entire spectrum of conscious and unconscious fantasy-feeling-idea-sentiment" through which people are driven to avoid "all things sensed as homosexual." In the new scholarship, homophobia isn't just a symptom; it's a system.

As Herek notes, people who come easily to the word *faggot* share other traits. For instance, they are older than the general population, more religious, and more traditional in their thinking about sexual roles. If this sounds like Trent Loft, so be it, but the most important variable is not membership in the Republican party or even the Christian right; it's gender itself.

Straight men "manifest higher levels of prejudice" against gays than do straight women, Herek writes. That's obvious, but Herek's conclusion is not. He maintains that homophobia serves to affirm male identity through a rejection of what is deemed either unmanly or negating the importance of males. This explains why effeminate men and butch women are the most common victims of antigay violence. They threaten the terms of masculinity.

By this standard, homophobia is nothing more than a tool to shape a social category by defining its boundaries. (It's worth noting that the homo/hetero dichotomy dates from only a century ago, when doctors invented both terms, thereby recasting as a duality what had previously been regarded as a wide variety of sexual attitudes and appetites.) Categories have their uses, especially when it comes to establishing hierarchy, and just as racism assigns value to whiteness, homophobia favors heterosexuality. Yet its major function is not to reward men for desiring women. As Sedgwick notes, male power over the "exchange of goods, persons, and meaning" depends on male bonding, and that solidarity is enforced by the threat of what she calls "homophobic blackmail." In other words, the fear of being perceived as gay holds guys together.

This is why boys in a playground police each other for signs of "sissiness," why adolescents conjure up elaborate codes in which wearing a certain color on a certain day labels the unwitting offender as a homo, and why the disingenuous *Seinfeld* punch line "not that there's anything wrong with being gay" is so funny. The obsession with homosexual signs—and the people who embody them—is the key to an order that ranks men by their invulnerability to same-sex desire.

It follows that a guy who is insecure about his place in the pack will panic when propositioned by another guy, and that the fiercest phobes are the most desperate for admission to the *bund*. But few men outgrow this febrile quest. "We're always proving our manhood in front of other men," says Stony Brook sociologist Michael Kimmel, the author of *Manhood in America: A Cultural History*. "Homophobia is the fear that someone might get the wrong idea."

In his lectures, Kimmel uses a routine to make this point: "I ask guys to tell me how they know a man is gay. The way they walk, the way they always dress so nicely, what they do for a living. The women mention the same things, but they also say, 'I get suspicious if a guy is listening too much in a bar, or he isn't coming on to me.' All these stereotypes become a negative rule book that keeps men enacting traditional ideas about masculinity; it keeps them hitting on women and dressing like shit, and it keeps women wearing uncomfortable shoes and showing no technical competence. You can see how homophobia maintains the most rigid gender roles."

The irony is that this heterosexual code of conduct has nothing to do with loving women. But it has everything to do with fear of femininity.

Perhaps the most perplexing figure in the Freudian pantheon is "the phallic mother." This is the primal parent as she is perceived by the infant not yet cognizant of gender. Regressing to a state of union with this figure is the ultimate desire. But for men, it is also the ultimate threat, since fusing with her means losing one's masculinity. What's more, it means incorporating the mother's desire for the father. The struggle against this unconscious fantasy is the root of homophobia.

This Oedipal model certainly helps explain the traditional association of homosexuals and that perilous condition known in some bars and Freudian circles as "failed masculinity." To be a gay man is to identify with mom, case closed. But what about those African cultures where homosex is a rite of passage, or those Greek city-states where it was the glue for an army of lovers? And what about lesbians? Does the specter of the primal parent in a strap-on explain why Barnard College recently found it necessary to brag that its graduates are more likely to marry and have children than are coed-college grads?

"Certainly the fear of lesbians is the fear of butch women," says Arlene Stein, the author of *Sex and Sensibility: Stories of a Lesbian Generation.* "But there's also the fear that women can be independent sexual actors, which is different from the issue with gay men. That doesn't mean the term *homophobia* can't apply to lesbians, but it has a different shape and tenor than when it's directed against men." Whatever the distinction, it isn't evident in the psychoanalytic literature on homophobia, which barely mentions lesbians even though about a third of the victims of antigay violence are women.

Clearly the Oedipal model is only a clue to homophobia, not the whole story. "For many men, masculinity is defined as that which is not female," says Nancy Chodorow, whose psychoanalytic training is tempered by a grounding in sociology. "But that's about separating from *mother*; it's not about the phallic mother. I think what's equally tenuous in male identity is how you identify with dad without loving him. In fact, the Oedipal boy does love his father; all identification is based in love. So what you get in homophobia is that you love dad but you're not supposed to love him."

This contradiction is compounded by the web of associations between male dominance and desire for women. Gay men, with their potential to be sexually passive, "threaten masculinity, which is supposed to be active," Chodorow notes. "And if we define gender by sexual orientation, which we do, then gender's at stake as well. To the extent that a man's heterosexuality is defensive and threatened, he's more likely to be homophobic. To the extent that his heterosexuality feels more secure, he can contain and live with his homoerotic desires. And if you want to talk about hate, then it's what happens when you are confronted with contradictions in yourself that you can't tolerate. You project the bad out, and then you want to destroy it."

Yet despite its grip, none of these scholars is willing to call homophobia innate. "What's innate is fear of the other," says Arlene Stein. Her sociologist's perspective tells her that even something as "natural" as sexuality is shaped by race, class, and gender. So, whatever its primal causes, why can't homophobia be changed?

What would have to happen for that to occur? No doubt it would be helpful if boys could fall in love with their fathers as easily as girls do. But that's just for starters. "Heterosexuality would have to change," says Suzanne Pharr, the author of *Homophobia: A Weapon of Sexism*. "It would have to give way to a more fluid sexuality, so that people might be engaged at different times with the same gender, or the other gender, or gender wouldn't be an issue for them at all."

This is not the latest incarnation of bisexual chic. A better term might be Eve Sedgwick's *allosexuality*, an arrangement of many erotic patterns in no particular hierarchy. In this scenario, sexuality would be seen as a kind of working compromise assembled from alternative impulses. If that seems like fun, welcome to the queer new world. If it seems scary, then you can imagine how difficult homophobia is to eradicate.

"Before we can imagine what heterosexuality would look like without homophobia, pschoanalysis has to figure out what normal, nondefensive masculinity is," says Chodorow. "The fact is that ordinary masculinity depends not just on heterosexuality but on male-dominant heterosexuality. So the question is, what would happen if that changed? To the extent that straight men can fold in passivity, receptivity, and vulnerability, I think both homophobia and male dominance would lessen."

Short of this transformation, perhaps the best weapon against homophobia is to acknowledge it. Straight or gay, we all fear the queer within—that can't be helped. But in understanding this primal rage, at least we can control it, and maybe even fight the power it creates.

# Part Six

# Moral/Rational Critiques
of Hate

# 20

# Is Racial Discrimination Arbitrary?

## Peter Singer

## INTRODUCTION

There is nowadays wide agreement that racism is wrong. To describe a
policy, law, movement, or nation as "racist" is to condemn it. It may
be thought that since we all agree that racism is wrong, it is unnecessary to speculate on exactly what it is and why it is wrong. This indifference to moral fundamentals could, however, prove dangerous. For one
thing, the fact that most people agree today that racism is wrong does
not mean that this attitude will always be so widely shared. Even if we
had no fears for the future, though, we need to have some understanding of what it is about racism that is wrong if we are to handle satisfac-
torily all the problems we face today. For instance, there is the contentious
issue of "reverse discrimination" or discrimination in favor of members
of oppressed minority groups. It must be granted that a university which
admits members of minority groups who do not achieve the minimum
standard that others must reach in order to be admitted is discriminating
on racial lines. Is such discrimination therefore wrong?

Or, to take another issue, the efforts of Arab nations to have the
United Nations declare Zionism a form of racism provoked an extremely
hostile reaction in nations friendly to Israel, particularly the United States,

but it led to virtually no discussion of whether Zionism is a form of racism. Yet the charge is not altogether without plausibility, for if Jews are a race, then Zionism promotes the idea of a state dominated by one race, and this has practical consequences in, for instance, Israel's immigration laws. Again, to consider whether this makes Zionsm a form of racism we need to understand what it is that makes a policy racist and wrong.

First it is necessary to get our terms clear. "Racism" is, as I have said, a word which now has an inescapable evaluative force, although it also has some descriptive content. Words with these dual functions can be confusing if their use is not specified. People sometimes try to argue: "X is a case of racial discrimination, therefore X is racist; racism is wrong, therefore X is wrong." This argument may depend on an equivocation in the meaning of "racist," the term being used first in a morally neutral, descriptive sense, and secondly in its evaluative sense.

To avoid this kind of confusion, I shall accept the usual evaluative force of the term "racist" and reserve it for practices that are judged to be wrong. Thus we cannot pronounce a policy, law, etc., "racist" unless we have decided that it is wrong. "Racial discrimination," on the other hand, I shall use in a descriptive, and morally neutral sense, so that to say that a policy or law discriminates racially is simply to point to the fact of discrimination based on race, leaving open the question of whether it can be justified. With this terminology it becomes possible to ask whether a given form of racial discrimination is racist; this is another way of asking whether it is justifiable.[1]

If we ask those who regard racial discrimination as wrong to say why it is wrong, it is commonly said that it is wrong to pick on race as a reason for treating one person differently from others, because race is irrelevant to whether a person should be given a job, the vote, higher education, or any benefits or burdens of this sort. The irrelevance of race, it is said, makes it quite arbitrary to give these things to people of one race while withholding them from those of another race. I shall refer to this account of what is wrong with racial discrimination as the "standard objection" to racial discrimination.

A sophisticated theory of justice can be invoked in support of this standard objection to racial discrimination. Justice requires, as Aristotle so plausibly said, that equals be treated equally and unequals be treated unequally. To this we must add the obvious proviso that the equalities or inequalities should be relevant to the treatment in question. Now when we consider things like employment, it becomes clear that the relevant inequalities between candidates for a vacant position are inequalities in their ability to carry out the duties of the position and, perhaps, inequalities in the extent to which they will benefit through being offered the position. Race does not seem to be relevant at all. Similarly with the vote, capacity for rational choice between candidates or policies might be held a relevant characteristic, but race should not be; and so on for other goods. It is hard to think of anything for which race in itself is a relevant characteristic, and hence to use race as a basis for discrimination is arbitrarily to single out an irrelevant factor, no doubt because of a bias or prejudice against those of a different race.[2]

As we shall see, this account of why racial discrimination is wrong is inadequate because there are many situations in which, from at least one point of view, the racial factor is by no means irrelevant, and therefore it can be denied that racial discrimination in these situations is arbitrary.

One type of situation in which race must be admitted to be relevant to the purposes of the person discriminating need not delay us at this stage; this is the situation in which those purposes themselves favor a particular race. Thus if the purpose of Hitler and the other Nazi leaders was, among other things, to produce a world in which there were no Jews, it was certainly not irrelevant to their purposes that those rounded up and murdered by the S.S. were Jews rather than so-called "Aryans." But the fundamental wrongness of the aims of the Nazis makes the "relevance" of race to those aims totally inefficacious so far as justifying Nazi racial discrimination is concerned. While their type of racial discrimination may not have been arbitrary discrimination in the usual sense, it was no less wrong for that. *Why* it was wrong is something that I hope will become clearer later in this [chapter]. Meanwhile I shall look at some less cataclysmic forms of racial discrimination, for too much contemporary discussion of racial discrimination has focused on the most blatant instances: Nazi Germany, South Africa, and the American "Deep South" during the period of legally enforced racial segregation.[3] These forms of racism are not the type that face us now in our own societies (unless we live in South Africa) and to discuss racial discrimination in terms of these examples today is to present an oversimplified picture of the problem of racial discrimination. By looking at some of the reasons for racial discrimination that might actually be offered today in countries all over the world I hope to show that the real situation is usually much more complex than consideration of the more blatant instances of racial discrimination would lead us to believe.

EXAMPLES

I shall start by describing an example of racial discrimination which may at first glance seem to be an allowable exception to a general rule that racial discrimination is arbitrary and therefore wrong; and I shall then suggest that this case has parallels with other cases we may not be so willing to allow as exceptions.

## Case 1

A film director is making a film about the lives of blacks living in New York's Harlem. He advertises for black actors. A white actor turns up, but the director refuses to allow him to audition, saying that the film is about blacks and there are no roles for whites. The actor replies that, with the appropriate wig and make-up, he can look just like a black; moreover he can imitate the mannerisms, gestures, and speech of Harlem blacks. Nevertheless the director refuses to consider him for the role, because it is essential to the director's conception of the film that the black experience be authentically portrayed, and however good a white actor might be, the director would not be satisfied with the authenticity of the portrayal.

The film director is discriminating along racial lines, yet he cannot be said to be discriminating arbitrarily. His discrimination is apt for his purpose. Moreover, his purpose is a legitimate one. So the standard objection to racial discrimination cannot be made in this instance.

Racial discrimination may be acceptable in an area like casting for films or the theater, when the race of a character in the film or play is important, because this is one of the seemingly few areas in which a person's race is directly relevant to his capacity to perform a given task. As such, it may be thought, these areas can easily be distinguished from other areas of employment, as well as from areas like housing, education, the right to vote, and so on, where race has no relevance at all. Unfortunately there are many other situations in which race is not as totally irrelevant as this view assumes.

## Case 2

The owner of a cake shop with a largely white and racially prejudiced clientele wishes to hire an assistant. The owner has no prejudice against blacks himself, but is reluctant to employ one, for fear that his customers will go elsewhere. If his fears were well-founded (and this is not impossible) then the race of a candidate for the position is, again, relevant to the purpose of the employer, which in this case is to maintain the profitability of his business.

What can we say about this case? We cannot deny the connection between race and the owner's purposes, and so we must recognize that the owner's discrimination is not arbitrary, and does not necessarily indicate a bias or prejudice on his part. Nor can we say that the owner's purpose is an illegitimate one, for making a profit from the sale of cakes is not generally regarded as wrong, at least if the amount of profit made is modest.

We can, of course, look at other aspects of the matter. We can object to the racial discrimination shown by customers who will search out shops staffed by whites only—such people do discriminate arbitrarily, for race is irrelevant to the quality of the goods and the proficiency of service in a shop—but is this not simply a fact that the shop owner must live with, however much he may wish he could change it? We might argue that by pandering to the prejudices of his customers, the owner is allowing those prejudices to continue unchallenged; whereas if he and other shopkeepers took no notice of them, people would eventually become used to mixing with those of another race, and prejudices would be eroded. Yet it is surely too much to ask an individual shop owner to risk his livelihood in a lone and probably vain effort to break down prejudice. Few of the most dedicated opponents of racism do as much. If there were national legislation which distributed the burden more evenly, by a general prohibition of discrimination on racial grounds (with some recognized exceptions for cases like casting for a film or play), the situation would be different. Then we could reasonably ask every shop owner to play his part. Whether there should be such legislation is a different question from whether the shop owner may be blamed for discriminating in the absence of legislation. I shall discuss the issue of legislation shortly, after we consider a different kind of racial discrimination that, again, is not arbitrary.

**Case 3**

A landlord discriminates against blacks in letting the accommodation he owns. Let us say that he is not so rigid as never to let an apartment to a black, but if a black person and a white person appear to be equally suitable as tenants, with equally good references and so on, the landlord invariably prefers the white. He defends his policy along the following lines:

> If more than a very small proportion of my tenants get behind in their
> rent and disappear without paying the arrears, I will be out of business.
> Over the years, I have found that more blacks do this than whites. I admit
> that there are many honest blacks (some of my best tenants have been
> black) and many dishonest whites, but, for some reason I do not claim
> to understand, the odds on a white tenant defaulting are longer than on
> a black doing so, even when their references and other credentials appear
> equally good. In this business you can't run a full-scale probe of every
> prospective tenant—and if I tried I would be abused for invading privacy
> —so you have to go by the average rather than the individual. That is
> why blacks have to have better indications of reliability than whites before
> I will let to them.

Now the landlord's impression of a higher rate of default among blacks
than among comparable whites may itself be the result of prejudice on
his part. Perhaps in most cases when landlords say this kind of thing,
there is no real factual basis to their allegations. People have grown up
with racial stereotypes, and these stereotypes are reinforced by a tendency
to notice occurrences which conform to the stereotype and to disregard
those which conflict with it. So if unreliability is part of the stereotype
of blacks held by many whites, they may take more notice of blacks who
abscond without paying the rent than of blacks who are reliable tenants;
and conversely they will take less notice of absconding whites and more
of those whites who conform to their idea of normal white behavior.

If it is prejudice that is responsible for the landlord's views about
black and white tenants, and there is no factual basis for his claims,
then the problem becomes one of eliminating this prejudice and getting
the landlord to see his mistake. This is by no means an easy task, but
it is not a task for philosophers, and it does not concern us here, for
we are interested in attempts to justify racial discrimination, and an attempted justification based on an inaccurate description of a situation
can be rejected without raising the deeper issue of justification.

On the other hand, the landlord's impression of a higher rate of default among black tenants *could* be entirely accurate. (It might be explic-
able in terms of the different cultural and economic circumstances in which
blacks are brought up.) Whether or not we think this likely, we need
to ask what its implications would be for the justifiability of the racial
discrimination exercised by the landlord. To refuse even to consider this
question would be to rest all one's objections to the landlord's practice
on the falsity of his claims, and thereby to fail to examine the possibility

that the landlord's practice could be open to objection even if his impressions on tenant reliability are accurate.

If the landlord's impressions were accurate, we would have to concede, once again, that racial discrimination in this situation is not arbitrary; that it is, instead, relevant to the purposes of the landlord. We must also admit that these purposes—making a living from letting property that one owns—are not themselves objectionable, provided the rents are reasonable, and so on. Nor can we, this time, locate the origin of the problem in the prejudices of others, except insofar as the problem has its origin in the prejudices of those responsible for the conditions of deprivation in which many of the present generation of blacks grew up— but it is too late to do anything to alter those prejudices anyway, since they belong to previous generations.

We have now looked at three examples of racial discrimination and can begin to examine the parallels and differences between them. Many people, as I have already said, would make no objection to the discriminatory hiring practice of the film director in the first of these cases. But we can now see that if we try to justify the actions of the film director in this case on the grounds that his purpose is a legitimate one and the discrimination he uses is relevant for his purpose, we will have to accept the actions of the cake-shop owner and the landlord as well. I suspect that many of those ready to accept the discriminatory practice in the first case will be much more reluctant about the other two cases. But what morally significant difference is there between them?

It might be suggested that the difference between them lies in the nature of what blacks are being deprived of, and their title to it. The argument would run like this: No one has a right to be selected to act in a film; the director must have absolute discretion to hire whomsoever he wishes to hire. After all, no one can force the director to make the film at all, and if he didn't make it, no one would be hired to play in it; if he does decide to make it, therefore, he must be allowed to make it on his own terms. Moreover, since so few people ever get the chance to appear in a film, it would be absurd to hold that the director violates someone's rights by not giving him something which most people will never have anyway. On the other hand, people do have a right to employment, and to housing. To discriminate against blacks in an ordinary employment situation, or in the letting of accommodation, threatens their basic rights and therefore should not be tolerated.

Plausible as it appears, this way of distinguishing the first case from the other two will not do. Consider the first and second cases: almost everything that we have said about the film director applies to the cake-shop owner as well. No one can force the cake-shop owner to keep his shop open, and if he didn't, no one would be hired to work in it. If in the film director's case this was a reason for allowing him to make the film on his own terms, it must be a reason for allowing the shop owner to run his shop on his own terms. In fact, such reasoning, which would allow unlimited discrimination in restaurants, hotels, and shops, is invalid. There are plenty of examples where we would not agree that the fact that someone did not have to make an offer or provide an opportunity at all means that if he does do it he must be allowed to make the offer or provide the opportunity on his own terms. The United States Civil Rights Act of 1964 certainly does not recognize this line of argument, for it prohibits those offering food and lodgings to the public from excluding customers on racial grounds. We may, as a society, decide that we shall not allow people to make certain offers, if the way in which the offers are made will cause hardship or offense to others. In so doing we are balancing people's freedom to do as they please against the harm this may do to others, and coming down on the side of preventing harm rather than enlarging freedom. This is a perfectly defensible position, if the harm is sufficiently serious and the restriction of freedom not grave.[4]

Nor does it seem possible to distinguish the first and second cases by the claim that since so few people ever get the chance to appear in a film, no one's rights are violated if they are not given something that most people will never have anyway. For if the number of jobs in cake shops was small, and the demand for such jobs high, it would also be true that few people would ever have the chance to work in a cake shop. It would be odd if such an increase in competition for the job justified an otherwise unjustifiable policy of hiring whites only. Moreover, this argument would allow a film director to discriminate on racial lines even if race was irrelevant to the roles he was casting; and that is quite a different situation from the one we have been discussing.

The best way to distinguish the situations of the film director and the shop owner is by reference to the nature of the employment offered, and to the reason why racial discrimination in these cases is not arbitrary. In casting for a film about blacks, the race of the actor auditioning is intrinsically significant, independently of the attitudes of those connected with the film. In the case of hiring a shop assistant, race is relevant only because of the attitudes of those connected (as customers) with the shop; it has nothing to do with the selling of cakes in itself, but only with the selling of cakes to racially prejudiced customers. This means that in the case of the shop assistant we could eliminate the relevance of race if we could eliminate the prejudices of the customers; by contrast there is no way in which we could eliminate the relevance of the race of an actor auditioning for a role in a film about blacks, without altering the nature of the film. Moreover, in the case of the shop owner racial discrimination probably serves to perpetuate the very prejudices that make such discrimination relevant and (from the point of view of the owner seeking to maintain his profits) necessary. Thus people who can buy all their cakes and other necessities in shops staffed only by whites will never come into the kind of contact with comparable blacks which might break down their aversion to being served by blacks; whereas if shop owners were to hire more blacks, their customers would no doubt become used to it and in time might wonder why they ever opposed the idea. (Compare the change of attitudes toward racial integration in the American South since the 1956 United States Supreme Court decision against segregated schools and subsequent measures against segregation were put into effect.[5])

Hence if we are opposed to arbitrary discrimination we have reason to take steps against racial discrimination in situations like Case 2, because such discrimination, while not itself arbitrary, both feeds on and gives support to discrimination by others which is arbitrary. In prohibiting it we would, admittedly, be preventing the employer from discriminating in a way that is relevant to his purposes; but if the causal hypothesis suggested in the previous paragraph is correct, this situation would only be temporary, and after some time the circumstances inducing the employer to discriminate racially would have been eliminated.

The case of the landlord presents a more difficult problem. If the facts he alleges are true, his nonarbitrary reasons for discrimination against blacks are real enough. They do not depend on present arbitrary discrimination by others, and they may persist beyond an interval in which there is no discrimination. Whatever the roots of hypothetical racial differences in reliability as tenants might be, they would probably go too deep to be eradicated solely by a short period in which there was no racial discrimination.

We should recognize, then, that if the facts are as alleged, to legislate against the landlord's racially discriminatory practice is to impose a long-term disadvantage upon him. At the very least, he will have to take greater care in ascertaining the suitability of prospective tenants. Perhaps he will turn to data-collecting agencies for assistance, thus contributing to the growth of institutions that are threats, potential or actual, to our privacy. Perhaps, if these methods are unavailable or unavailing, the landlord will have to take greater losses than he otherwise would have, and perhaps this will lead to increased rents or even to a reduction in the amount of rentable housing available.

None of this forces us to conclude that we should not legislate against the landlord's racial discrimination. There are good reasons why we should seek to eliminate racial discrimination even when such discrimination is neither arbitrary in itself, nor relevant only because of the arbitrary prejudices of others. These reasons may be so important as to make the disadvantage imposed on the landlord comparatively insignificant.

An obvious point that can be made against the landlord is that he is judging people, at least in part, as members of a race rather than as individuals. The landlord does not deny that some black prospective tenants he turns away would make better tenants than some white prospective tenants he accepts. Some highly eligible black prospective tenants are refused accommodation simply because they are black. If the landlord assessed every prospective tenant as an individual, this would not happen.

A similar point is often made in the debate over alleged differences between blacks and whites in America in whatever is measured by IQ tests. Even if, as Jensen and others have suggested, there is a small inherited difference in IQ between blacks and whites, it is clear that this difference shows up only when we compare averages, and not when we compare individuals. Even if we accept the controversial estimates that the average IQ of American blacks is 15 points lower than the average IQ of American whites, there is still a tremendous amount of overlap between the IQs of blacks and whites, with many whites scoring lower than the majority of blacks. Hence the difference in averages between the races would be of limited significance. For any purpose for which IQ mattered—like entrance into higher levels of education—it would still be essential to consider each applicant individually, rather than as a member of a certain race.

There are plenty of reasons why in situations like admitting people to higher education or providing them with employment or other benefits we should regard people as individuals and not as members of some larger group. For one thing we will be able to make a selection better suited for our own purposes, for selecting or discarding whole groups of people will generally result in, at best, a crude approximation to the results we hope to achieve. This is certainly true in an area like education. On the other hand it must be admitted that in some situations a crude approximation is all that can be achieved anyway. The landlord claims that his situation is one of these, and that as he cannot reliably tell which individuals will make suitable tenants, he is justified in resorting to so crude a means of selection as race. Here we need to turn our attention from the landlord to the prospective black tenant.

To be judged merely as a member of a group when it is one's individual qualities on which the verdict should be given is to be treated as less than the unique individual that we see ourselves as. Even where our individual qualities would merit less than we receive as a member of a group—if we are promoted over better-qualified people because we went to the "right" private school—the benefit is usually less welcome than it would be if it had been merited by our own attributes. Of course in this case qualms are easily stilled by the fact that a benefit has been received, never mind how. In the contrary case, however, when something of value has been lost, the sense of loss will be compounded by the feeling that one was not assessed on one's own merits, but merely as a member of a group.

To this general preference for individual as against group assessment must be added a consideration arising from the nature of the group. To be denied a benefit because one was, say, a member of the Communist party would be unjust and a violation of basic principles of political liberty, but if one has chosen to join the Communist party, then one is, after all, being assessed for what one has done, and one can choose between living with the consequences of continued party membership or leaving the party.[6] Race, of course, is not something that one chooses to adopt or that one can ever choose to give up. The person who is denied advantage because of his race is totally unable to alter this particular circumstance of his existence and so may feel with added sharpness that his life is clouded, not merely because he is not being judged as an individual, but because of something over which he has no control at all. This makes racial discrimination peculiarly invidious.

So we have the viewpoint of the victim of racial discrimination to offset against the landlord's argument in favor, and it seems that the victim has more at stake and hence should be given preference, even if the landlord's reason for discriminating is nonarbitrary and hence in a sense legitimate. The case against racial discrimination becomes stronger still when we consider the long-term social effects of discrimination.

When members of a racial minority are overwhelmingly among the poorest members of a society, living in a deprived area, holding jobs low in pay and status, or no jobs at all, and less well-educated than the average member of the community, racial discrimination serves to perpetuate a divided society in which race becomes a badge of a much broader inferiority. It is the association of race with economic status and educational disadvantages which in turn gives rise to the situation in which there could be a coloring of truth to the claim that race is a relevant ground for discriminating between prospective tenants, applicants for employment, and so on. Thus there is, in the end, a parallel between the situation of the landlord and the cake-shop owner, for both, by their discrimination, contribute to the maintenance of the grounds for claiming that this discrimination is nonarbitrary. Hence prohibition of such discrimination can be justified as breaking this circle of deprivation and discrimination. The difference between the situations, as I have already said, is that in the case of the cake-shop owner it is only a prejudice against contact with blacks that needs to be broken down, and experience has shown that such prejudices do evaporate in a relatively short period of time. In the case of the landlord, however, it is the whole social and economic position of blacks that needs to be changed, and while overcoming discrimination would be an essential part of this process it may not be sufficient. That is why, if the facts are as the landlord alleges them to be, prohibition of racial discrimination is likely to impose more of a long-term disadvantage on the landlord than on the shop owner—a disadvantage which is, however, outweighed by the costs of continuing the circle of racial discrimination and deprivation for those discriminated against; and the costs of greater social inequality and racial divisiveness for the community as a whole.

## A BASIC PRINCIPLE

If our discussion of the three examples has been sound, opposition to racial discrimination cannot rely on the standard objection that racial discrimination is arbitrary because race is irrelevant to employment, housing, and other things that matter. While this very often will be true, it will not always be true. The issue is more complicated than that appealing formula suggests, and has to do with the effect of racial discrimination on its victims, and on society as a whole. Behind all this, however, there is a more basic moral principle, and at this more basic level the irrelevance of race and the arbitrariness of racial discrimination reappear and help to explain why racism is wrong. This basic moral principle is the principle of equal consideration of interests.

The principle of equal consideration of interests is easy to state, though difficult to apply. Bentham's famous "each to count for one and none for more than one" is one way of putting it, though not free from ambiguity; Sidgwick's formulation is more precise, if less memorable: "The good of any one individual is of no more importance, from the point of view (if I may say so) of the Universe, than the good of any other."[7] Perhaps the best way of explaining the effect of the principle is to follow C. I. Lewis's suggestion that we imagine ourselves living, one after the other, the lives of everyone affected by our actions; in this way we would experience all of their experiences as our own.[8] R. M. Hare's insistence that moral judgments must be universalizable comes to much the same thing, as he has pointed out.[9] The essence of the principle of equal consideration of interests is that we give equal weight in our moral deliberations to the like interests of all those affected by our actions. This means that if only X and Y would be affected by a possible act, and if X stands to lose more than Y stands to gain (for instance, X will lose his job and find it difficult to get another, whereas Y will merely get a small promotion) then it is better not to do the act. We cannot, if we accept the principle of equal consideration of interests, say that doing the act is better, despite the facts described, because we are more concerned about Y than we are about X. What the principle is really saying is that an interest is an interest, whoever's interest it may be.

We can make this more concrete by considering a particular interest, say the interest we have in the relief of pain. Then the principle says that the ultimate moral reason for relieving pain is simply the undesirability of pain as such, and not the undesirability of X's pain, which might be different from the undesirability of Y's pain. Of course, X's pain might be more undesirable than Y's pain because it is more painful, and then the principle of equal consideration would give greater weight to the relief of X's pain. Again, even where the pains are equal, other factors might be relevant, especially if others are affected. If there has been an earthquake we might give priority to the relief of a doctor's pain so that he can treat other victims. But the doctor's pain itself counts only once, and with no added weighting. The principle of equal consideration of interests acts like a pair of scales, weighing interests impartially. True scales favor the side where the interest is stronger, or where several interests combine to outweigh a smaller number of similar interests; but they take no account of whose interests they are weighing.

It is important to understand that the principle of equal consideration of interests is, to adopt Sidgwick's suggestive phrase, a "point of view of the universe" principle. The phrase is, of course, a metaphor. It is not intended to suggest that the universe as a whole is alive, or conscious, or capable of having a point of view; but we can, without getting involved in any pantheist suppositions, imagine how matters would be judged by a being who was able to take in all of the universe, viewing all that was going on with an impartial benevolence.[10]

It is from this universal point of view that race is irrelevant to the consideration of interests; for all that counts are the interests themselves. To give less consideration to a specified amount of pain because that pain was experienced by a black would be to make an arbitrary distinction.

Why pick on race? Why not on whether a person was born in a leap year? Or whether there is more than one vowel in his surname? All these characteristics are equally irrelevant to the undesirability of pain from the universal point of view. Hence the principle of equal consideration of interests shows straightforwardly why the most blatant forms of racism, like that of the Nazis, are wrong. For the Nazis were concerned only for the welfare of members of the "Aryan" race, and the sufferings of Jews, Gypsies, and Slavs were of no concern to them.

That the principle of equal consideration of interests is a "point of view of the universe" principle allows us to account for the fact that it is a principle upon which it seems virtually impossible to act. Who of us can live as if our own welfare and that of our family and friends were of no more concern to us than the welfare of anonymous individuals in faraway countries, of whom we know no more than the fact of their existence? Only a saint or a robot could live in this way; but this does not mean that only a saint or a robot can live in accordance with the principle of equal consideration of interests, for a principle which is valid from a universal point of view may yield subordinate principles to be acted upon by those who have limited resources and are involved in a particular segment of the world, rather than looking down on the whole from a position of impartiality.

So subordinate principles giving members of families responsibility for the welfare of others in the family, or giving national governments responsibility for the welfare of their citizens, will be derivable from the principle of equal consideration, if everyone's interests are best promoted by such arrangements; and this is likely to be the case if, first, people are more knowledgeable about the interests of those close to them and more inclined to work to see that these interests are catered for, and, second, if the distribution of resources between families and between na-tions is not so unequally distributed that some families or nations are simply unable to provide for themselves the means to satisfying interests that could be satisfied with ease by other families or nations. In the world as it is presently constituted the first condition seems to hold, but not the second. For that reason I do not think that the subordinate princi-ples mentioned correctly set out our present moral responsibilities, though they could do so if resources were more evenly distributed. Until then, we ought to strive to be more saint-like.[11]

Subordinate principles based on race, giving each race responsibility for the welfare of other members of that race are, I think, considerably less likely to be derivable from the principle of equal consideration than subordinate principles based on family or membership of a nation. For where they are not living together as a nation, races tend to be widely scattered; there is usually little knowledge of the circumstances of other members of one's race in different parts of the world, and there is nobody with the capacity to look after all members of a race as a national government can look after the interests of its citizens. There is, admittedly, often a degree of sentiment connecting members of a race, however widely they are separated. The contributions of American Jews to the support of members of their race in Israel is a well-known example of this, and there are many others. But the intermingling of races still makes it very doubtful that interests could be generally promoted by dividing responsibilities along racial lines.

The fundamental principle of equal consideration of interests, then, pays no regard to the race of those whose interests are under consideration; nor can we plausibly derive from the basic principle a subordinate principle enjoining us to consider the interests of members of our own race before we consider the interests of others; yet it cannot be said that the principle rules out racial discrimination in all circumstances. For the principle is an abstract one, and can only be applied in a concrete situation, in which the facts of the situation will be relevant. For instance, I have heard it said that somewhere in ancient Hindu writings members of the Brahmin or priestly caste are claimed to be so much more sensitive than members of the lower castes that their pleasures and pains are twenty times as intense as those of lesser human beings. We would, of course, do well to be suspicious of such a claim, particularly as the author of the document would no doubt have been a Brahmin himself. But let us assume that we somehow discovered that this extraordinary difference in sensitivity did in fact exist; it would follow that Brahmins have a greater interest in having access to a source of pleasure, and in avoiding a source of pain, than others. It would be as if when a Brahmin scratches his finger he feels a pain similar to that which others feel when they dislocate their shoulder. Then, consistently with the principle of equal consideration of interests, if a Brahmin and an ordinary person have both scratched their fingers, and we have only enough soothing ointment to cover one scratch, we should favor the Brahmin—just as, in the case of two normal people, if one had scratched a finger while the other had dislocated a shoulder we should favor the person with the more painful injury.

Needless to say, the example is a fanciful one, and intended to show only how, within the confines of the principle of equal consideration of interests, factual differences could be relevant to racial discrimination. In the absence of any real evidence of racial differences in sensitivity to pleasure and pain, the example has no practical relevance. Other differences between races—if they were differences between all members of races, and not differences which showed up only when averages were taken—could also justify forms of discrimination which ran parallel to the boundary of race. Examples would be substantial differences in intelligence, educability, or the capacity to be self-governing. Strictly, if there were such differences then discrimination based on them would not be *racial* discrimination but rather discrimination on the ground of differences which happened to coincide with racial differences. But perhaps this is hair-splitting, since it would certainly be popularly known as racial discrimination. The kind of discrimination that such difference would justify would be only that to which these differences were relevant. For instance a respectable argument for benevolent colonialism could be mounted if it really were true that certain races were so incapable of self-government as to be obviously better off on the whole when ruled by people of a different race. I hasten to add that the historical record gives no support to such a hypothesis but rather suggests the contrary. Again, this fictional example shows only that, given peculiar enough factual assumptions, any acceptable principle of equality can lead to racial discrimination.

On the other hand, the principle of equal consideration of interests does underpin the decisions we reached when considering the three more realistic examples of racial discrimination in the preceding section of this article. Although the principle is too general to allow the derivation of straightforward and indisputable conclusions from it in complex situations, it does seem that an impartial consideration of the interests of all involved would, for reasons already discussed, rule out discrimination by the shop owner and the landlord, though allowing that of the film director. Hence it is the arbitrariness of racial discrimination at the level of the principle of equal consideration of interests, rather than at the level of the particular decision of the person discriminating, that governs whether a given act of racial discrimination is justifiable.

This conclusion may be applied to other controversial cases. It suggests, for instance, that the problem of "reverse discrimination" or "compensatory discrimination" which arise when a university or employer gives preference to members of minority groups should be discussed by asking not whether racial discrimination is always and intrinsically wrong, but whether the proposal is, on balance, in the interests of all those affected by it. This is a difficult question, and not one that can be answered generally for all types of reverse discrimination. For instance, if white communities have a far better doctor-patient ratio than black communities because very few blacks are admitted to medical school and white doctors tend to work in white communities, there is a strong case for admitting some black candidates to medical school ahead of whites who are better qualified by the standard entry procedures, provided, of course, that the blacks admitted are not so poorly qualified as to be unable to become competent doctors. The case for separate and easier entry would be less strong in an area where there is no equivalent community need, for instance, in philosophy. How much would depend on whether black students who would not otherwise have been admitted were able to make up ground and do as well as whites with higher ratings on standard entry procedures. If so, easier entry for blacks could be justified in terms of the conventional goal of admitting those students most likely to succeed in their course; taking into account a student's race would merely be a way of correcting for the failure of standard tests to allow for the disadvantages that face blacks in competing with whites on such tests. If, on the other hand, blacks admitted under easier entry in a field like philosophy did not do as well as the whites they displaced could have been expected to do, discrimination in their favor would be much harder to justify.

Immigration policy, too, is an area in which the principle of equal consideration of interests suggests the kinds of facts we should look for, instead of giving a definite answer. The relevant questions are the extent to which an immigrant will be benefited by admission, and the extent to which the admitting nation will be benefited. Race certainly does not provide an answer to the first of these questions. A country which chooses to give only those of a certain race the benefit of permanent residence fails to give equal consideration to those not of the favored race who may have a greater interest in leaving their present country than those who are accepted because of their race. While this kind of racial discrimination would in itself be unjustifiable, it has been defended on the grounds that the alternative would be disastrous for citizens of the admitting nation, and ultimately for those admitted, too. An extreme version of this kind of defense is the line taken by the British politician Enoch Powell, who prophesied "rivers of blood" if black immigration was not stopped and blacks who had already arrived were not encouraged to go back to where they had come from.[12] Here again, the facts are relevant. If Powell's claims had been soundly based, if it really were impossible for blacks and whites to live together without widespread bloodshed, then continued immigration would have been in the interests of neither blacks nor whites, and stopping immigration would not have been condemned as racist—though the epithet could have been applied to those Britons who were so hostile to blacks as to produce the situation Powell predicted. Despite occasional racial disturbances in Britain, however, there is no sign that Powell's predictions will come true. While a sudden influx of large numbers of immigrants of a different racial (or ethnic) group may cause problems, it is clear that people of different races can live together without serious strife. This being so, there is no justification for immigration policies that impose blanket prohibitions on people of a different race from that of the residents of the country. The most that can be defended in terms of the principle of equal consideration of interests is a quota system that leads to a gradual adjustment in the racial composition of a society.[13]

## NOTES

1. In popular usage, even the term "discrimination" is often used to suggest that the practice referred to is wrong; this is, of course, an abuse of language, for to discriminate is merely to distinguish, or differentiate, and we could hardly get along without doing that.

2. For a brief and clear statement of this idea of justice, see H. L. A. Hart, *The Concept of Law* (Oxford: Clarendon Press, 1961), pp. 156–58; see also Joel Feinberg, *Social Philosophy* (Englewood Cliffs, N.J.: Prentice-Hall, 1973), ch. 7.

3. See, for instance, R. M. Hare, *Freedom and Reason* (Oxford: Clarendon Press, 1963), chs. 9, 11; Richard Wasserstrom, "Rights, Human Rights, and Racial Discrimination," *Journal of Philosophy* 61 (1964), and reprinted in James Rachels, ed., *Moral Problems* (New York: Harper and Row, 1975).

4. See Feinberg, *Social Philosophy,* p. 78.

5. In most southern communities . . . the adjustment to public desegregation following the enactment of the 1964 Civil Rights Act was amazing. Lewis M. Killian, *White Southerners* (New York: Random House, 1970). Similar comments have been made by many other observers; for a more recent report, see *Time,* September 27, 1976, especially the favorable comments of northern blacks who have recently moved to the South (p. 44). That contact with those of another race helps to reduce racial prejudice had been demonstrated as early as 1949, when a study of U.S. soldiers showed that the more contact white soldiers had with black troops, the more favorable were their attitudes to integration. See Samuel Stouffer et al., *The American Soldier: Adjustment During Army Life* (Princeton: Princeton University Press, 1949), p. 594. This finding was supported by a later study, "Project Clear," reported by Charles Moskos, Jr., "Racial Integration in the Armed Forces," *American Journal of Sociology* 72 (1966): 132–48.

6. The situation is different if it is because of a past rather than a present political connection that one is subjected to disadvantages. Perhaps this is why the hounding of ex-Communists in the McCarthy era was a particularly shameful episode in American history.

7. Henry Sidgwick, *The Methods of Ethics,* 7th ed. (London: Macmillan, 1907), p. 382.

8. C. I. Lewis, *Analysis of Knowledge and Valuation* (La Salle, 1946), p. 547; I owe this reference to R. M. Hare.

9. See Hare, "Rules of War and Moral Reasoning," *Philosophy and Public Affairs* 1 (1972).

10. See the discussion of the Ideal Observer theory in Roderick Firth, "Ethical Absolutism and the Ideal Observer," *Philosophy and Phenomenological Research* 12 (1952), and the further discussion in the same journal by Richard Brandt, 15 (1955).

11. For a general discussion of this issue, see Sidgwick, *The Methods of Ethics,* pp. 432–33; for considerations relevant to the present distribution of resources, see my "Famine, Affluence and Morality," *Philosophy and Public Affairs* 1 (1972) and reprinted in James Rachels, ed., *Understanding Moral Philosophy* (Encino, Calif.: Dickinson, 1976) and Paula and Karsten Struhl, eds., *Philosophy Now* (New York: Random House, 2d ed., 1975).

12. *The Times* (London) April 21, 1968.

# 21

# Gay Basics: Some Questions, Facts, and Values

## Richard D. Mohr

### I. WHO ARE GAYS ANYWAY?

A recent Gallup poll found that only one in five Americans reports having a gay or lesbian acquaintance.[1] This finding is extraordinary given the number of practicing homosexuals in America. Alfred Kinsey's 1948 study of the sex lives of 12,000 white males shocked the nation: 37 percent had at least one homosexual experience to orgasm in their adult lives; an additional 13 percent had homosexual fantasies to orgasm; 4 percent were exclusively homosexual in their practices; another 5 percent had virtually no heterosexual experience; and nearly 20 percent had at least as many homosexual as heterosexual experiences.[2]

Two out of five men one passes on the street have had orgasmic sex with men. Every second family in the country has a member who is essentially homosexual and many more people regularly have homosexual experiences. Who are homosexuals? They are your friends, your minister, your teacher, your bank teller, your doctor, your mail carrier, your officemate, your roommate, your congressional representative, your sibling, parent, and spouse. They are everywhere, virtually all ordinary, virtually all unknown.

Several important consequences follow. First, the country is profoundly ignorant of the actual experience of gay people. Second, social attitudes and practices that are harmful to gays have a much greater overall harmful impact on society than is usually realized. Third, most gay people live in hiding—in the closet—making the "coming out" experience the central figure of gay consciousness and invisibility the chief characteristic of the gay community.

## II. IGNORANCE, STEREOTYPE, AND MORALITY

Ignorance about gays, however, has not stopped people from having strong opinions about them. The void which ignorance leaves has been filled with stereotypes. Society holds chiefly two groups of anti-gay stereotypes; the two are an oddly contradictory lot. One set of stereotypes revolves around alleged mistakes in an individual's gender identity; lesbians are women who want to be, or at least look and act like, men—bull dykes, diesel dykes; while gay men are those who want to be, or at least look and act like, women—queens, fairies, limp-wrists, nellies. These stereotypes of mismatched genders provide the materials through which gays and lesbians become the butts of ethniclike jokes. These stereotypes and jokes, though derisive, basically view gays and lesbians as ridiculous.

Another set of stereotypes revolves around gays as a pervasive, sinister, conspiratorial threat. The core stereotype here is the gay person as child molester, and more generally, as sex-crazed maniac. These stereotypes carry with them fears of the very destruction of family and civilization itself. Now, that which is essentially ridiculous can hardly have such a staggering effect. Something must be afoot in this incoherent amalgam.

Sense can be made of this incoherence if the nature of stereotypes is clarified. Stereotypes are not *simply* false generalizations from a skewed sample of cases examined. Admittedly, false generalizing plays some part in the stereotypes a society holds. If, for instance, one takes as one's sample homosexuals who are in psychiatric hospitals or prisons, as was done in nearly all early investigations, not surprisingly one will probably find homosexuals to be of a crazed and criminal cast. Such false generalizations, though, simply confirm beliefs already held on independent grounds, ones that likely led the investigator to the prison and psychiatric ward to begin with. Evelyn Hooker, who in the late fifties carried out the first rigorous studies to use nonclinical gays, found that psychiatrists, when presented with case files including all the standard diagnostic psychological profiles—but omitting indications of sexual orientation—were unable to distinguish files of gays from those of straights, even though they believed gays to be crazy and supposed themselves to be experts in detecting craziness.[3] These studies proved a profound embarrassment to the psychiatric establishment, the financial well-being of which has been substantially enhanced by "curing" allegedly insane gays. The studies led the way to the American Psychiatric Association finally in 1973 dropping homosexuality from its registry of mental illness.[4] Nevertheless, the stereotype of gays as sick continues apace in the mind of America.

False generalizations *help maintain* stereotypes; they do not *form* them. As the history of Hooker's discoveries shows, stereotypes have a life beyond facts; their origin lies in a culture's ideology—the general system of beliefs by which it lives—and they are sustained across generations by diverse cultural transmissions, hardly any of which, including slang and jokes, even purport to have a scientific basis. Stereotypes, then, are not the products of bad science but are social constructions that perform central functions in maintaining society's conception of itself.

On this understanding, it is easy to see that the anti-gay stereotypes surrounding gender identification are chiefly means of reinforcing still powerful gender roles in society. If, as this stereotype presumes and condemns, one is free to choose one's social roles independently of gender, many guiding social divisions, both domestic and commercial, might be threatened. The socially gender-linked distinctions between breadwinner and homemaker, boss and secretary, doctor and nurse, protector and protected would blur. The accusations "dyke" and "fag" exist in significant part to keep women in their place and to prevent men from breaking ranks and ceding away theirs.

The stereotypes of gays as child molesters, sex-crazed maniacs, and civilization destroyers function to displace (socially irresolvable) problems from their actual source to a foreign (and so, it is thought, manageable) one. Thus the stereotype of child molester functions to give the family unit a false sheen of absolute innocence. It keeps the unit from being examined too closely for incest, child abuse, wife-battering, and the terrorism of constant threats. The stereotype teaches that the problems of the family are not internal to it, but external.[5]

One can see these cultural forces at work in society's and the media's treatment of current reports of violence, especially domestic violence. When a mother kills her child or a father rapes his daughter—regular Section B fare even in major urban papers—this is never taken by reporters, columnists, or pundits as evidence that there is something wrong with heterosexuality or with traditional families. These issues are not even raised. But when a homosexual child molestation is reported it is taken as con-

firming evidence of the way homosexuals are. One never hears of heterosexual murders, but one regularly hears of "homosexual" ones. Compare
the social treatment of Richard Speck's sexually motivated mass murder
of Chicago nurses with that of John Wayne Gacy's murders of Chicago
youths. Gacy was in the culture's mind taken as symbolic of gay men
in general. To prevent the possibility that The Family was viewed as anything but an innocent victim in this affair, the mainstream press know-
ingly failed to mention that most of Gacy's adolescent victims were home-
less hustlers. That knowledge would be too much for the six o'clock news
and for cherished beliefs.

Because "the facts" largely don't matter when it comes to the generation and maintenance of stereotypes, the effects of scientific and academic
research and of enlightenment generally will be, at best, slight and gradual
in the changing fortunes of lesbians and gay men. If this account of
stereotypes holds, society has been profoundly immoral. For its treatment
of gays is a grand-scale rationalization, a moral sleight-of-hand. The problem is not that society's usual standards of evidence and procedure in
coming to judgments of social policy have been misapplied to gays; rather
when it comes to gays, the standards themselves have simply been ruled
out of court and disregarded in favor of mechanisms that encourage unex-
amined fear and hatred.


### III.  ARE GAYS DISCRIMINATED AGAINST? DOES IT MATTER?

Partly because lots of people suppose they don't know any gay people
and partly through willful ignorance of its own workings, society at large
is unaware of the many ways in which gays are subject to discrimination
in consequence of widespread fear and hatred. Contributing to this social
ignorance of discrimination is the difficulty for gay people, as an invisible
minority, even to complain of discrimination. For if one is gay, to register
a complaint would suddenly target one as a stigmatized person, and so
in the absence of any protections against discrimination, would simply
invite additional discrimination. Further, many people, especially those who
are persistently downtrodden and so lack a firm sense of self to begin
with, tend either to blame themselves for their troubles or to view injustice as a matter of bad luck rather than as indicating something wrong
with society. The latter recognition would require doing something to rec-
tify wrong, and most people, especially the already beleaguered, simply
aren't up to that. So for a number of reasons discrimination against gays,
like rape, goes seriously underreported.

First, gays are subject to violence and harassment based simply on their perceived status rather than because of any actions they have performed. A recent extensive study by the National Gay Task Force found that over 90 percent of gays and lesbians had been victimized in some form on the basis of their sexual orientation.[6] Greater than one in five gay men and nearly one in ten lesbians had been punched, hit, or kicked; a quarter of all gays had had objects thrown at them; a third had been chased; a third had been sexually harassed; and 14 percent had been spit on—all just for being perceived as gay.

The most extreme form of anti-gay violence is "queer bashing"—where groups of young men target a person who they suppose is a gay man and beat and kick him unconscious and sometimes to death amid a torrent of taunts and slurs. Such seemingly random but in reality socially encouraged violence has the same social origin and function as lynchings of blacks—to keep a whole stigmatized group in line. As with lynchings in the recent past, the police and courts have routinely averted their eyes, giving their implicit approval to the practice.

Few such cases with gay victims reach the courts. Those that do are marked by inequitable procedures and results. Frequently judges will describe "queerbashers" as "just all-American boys." Recently a District of Columbia judge handed suspended sentences to queerbashers whose victim had been stalked, beaten, stripped at knife point, slashed, kicked, threatened with castration, and pissed on, because the judge thought the bashers were good boys at heart—after all, they went to a religious prep school.[7]

Police and juries will simply discount testimony from gays; they typically construe assaults and murders of gays as "justified" self-defense— the killer need only claim his act was a panicked response to a sexual overture. Alternatively, when guilt seems patent, juries will accept highly implausible "diminished capacity" defenses, as in the case of Dan White's 1978 assassination of openly gay San Francisco city councilman Harvey Milk; Hostess Twinkies made him do it.[8]

These inequitable procedures and results collectively show that the life and liberty of gays, like those of blacks, simply count for l ss than the life and liberty of members of the dominant culture.

The equitable rule of law is the heart of an orderly society. The collapse of the rule of law for gays shows that society is willing to perpetrate the worst possible injustices against them. Conceptually there is only a difference in degree between the collapse of the rule of law and systematic extermination of members of a population simply for having some group status independent of any act an individual has performed. In the

Nazi concentration camps, gays were forced to wear pink triangles as identifying badges, just as Jews were forced to wear yellow stars. In remembrance of that collapse of the rule of law, the pink triangle has become the chief symbol of the gay rights movement.[9]

Gays are subject to widespread discrimination in employment—the very means by which one puts bread on one's table and one of the chief means by which individuals identify themselves to themselves and achieve personal dignity. Governments are leading offenders here. They do a lot of discriminating themselves, requiring that others do it (e.g., government contractors), and set precedents favoring discrimination in the private sector. The federal government explicitly discriminates against gays in the armed forces, the CIA, FBI, National Security Agency, and the state department. The federal government refuses to give security clearances to gays and so forces the country's considerable private sector military and aerospace contractors to fire known gay employees. State and local governments regularly fire gay teachers, policemen, firemen, social workers, and anyone who has contact with the public. Further, through licensing laws states officially bar gays from a vast array of occupations and professions—everything from doctors, lawyers, accountants, and nurses to hairdressers, morticians, and used car dealers. The American Civil Liberties Union's handbook *The Rights of Gay People* lists 307 such prohibited occupations.[10]

Gays are subject to discrimination in a wide variety of other ways, including private-sector employment, public accommodations, housing, immigration and naturalization, insurance of all types, custody and adoption, and zoning regulations that bar "singles" or "nonrelated" couples. All of these discriminations affect central components of a meaningful life; some even reach to the means by which life itself is sustained. In half the states, where gay sex is illegal, the central role of sex to meaningful life is officially denied to gays.

All these sorts of discriminations also affect the ability of people to have significant intimate relations. It is difficult for people to live together as couples without having their sexual orientation perceived in the public realm and so becoming targets for discrimination. Illegality, discrimination, and the absorption by gays of society's hatred of them all interact to impede or block altogether the ability of gays and lesbians to create and maintain significant personal relations with loved ones. So every facet of life is affected by discrimination. Only the most compelling reason could justify it.

IV. BUT AREN'T THEY IMMORAL?

Many people think society's treatment of gays is justified because they think gays are extremely immoral. To evaluate this claim, different senses of "moral" must be distinguished. Sometimes by "morality" is meant the overall beliefs affecting behavior in a society—its mores, norms, and customs. On this understanding, gays certainly are not moral: lots of people hate them and social customs are designed to register widespread disapproval of gays. The problem here is that this sense of morality is merely a *descriptive* one. On this understanding *every* society has a morality—even Nazi society, which had racism and mob rule as central features of its "morality," understood in this sense. What is needed in order to use the notion of morality to praise or condemn behavior is a sense of morality that is *prescriptive* or *normative*—a sense of morality whereby, for instance, the descriptive morality of the Nazis is found wanting.

As the Nazi example makes clear, that something is descriptively moral is nowhere near enough to make it normatively moral. A lot of people in a society saying something is good, even over eons, does not make it so. Our rejection of the long history of socially approved and state-enforced slavery is another good example of this principle at work. Slavery would be wrong even if nearly everyone liked it. So consistency and fairness require that we abandon the belief that gays are immoral simply because most people dislike or disapprove of gays or gay acts, or even because gay sex acts are illegal.

Furthermore, recent historical and anthropological research has shown that opinion about gays has been by no means universally negative. Historically, it has varied widely even within the larger part of the Christian era and even within the church itself.[11] There are even societies—current ones—where homosexuality is not only tolerated but a universal compulsory part of social maturation.[12] Within the last thirty years, American society has undergone a grand turnabout from deeply ingrained, near total condemnation to near total acceptance on two emotionally charged "moral" or "family" issues: contraception and divorce. Society holds its current descriptive morality of gays not because it has to, but because it chooses to.

If popular opinion and custom are not enough to ground moral condemnation of homosexuality, perhaps religion can. Such argument proceeds along two lines. One claims that the condemnation is a direct revelation of God, usually through the Bible; the other claims to be able to detect condemnation in God's plan as manifested in nature.

One of the more remarkable discoveries of recent gay research is that the Bible may not be as univocal in its condemnation of homosexuality as has been usually believed.[13] Christ never mentions homosexuality. Recent interpreters of the Old Testament have pointed out that the story of Lot at Sodom is probably intended to condemn inhospitality rather than homosexuality. Further, some of the Old Testament condemnations of homosexuality seem simply to be ways of tarring those of the Israelites' opponents who happened to accept homosexual practices when the Israelites themselves did not. If so, the condemnation is merely a quirk of history and rhetoric rather than a moral precept.

What does seem clear is that those who regularly cite the Bible to condemn an activity like homosexuality do so by reading it selectively. Do ministers who cite what they take to be condemnations of homosexuality in Leviticus maintain in their lives all the hygienic and dietary laws of Leviticus? If they cite the story of Lot at Sodom to condemn homosexuality, do they also cite the story of Lot in the cave to praise incestuous rape? It seems then not that the Bible is being used to ground condemnations of homosexuality as much as society's dislike of homosexuality is being used to interpret the Bible.[14]

Even if a consistent portrait of condemnations could be gleaned from the Bible, what social significance should it be given? One of the guiding principles of society, enshrined in the Constitution as a check against the government, is that decisions affecting social policy are not made on religious grounds. If the real ground of the alleged immorality invoked by governments to discriminate against gays is religious (as it has explicitly been even in some recent court cases involving teachers and guardians), then one of the major commitments of our nation is violated.


## V.  BUT AREN'T THEY UNNATURAL?

The most noteworthy feature of the accusation of something being unnatural (where a moral rather than an advertising point is being made) is that the plaint is so infrequently made. One used to hear the charge leveled against abortion, but that has pretty much faded as anti-abortionists have come to lay all their chips on the hope that people will come to view abortion as murder. Incest used to be considered unnatural but discourse now usually assimilates it to the moral machinery of rape and violated trust. The charge comes up now in ordinary discourse only against homosexuality. This suggests that the charge is highly idiosyncratic and has little, if any, explanatory force. It fails to put homosexuality in a class with anything else so that one can learn by comparison with clear cases of the class just exactly what it is that is allegedly wrong with it.

Though the accusation of unnaturalness looks whimsical, in actual ordinary discourse when applied to homosexuality, it is usually delivered with venom aforethought. It carries a high emotional charge, usually expressing disgust and evincing queasiness. Probably it is nothing but an emotional charge. For people get equally disgusted and queasy at all sorts of things that are perfectly natural—to be expected in nature apart from artifice—and that could hardly be fit subjects for moral condemnation. Two typical examples in current American culture are some people's responses to mothers' suckling in public and to women who do not shave body hair. When people have strong emotional reactions, as they do in these cases, without being able to give good reasons for them, we think of them not as operating morally, but rather as being obsessed and manic. So the feelings of disgust that some people have to gays will hardly ground a charge of immorality. People fling the term "unnatural" against gays in the same breath with the same force as when they call gays "sick" and "gross." When they do this, they give every appearance of being neurotically fearful and incapable of reasoned discourse.

When "nature" is taken in *technical* rather than ordinary usages, it looks like the notion also will not ground a charge of homosexual immorality. When unnatural means "by artifice" or "made by humans," it need only be pointed out that virtually everything that is good about life is unnatural in this sense, that the chief feature that distinguishes people from other animals is their very ability to make over the world to meet their needs and desires, and that their well-being depends upon these departures from nature. On this understanding of human nature and the natural, homosexuality is perfectly unobjectionable.

Another technical sense of natural is that something is natural and so, good, if it fulfills some function in nature. Homosexuality on this view is unnatural because it allegedly violates the function of genitals, which is to produce babies. One problem with this view is that lots of bodily parts have lots of functions and just because some one activity can be fulfilled by only one organ (say, the mouth for eating) this activity does not comdemn other functions of the organ to immorality (say, the mouth for talking, licking stamps, blowing bubbles, or having sex). So the possible use of the genitals to produce children does not, without more, condemn the use of the genitals for other purposes, say, achieving ecstasy and intimacy.

The functional use of nature will only provide a morally condemnatory sense to the unnatural if a thing which might have many uses has but one proper function to the exclusion of other possible functions. But whether this is so cannot be established simply by looking at the thing. For what is seen is all its possible functions. The notion of function seemed like it might ground moral authority, but instead it turns out that moral authority is needed to define proper function. Some people try to fill in this moral authority by appeal to the "design" or "order" of an organ, saying, for instance, that the genitals are designed for the purpose of procreation. But these people cheat intellectually if they do not make explicit *who* the designer and orderer is. If it is God, we are back to square one—holding others accountable for religious beliefs.

Further, ordinary moral attitudes about childbearing will not provide the needed supplement which in conjunction with the natural function view of bodily parts would produce a positive obligation to use the genitals for procreation. Society's attitude toward a childless couple is that of pity not censure—even if the couple could have children. This pity may be an unsympathetic one, that is, not registering a course one would choose *for oneself*, but this does not make it a course one would *require* of others. The couple who discovers they cannot have children are viewed not as having thereby had a debt canceled, but rather as having to forgo some of the richness of life, just as a quadriplegic is viewed not as absolved from some moral obligation to hop, skip, and jump, but as missing some of the richness of life. Consistency requires then that, at most, gays who do not or cannot have children are to be pitied rather than condemned. What *is* immoral is the willful preventing of people from achieving the richness of life. Immorality in this regard lies with those social customs, regulations, and statutes that prevent lesbians and gay men from establishing blood or adoptive families, not with gays themselves.

Sometimes people attempt to estabish authority for a moral obligation to use bodily parts in a certain fashion simply by claiming that moral laws are natural laws and vice versa. On this account, inanimate objects and plants are good in that they follow natural laws by necessity, animals by instinct, and persons by a rational will. People are special in that they must first discover the laws that govern them. Now, even if one believes the view—dubious in the post-Newtonian, post-Darwinian world—that natural laws in the usual sense ($E = mc^2$, for instance) have some moral content, it is not at all clear how one is to discover the laws in nature that apply to people.

On the one hand, if one looks to people themselves for a model—and looks hard enough—one finds amazing variety, including homosexuality as a social ideal (upper-class fifth-century Athens) and even as socially mandatory (Melanesia today). When one looks to people, one is simply unable to strip away the layers of social custom, history, and taboo in order to see what's really there to any degree more specific than that people are the creatures that make over their world and are capable of abstract thought. That this is so should raise doubts that neutral principles are to be found in human nature that will condemn homosexuality.

On the other hand, if one looks to nature apart from people for models, the possibilities are staggering. There are fish that change gender over their lifetimes: should we "follow nature" and be operative transsexuals? Orangutans, genetically our next of kin, live completely solitary lives without social organization of any kind: ought we to "follow nature" and be hermits? There are many species where only two members per generation reproduce: should we be bees? The search in nature for people's purpose, far from finding sure models for action, is likely to leave one morally rudderless.

## VI. BUT AREN'T GAYS WILLFULLY THE WAY THEY ARE?

It is generally conceded that if sexual orientation is something over which an individual—for whatever reason—has virtually no control, then discrimination against gays is especially deplorable, as it is against racial and ethnic classes, because it holds people accountable without regard for anything they themselves have done. And to hold a person accountable for that over which the person has no control is a central form of prejudice.

Attempts to answer the question whether or not sexual orientation is something that is reasonably thought to be within one's own control usually appeal simply to various claims of the biological or "mental" sciences. But the ensuing debate over genes, hormones, twins, early childhood development, and the like, is as unnecessary as it is currently inconclusive.[15] All that is needed to answer the question is to look at the actual experience of gays in current society and it becomes fairly clear that sexual orientation is not likely a matter of choice. For coming to have a homosexual identity simply does not have the same sort of structure that decision making has.

On the one hand, the "choice" of the gender of a sexual partner does not seem to express a trivial desire that might be as easily well fulfilled by a simple substitution of the desired object. Picking the gender of a sex partner is decidedly dissimilar, that is, to such activities as picking a flavor of ice cream. If an ice-cream parlor is out of one's flavor, one simply picks another. And if people were persecuted, threatened with jail terms, shattered careers, loss of family and housing, and the like, for eating, say, rocky road ice cream, no one would ever eat it; everyone would pick another easily available flavor. That gay people abide in being gay even in the face of persecution shows that being gay is not a matter of easy choice.

On the other hand, even if establishing a sexual orientation is not like making a relatively trivial choice, perhaps it is nevertheless relevantly like making the central and serious life choices by which individuals try to establish themselves as being of some type. Again, if one examines gay experience, this seems not to be the case. For one never sees anyone setting out to become a homosexual, in the way one does see people setting out to become doctors, lawyers, and bricklayers. One does not find "gays-to-be" picking some end—"At some point in the future, I want to become a homosexual"—and then setting about planning and acquiring the ways and means to that end, in the way one does see people deciding that they want to become lawyers, and then sees them plan what courses to take and what sort of temperament, habits, and skills to develop in order to become lawyers. Typically, gays-to-be simply find themselves having homosexual encounters and yet at least initially resisting quite strongly the identification of being homosexual. Such a person even very likely resists having such encounters, but ends up having them anyway. Only with time, luck, and great personal effort, but sometimes never, does the person gradually come to accept his or her orientation, to view it as a given material condition of life, coming as materials do with certain capacities and limitations. The person begins to act in accordance with his or her orientation and its capacities, seeing its actualization as a requisite for an integrated personality and as a central component of personal well-being. As a result, the experience of coming out to oneself has for gays the basic structure of a discovery, not the structure of a choice. And far from signaling immorality, coming out to others affords one of the few remaining opportunities in ever more bureaucratic, mechanistic, and socialistic societies to manifest courage.

## VII. HOW WOULD SOCIETY AT LARGE BE CHANGED IF GAYS WERE SOCIALLY ACCEPTED?

Suggestions to change social policy with regard to gays are invariably met with claims that to do so would invite the destruction of civilization itself: after all, isn't that what did Rome in? Actually Rome's decay paralleled not the flourishing of homosexuality but its repression under the later Christianized emperors.[16] Predictions of American civilization's imminent demise have been as premature as they have been frequent. Civilization has shown itself rather resilient here, in large part because of the country's traditional commitments to a respect for privacy, to individual liberties, and especially to people minding their own business. These all give society an open texture and the flexibility to try out things to see what works. And because of this one now need not speculate about what changes reforms in gay social policy might bring to society at large. For many reforms have already been tried.

Half the states have decriminalized homosexual acts. Can you guess which of the following states still have sodomy laws: Wisconsin, Minnesota; New Mexico, Arizona; Vermont, New Hampshire; Nebraska, Kansas. One from each pair does and one does not have sodomy laws. And yet one would be hard pressed to point out any substantial difference between the members of each pair. (If you're interested it is the second of each pair with them.) Empirical studies have shown that there is no increase in other crimes in states that have decriminalized.[17] Further, sodomy laws are virtually never enforced. They remain on the books not to "protect society" but to insult gays, and for that reason need to be removed.

Neither has the passage of legislation barring discrimination against gays ushered in the end of civilization. Some 50 counties and municipalities, including some of the country's largest cities (like Los Angeles and Boston), have passed such statutes and among the states and colonies Wisconsin and the District of Columbia have model protective codes. Again, no more brimstone has fallen in these places than elsewhere. Staunchly anti-gay cities, like Miami and Houston, have not been spared the AIDS crisis.

Berkeley, California, has even passed domestic partner legislation giving gay couples the same rights to city benefits as married couples, and yet Berkeley has not become more weird than it already was.

Seemingly hysterical predictions that the American family would collapse if such reforms would pass proved false, just as the same dire predictions that the availability of divorce would lessen the ideal and desirability of marriage proved completely unfounded. Indeed if current discriminations, which drive gays into hiding and into anonymous relations, were lifted, far from seeing gays raze American families, one would see gays forming them.

Virtually all gays express a desire to have a permanent lover. Many would like to raise or foster children—perhaps those alarming numbers of gay kids who have been beaten up and thrown out of their "families" for being gay. But currently society makes gay coupling very difficult. A life of hiding is a pressure-cooker existence not easily shared with another. Members of non-gay couples are here asked to imagine what it would take to erase every trace of their own sexual orientation for even just a week.

Even against oppressive odds, gays have shown an amazing tendency to nest. And those gay couples who have survived the odds show that the structure of more usual couplings is not a matter of destiny but of personal responsibility. The so-called basic unit of society turns out not to be a unique immutable atom, but can adopt different parts, be adapted to different needs, and even be improved. Gays might even have a thing or two to teach others about division of labor, the relation of sensuality and intimacy, and stages of development in such relations.

If discrimination ceased, gay men and lesbians would enter the mainstream of the human community openly and with self-respect. The energies that the typical gay person wastes in the anxiety of leading a day-to-day existence of systematic disguise would be released for use in personal flourishing. From this release would be generated the many spinoff benefits that accrue to a society when its individual members thrive.

Society would be richer for acknowledging another aspect of human richness and diversity. Families with gay members would develop relations based on truth and trust rather than lies and fear. And the heterosexual majority would be better off for knowing that they are no longer trampling on their gay friends and neighbors.

Finally and perhaps paradoxically, in extending to gays the rights and benefits it has reserved for its dominant culture, America would confirm its deeply held vision of itself as a morally progressing nation, a nation itself advancing and serving as a beacon for others—especially with regard to human rights. The words with which our national pledge ends —"with liberty and justice for all"—are not a description of the present but a call for the future. Ours is a nation given to a prophetic political rhetoric which acknowledges that morality is not arbitrary and that justice is not merely the expression of the current collective will. It is this vision that led the black civil rights movement to its successes. Those congressmen who opposed that movement and its centerpiece, the 1964 Civil Rights Act, on obscurantist grounds, but who lived long enough and were noble enough, came in time to express their heartfelt regret and shame at what they had done. It is to be hoped and someday to be expected that those who now grasp at anything to oppose the extension of that which is best about America to gays will one day feel the same.

NOTES

1. "Public Fears—And Sympathies," *Newsweek,* August 12, 1985, p. 23.
2. Alfred C. Kinsey, *Sexual Behavior in the Human Male* (Philadelphia: Saunders, 1948), pp. 650–51. On the somewhat lower incidences of lesbianism,

see Alfred C. Kinsey, *Sexual Behavior in the Human Female* (Philadelphia: Saunders, 1953), pp. 472–75.

3. Evelyn Hooker, "The Adjustment of the Male Overt Homosexual," *Journal of Projective Techniques* 21 (1957): 18–31, reprinted in Hendrik M. Ruitenbeck, ed., *The Problem of Homosexuality* (New York: Dutton, 1963), pp. 141–61.

4. See Ronald Bayer, *Homosexuality and American Psychiatry* (New York: Basic Books, 1981).

5. For studies showing that gay men are no more likely—indeed, are less likely—than heterosexuals to be child molesters and that the largest groups of sexual abusers of children and the people more persistent in their molestation of children are the children's fathers or stepfathers or mother's boyfriends, see Vincent De Francis, *Protecting the Child Victim of Sex Crimes Committed by Adults* (Denver: The American Humane Association, 1969), pp. vii, 38, 69–70; A. Nicholas Groth, "Adult Sexual Orientation and Attraction to Underage Persons," *Archives of Sexual Behavior* 7 (1978): 175–81; Mary J. Spencer, "Sexual Abuse of Boys," *Pediatrics* 78, no. 1 (July 1986): 133–38.

6. See National Gay Task Force, *Anti-Gay/Lesbian Victimization* (New York: NGTF, 1984).

7. "2 St. John's Students Given Probation in Assault on Gay," *The Washington Post,* May 15, 1984, p. 1.

8. See Randy Shilts, *The Mayor of Castro Street: The Life and Times of Harvey Milk* (New York: St. Martin's, 1982), pp. 308–25.

9. See Richard Plant, *The Pink Triangle: The Nazi War Against Homosexuals* (New York: Holt, 1986).

10. E. Carrington Boggan, *The Rights of Gay People: The Basic ACLU Guide to a Gay Person's Rights* (New York: Avon, 1975), pp. 211–35.

11. John Boswell, *Christianity, Social Tolerance and Homosexuality: Gay People in Western Europe from the Beginning of the Christian Era to the Fourteenth Century* (Chicago: University of Chicago Press, 1980).

12. See Gilbert Herdt, *Guardians of the Flute: Idioms of Masculinity* (New York: McGraw-Hill, 1981), pp. 232–39, 284–88; and see generally Gilbert Herdt, ed., *Ritualized Homosexuality in Melanesia* (Berkeley: University of California Press, 1984). For another eye-opener, see Walter L. Williams, *The Spirit and the Flesh: Sexual Diversity in American Indian Culture* (Boston: Beacon, 1986).

13. See especially Boswell, *Christianity,* ch. 4.

14. For Old Testament condemnations of homosexual acts, see Leviticus 18:22, 21:3. For hygienic and dietary codes, see, for example, Leviticus 15:19–27 (on the uncleanliness of women) and Leviticus 11:1–47 (on not eating rabbits, pigs, bats, finless water creatures, legless creeping creatures, etc.). For Lot at Sodom, see Genesis 19:1–25. For Lot in the cave, see Genesis 19:30–38.

15. The preponderance of the scientific evidence supports the view that homosexuality is either genetically determined or a permanent result of early childhood development. See the Kinsey Institute's study by Alan Bell, Martin Weinberg, and Sue Hammersmith, *Sexual Preference: Its Development in Men*

*and Women* (Bloomington: Indiana University Press, 1981); Frederick Whitam and Robin Mathy, *Male Homosexuality in Four Societies* (New York: Praeger, 1986), ch. 7.

16. See Boswell, *Christianity,* ch. 3.

17. See Gilbert Geis, "Reported Consequences of Decriminalization of Consensual Adult Homosexuality in Seven American States," *Journal of Homosexuality* 1, no. 4 (1976): 419–26; Ken Sinclair and Michael Ross, "Consequences of Decriminalization of Homosexuality: A Study of Two Australian States," *Journal of Homosexuality* 12, no. 1 (1985): 119–27.

# 22

# A Classical Case for Gay Studies

## Martha Nussbaum

In *The Clouds,* Aristophanes' great comedy about Socrates, a young man
eager for the new learning goes to the Think-Academy run by that strange
and notorious figure. A debate is staged for him, contrasting the merits
of traditional education with those of the new discipline of argument. The
spokesman for the old education is a he-man. He favors a tough military
regimen, including lots of gymnastics and not much questioning. (Never
mind if he does dwell a bit on the beauty of naked youths sitting in the
sand; we know that he is no pathic, that his pleasures are not passive,
but active and insertive.) His idea of art is the song "Pallas, glorious sacker
of cities." His idea of culture is the recitation of the great works of the
past by a chorus of boys, with no interrogation and no innovation. Study
with me, he booms, and you will come to have a small tongue, a broad
chest, a firm ass, and a small prick (a plus in those days, symbolic of
manly control).

His opponent, Socrates' representative in this scene, is a seductive
softie, a man of words and arguments, a tongue man. He promises the
youth that he will learn to talk critically about the social origins of apparently timeless moral norms, about the distinction between convention and
nature. He will learn to construct arguments on his own, heedless of authority. He won't do much marching. Study with me, he concludes, and you

Originally published as "The Softness of Reason." Reprinted by permission of *The New
Republic.* Copyright © 1992, the New Republic, Inc.

will come to have a big tongue, a narrow chest, a soft ass, and a big prick (a minus in those days, symbolic of lack of control over one's appetites)—and possibly, even, a widely stretched asshole.

This self-advertisement, of course, is being slyly scripted by the conservative enemy. The message? The new education will subvert manly self-control, turn young people into sex-obsessed pathics, and destroy the city. The Think-Academy soon gets burned to the ground by an angry parent. And twenty-four years later, Socrates, on trial for corrupting the young, cites this play as a major source of prejudice against him.

New forms of study, subversive of cultural conventions, urging the critical scrutiny of what had previously seemed natural and inevitable, are once again under attack. And once again the conservative assault charges them with weakening time-honored sources of manliness, of political motives, of a dangerous corruption of the character of the young. Once again, coupled to these explicit charges is the insinuation that these new Think-Academicians are all really after sex, and are in some sense all about sex—especially sex of a passive, soft, dangerously unpatriotic variety.

My focus will be on controversies about gays and gay studies. But this controversy, I shall argue, is part of a larger history, in which women and women's studies play a parallel and earlier role. The best way I know to approach this connection is to tell some true stories.

Last year I gave a series of lectures, on the role of emotions in legal reasoning and on issues pertaining to gay civil rights, at a major law school. From that experience I report two incidents, involving norms of manliness and the new education. At the dinner that followed my lectures, the nonlawyer wife of one of the lawyers showed surprise and perplexity on being introduced to me. When I inquired about this, she explained that her husband had come home and reported that there was a woman lecturing who looked "just like Madonna." (I do not resemble Madonna.) We laughed at our discovery of a view of the legal academy in which there are just two boxes for women: the gray-suited woman who looks like a male lawyer, and the subversive, the wet, the dangerous woman. The latter, of course, is the one who talks about emotion, gender, and gay rights. And the statements that she makes about legal rationality are not arguments, they are seductions, an elaborate game of Truth or Dare.

In my final lecture I discussed *Bowers* v. *Hardwick,* criticizing the reasoning in the Supreme Court opinions that denied due process rights to a gay man. A third-year law student came up to me afterward and said he was gay, and wanted to thank me for treating that case "with dignity." I pondered the implications of his comment for the contents and tone of his previous legal education. Was this not an academic institution? And weren't academic institutions places where one learned about the history and the experience of people similar to *and* different from oneself, all in an atmosphere of dignity? And weren't schools of law, just maybe, especially concerned with knowledge about the lives of excluded minorities, and their dignity? But it appeared that such knowledge had been warded off in that law school, as in the Supreme Court opinions themselves, which show no curiosity about the history of homosexuality, and treat the gay man Michael Hardwick as a weird and dangerous being, altogether unlike other human beings who wish to make their own sexual choices in the privacy of their own bedrooms.

Madonna, the study of emotion, the study of gender and sexuality, Michael Hardwick—these soft and dangerous, sticky and subversive things, these threats to order and morals, were being evaded, carefully moved away, and their knowledge with them.

There is a norm of manliness in our society (much as there was in fifth-century Athens) that is deeply hostile to reason and learning. Its enforcers frequently wear the mantle of reason and learning. They speak of upholding standards, of time-honored educational values. But unlike true Socratic reasoners, they are unwilling to be penetrated by new factual information, new forms of interpretation, unwilling to commit themselves to following the argument and the facts anywhere they lead. To follow reason in the Socratic way requires a form of vulnerability and even passivity. It means dropping the pose that one is always adequate to any occasion, always on top, always hard. It means letting reputation and mastery wait on the outcome of impersonal logic and factual discovery; searching with humility for the truth that will refute what one most holds dear. As Callicles remarked to Socrates in Plato's *Gorgias,* that form of life is not for the he-man—although, as the Platonic dialogues amply attest, self-defensive he-men love to ape the give-and-take of argument, so long as their manly control is guaranteed.

To people who define themselves in this way, and who think of education accordingly, certain minorities seem especially dangerous and subversive—both by their physical presence and by the stimulus of knowledge about them. They stand for vulnerability and emotionality, forms of passivity so seductive that they must be relentlessly scrutinized and chastened. In the nineteenth century this scrutiny targeted the Jew and the woman— and it became a common stratagem of anti-Semitic rhetoric to portray the Jew as a dangerously effeminate being, whose inclusion in the academy, and in the polity in general, would spread both intellectual and sexual corruption. The link between the Jew and the woman—and between both and the "effeminate" male—was made in an especially vivid and influential form in the twisted arguments of Otto Weininger, a Jew and a closeted homosexual, whose rhetoric portrayed both women and Jews as beings obscenely emotional, soft, open, slimy, hence parasitic and subversive of intellectual creation.

By now the mantle of culpable and corrupting softness has to some extent shifted in American academic life from Jews to gay males—though all women still must wear it, especially when their presence is a reminder of desire. The academy, today as earlier, is not happy to have strange beings, reminders of desire and emotion, around; it views them—and studies about them—as corruptors of the intellectual life. This resistance appears to have deep roots. (As Schopenhauer perceptively if misogynistically argued, the female is a constant reminder of the intellect's lack of self-sufficiency, the unassuageable nature of desire, the limits of the body, the proximity of death.) And thus the rhetoric of resistance to these forms of "corruption" has changed relatively little—whether it takes the form of the charge that "Madonna" will subvert the purity of legal analysis, or that gay men, in positions of instruction, will corrupt their young charges by attempting to convert them to their own sexuality. In short: those who want to add such people and such forms of study to the curriculum are interested in just one thing—in having sex with them, or their students, or their children; in turning the pure Think-Academy into a den of vice. And so, as the Aristophanic chorus says to the audience, insofar as you listen to this stuff you are all wide-assholes, every one of you.

The past two decades have seen a considerable transformation in humanistic research and teaching, both in studies concerning women and in the study of lesbian and gay minorities. But these new studies are increasingly under attack from conservative critics, who charge that they have little scholarly legitimacy, entail the lowering of traditional standards, and are introduced only out of some sort of illegitimate "political motivation," which, in Dinesh D'Souza's words, defines a "shared orthodoxy for . . . the entire field." Although many scholars in these new areas have successful careers, many still face suspicion and hostility. So one must confront the question: Why should the academy add to its rich repertory the new disciplines of women's studies and lesbian and gay studies?

I suggest, as the beginning of an answer, that there are two central goals of an undergraduate college education in the liberal arts: to produce students who can reason and argue for themselves, conducting a Socratically "examined life," and also to produce students who are, to use the old Stoic term, "citizens of the entire world."

The first idea speaks for itself. It demands the searching criticism of traditional belief, conducted in an atmosphere of open debate and genuine receptivity. Indeed, the Socratic commitment to the life of reason not only does not require reverence for traditional norms, it requires their most vigilant scrutiny, and a determined openness to new argument and new evidence. And far from requiring the abandonment of logic and standards of rigor, as some conservatives charge, this critical posture of the mind rests precisely upon logic and a respect for standards of argumentation— a point that some anti-traditionalists on the left have not always sufficiently grasped.

The second idea holds that we live in a world that is complex and various, that has a history of still greater complexity—and that in order to be good citizens in such a world, we must make ourselves competent in that complexity, able to grapple with that variety and historical many-sidedness. We will need to know, in other words, whatever is required in order to converse and to argue intelligently with people who come from ways of life other than our own. We will also need to be able to convey our respect for our fellow world-citizens by taking them and their lives seriously. Our students will go out to take many roles in this world, participating in discussions where progress can be made only with information, sensitivity, and sound argument. They must be pedagogically prepared for this, both by learning many things and by coming to know what they don't know.

Before the field of women's studies began to be represented on university campuses, neither students nor faculty had much knowledge about the history and the lives of the world's women. It seemed perfectly normal and neutral to study the history, the lives, and the achievements of men; and any change in that status quo seemed like a radical departure, motivated by political concerns. But of course the status quo was far from neutral or apolitical. Indeed, it undermined the integrity of historical understanding by taking entire groups off the agenda of the humanistic professions, preventing generations of students from learning anything about approximately half of the people with whom they would deal in their lives. It comes as no surprise to find that this failure of attention coincided with the exclusion of women from many of the rights and privileges of the academy.

In order to change the status quo, it was necessary not only to add new content to the curriculum, but also to introduce and to refine new methods of research. In history, for example, research into the lives of women could not be well done with the methods customary for writing the history of the political leadership. Discovering how the excluded and the often illiterate lived is a difficult business, requiring demographic and statistical methods, and often interdisciplinary cooperation.

A distinguished example of this can be found in the career of the late David Herlihy, one of the most eminent medievalists of his generation, and at his death in 1991 the president of the American Historical Association. Herlihy was one of the founding members of the Women's Studies Committee at Harvard University; years earlier he had called for the establishment of this new disicpline in a famous lecture that transformed the field. He also gave a founding impetus to lesbian and gay studies, when he encouraged his doctoral student John Boswell to write his massive study of homosexuality and the Christian Church—at a time when gay people found almost nobody in the academy willing to speak their name. I had the good fortune to be an associate of Herlihy's, and at Brown we worked together on the founding of lesbian and gay studies. I always note with interest the absence of this distinguished name from the conservative attacks on women's and gay studies, since he was a pioneer in both, and a man universally respected for his learning and for his integrity.

What led Herlihy and others to propose radical changes in their own professions, and to follow them up with political action aimed at founding interdisciplinary programs to pursue the new studies further? Above all, a passion for truth and understanding. It seemed ludicrous that we knew nothing about the lives of women in the periods on which he worked. It seemed shameful, too, that we did not care to know and to teach views of sexuality along with everything else we knew and taught about the medieval world. And it seemed, too, that this was connected to the fact that neither women nor gays enjoyed equality in the academy. Surely greater equality of these groups in the historical record might contribute to their equality in the larger society. That was Herlihy's political agenda—radical enough for Harvard in the 1960s, when there were no tenured women on the faculty, and no noncloseted gay men. Herlihy was a conservative man, a religious Catholic, dedicated to home and family. But in his preference for the openness of reason over exclusionary scholarship, he was a true radical.

Introducing the study of women was difficult enough, but the effort to introduce the study of homosexuality into the curriculum has proved more difficult by far. Let me adduce my own experience at Brown, and the efforts made to incorporate the study of lesbians and gays into the curriculum. In 1985, as chair of a special committee on Minority Perspectives in the Curriculum, charged with describing the resources the curriculum offered for the study of various minority groups, I recommended adding the study of lesbian and gay minorities to our fact-finding task. The then dean of the college opposed my suggestion, on the grounds that these groups and their goals were controversial and troubling in a way that racial and ethnic minorities were not. I pressed, arguing above all that this was a legitimate and important area of scholarship. I also suggested that our failure to inquire as scholars in this area might be connected to the fact that we were the only remaining Ivy League university that had not adopted a statement of nondiscrimination for sexual orientation. Nor had we even seriously debated this question. It appeared that we had not been eager to confront the topic of homosexuality, either in the classroom or in the formation of university policy. I eventually succeeded in securing the formation of a separate fact-finding committee, devoted to the curricular treatment of sexual orientation. But then an odd thing happened.

An old friend of the dean's, a professor of medicine, invited me to lunch. After much general discussion, it emerged that what he really wanted was to discover my real motivation for this keen interest in sexual minorities. He began asking numerous questions about my personal life—attempting to ascertain whether my political activity was motivated by a minority sexual orientation. How odd, I thought, this scrutiny was. For it appeared we were talking about two things: the curriculum, and social justice. Could I really infer this gentleman held principles of the following sort:

(1) For all x and all y, if y defends x as a legitimate area of study, y is (whether openly or secretly) a member of x; and (2) For all x and all y, if y defends a claim of justice involving a member of x, y is (whether openly or secretly) a member of x?

If (1) is true, I thought, we have in our university many more fascists than I knew, many more criminals and psychopaths, many more saints, many more heroes. If (2) is true, then we have many more blacks on our faculty than anyone has known, and we can now unmask all those secret Jews who oppose the Holocaust, along with those extremely well-disguised rabbits who oppose product testing.

It is a dogma of American life, of course, that all actions are motivated by self-interest. But this dogma is false. There *are* claims of justice, and there *are* people who pursue them for their own sake. On this one issue of sexual orientation, however, the straight academy's (and above all the straight male academy's) fear of contagion was so deep that it was rare indeed to find support for those claims of justice, or for the closely related claims of scholarly inclusiveness. Straight men who had risked their lives in the civil rights movement shrank from taking any stand on this issue, and they thought it mighty odd that I would do so.

In the aftermath of that lunch, I lived for some months on campus as a person of undisclosed sexual orientation, "out" as a heterosexual to my friends but the object of surveillance by others. I understood, in that very brief time, the intensity of the scrutiny to which a lesbian or gay person in the university, or a person who is suspected of being gay, is subjected throughout his or her career, as though no conversation about any topic can begin until we first define "who you really are." The criticisms I had made of Foucault in my writing came to haunt me, as I experienced the truth of his claim that modern society makes questions of sexual orientation fundamental to all its dealings with a person, more fundamental than kindness, or excellence, or justice. I surrendered my public pose of ambiguity only when it became clear that students wanted to know whether the person in whom they wished to confide shared their experiences—a context in which my experiment in pursuing the educational issue without personal declaration seemed misguided.

The scrutiny I encountered was trivial. It caused me mild embarrassment, but no real damage to my activity as a teacher and a scholar. The opposition, however, can take a far more pernicious form, impugning the personal integrity of leading scholars in gay studies as a way of attacking their academic programs. Take the lawsuit recently brought against MIT by Professor Cynthia Griffin Wolff, a member of that university's literature department. Wolff seeks damages from the university because of the unpleasantness to which she has been subjected by the curricular efforts and the departmental politics of some of her associates. Her lawsuit has received wide publicity, and her efforts have been praised by some well-known conservative opponents of women's studies and gay studies. Wolff's suit is about to go to court.

The substance of her allegation is that MIT, by cooperating in the efforts of some of her colleagues to diversify the curriculum by adding material dealing with women and gays to the existing core of study, has subverted standards of scholarship and supported an agenda that is "politically motivated," by which she seems to mean subversive and bad. In the process, she made some unsubstantiated allegations against the professional integrity of David Halperin, a prominent figure in gay studies, a founder of the gay studies program at MIT, and an outspoken political activist. Halperin's own homosexuality makes him peculiarly vulnerable to an Artistophanic attack.

Wolff makes two serious charges against Halperin, in close connection with her opposition to the gay studies program. The first charge is that twice, in two different years, Professor David Halperin, an outspoken advocate of gay and lesbian views, demanded that the Section interview a specific candidate because he said he was "in love" with the candidate. When Professors Wolff and Taylor expressed opposition to this rationale for hiring, Professor Halperin verbally attacked them for expressing "homophobic" attitudes.

This story has all the hallmarks of the Aristophanic pattern I have tried to describe: someone who advocates "gay and lesbian views" must be all about sex, and his every professional act reveals a sexual motive. However, an affidavit from Professor Louis Kampf, who was one of the few of Wolff's colleagues whom she does not accuse of anything, tells a very different story. According to Kampf, all present at the meeting understood that Halperin was declaring a potential conflict of interest with respect to the candidate, for whom he had some erotic feeling (not an erotic relationship). "He wanted to make sure that everything was above board." The candidate was later offered the job by the unanimous vote of the department, though he declined to take it. The story of a homosexual plot to foist on the department a sexual pal instead of the best candidate is thus false in more than one way.

Wolff's second charge is more elusive, but it is from this charge that her link to the Old Education emerges most clearly. Wolff speaks of her belief that Halperin had subjected a colleague to "sexual harassment." What is interesting here is not simply that no formal charge of harassment against Halperin was ever brought or adjudicated; or that Halperin was never formally asked to defend himself against any charge; but that Wolff went on to argue that he "could readily be harassing undergraduates, especially as Professor Halperin had been charged and funded by the administration to create an undergraduate program in gay and lesbian studies." It is as good an example as one can find of the Aristophanic syndrome.

But let us now return to Brown and to the struggle for curriculum reform. At Brown, our committee looked at the curriculum to ascertain what resources it offered for any person who wished to understand the phenomenon of homosexuality in history or psychology or biology or literature. We sent a questionnaire to all departments and programs, with three questions: (1) Did they have any courses that dealt with homosexuality? (2) Did they have any plans for course development in that area? (3) Did they have any faculty member who could advise students who wished to do reading and research in that area? The following departments, among many others, answered all three questions in the negative:

Psychology, Sociology, History, Japanese Literature, German, French. Only Religious Studies and Biology (a subsection of a single course in each case) had any formal curricular offerings. When individual faculty members were named as competent to advise work in the area, odd disclaimers tended to be attached, protecting the person's straight reputation against the suspicion of a personal connection to the topic. To want to know something about this suspect form of life calls for explanation; and it is assumed that the explanation is a confession, unless a disclaimer (never fully convincing) is explicitly entered.

In short, our students' knowledge of psychology and literature and history was not well served. And this refusal of knowledge—for that is what the opposition to the study of homosexuality was—came linked with prejudice and injustice, as both cause and effect. Lesbian and gay students reported the feelings that seized them when, as so often happened, an instructor arrived at a portion of a historical event, or a literary text, in which the issue of homosexuality arose—and passed over it with embarrassment, or even disgust, as if to say that we all know what *that* is. Well, we did not know, and do not know; and on the whole do not want to know. For in this case, to want to know is to be tainted. We were not far, and in many cases still are not far, from the moment in E. M. Forster's *Maurice* when, as the undergraduates prepare to translate a Greek text, their tutor "observed in a flat toneless voice: 'Omit: a reference to the unspeakable vice of the Greeks.'"

This, then, is the primary rationale for gay studies, as for women's studies: the completeness of knowledge itself demands their promotion. And the completeness of knowledge, openness to the facts of history and to arguments about history, is an ideal that conservative opponents of these new forms of study cannot consistently repudiate and still claim to be honoring the time-honored norms of the Western philosophical tradition.

It is also true that this knowledge can help produce students who are more fully "citizens of the entire world." This knowledge will, of course, have a special meaning for those whose very identity has previously been excluded from the precincts of knowledge. (Hearing his first real discussion of Greek homosexuality, Forster's Maurice is transformed: "He hadn't known it could be mentioned, and when Durham did so in the middle of the sunlit court a breath of liberty touched him.") But to know about the lives of one's fellow citizens and to understand their history is essential also for those who are not lesbian or gay. As the legal theorist Richard Posner has recently argued, a great deal more knowledge about sexuality, and especially about homosexuality, is essential if we are to have a well-informed judiciary and, in general, a humane and just society.

To strive for a citizenry of this sort is, of course, a certain sort of political agenda. But is this really a bad thing? Political motivations have been explicit in many of the greatest works of moral and political thought—within the Western tradition, in Plato, Aristotle, Seneca, Spinoza, Kant, and Rawls, to name just a few. Since Aristotle, indeed, it has been common to argue that the end of inquiry into areas touching on ethics and the conduct of life ought to be not just theoretical understanding, but also the improvement of political life. Thucydides argued that this was also true of the study of history, and many great historians have followed him. That literary study also may have a social goal has been more controversial; but many leading theorists, from Plato and Aristotle to Wayne Booth, have argued that it can and should.

So what do the critics of gay studies and women's studies mean when they say that these studies are "politically motivated"? Surely not just that the proponents side with Plato and Aristotle—or with Leavis, Trilling, and Booth—against more formalist or aestheticizing humanists. That could hardly be a point against their inclusion in the academy. Perhaps they mean that these studies are pursued because they advance a political goal that is improperly related to the goals of scholarly study itself. But what could such a goal be? It was evident enough at Brown that we connected scholarship to goals of equal respect, arguing that silence about a group undermines its dignity. But this seems a cogent argument and one would hardly have to be a radical to endorse it.

What assailants of the new studies might mean, by their claims of "political motivation," is that there is no inquiry here, and no reasoned debate, but only the dogmatic imposition of a single viewpoint. But the nature of lesbian and gay studies in the academy today bears little resemblance to this stereotype. Indeed, what is most striking about the field is its variety, in both its subject matter and its methodology. Where ancient Greece is concerned, the tight-lipped omissions described by Forster have been replaced by a wide variety of scholarly accounts of Greek homosexuality, from which a student may now learn what the historical, literary, and artistic evidence shows about ancient sexual life. The pioneering work was *Greek Homosexuality* by Kenneth Dover, one of the century's leading ancient historians, and among the least likely to be accused of lowering standards of scholarship for the sake of a political end. (Despite Dover's prominence, he had difficulty finding a major press that would undertake the job.) Michel Foucault then made a major theoretical step forward by pointing out that our modern categories of the heterosexual and the homosexual have no precise equivalent in classical antiquity. The fundamental distinction for males was that between the active and the passive roles, and so long as one took the active role, the gender of the partner was not considered a matter of great importance. David Halperin's work has advanced this inquiry further. Many other scholars are by now contributing to the investigation on many fronts.

Much the same situation obtains across the humanities. "Lesbian and gay studies" are sometimes pursued in separate programs, though far more often within existing departments of history, literature, art, philosophy (where ethical and legal issues concerning homosexuality are vigorously debated). It is as if an entire new continent for scholarship has just been opened up, and younger scholars can feel the exhilaration of uncharted territory. Conservative critics paint a picture of narrow political uniformity. They suggest, for example, that all scholars in this field are themselves gay or lesbian, and are all either deconstructionist literary theorists or uncritical followers of Foucault. But the projects undertaken in gay studies are too varied to be captured in such glib generalizations. Although, as with any study connected to deep concerns about identity, many in this field have been lesbian and gay, they are, like heterosexual scholars, tremendously varied in their style of life, their politics, their religious attitudes and practices; and some leading writers in the field are not homosexual at all. It is, after all, as I have argued, an important area of knowledge for all of us.

About the central methodological questions raised by Foucault's work, moreover, there has been a lively and sometimes heated debate. The historian John Boswell and the philosopher Richard Mohr stress the underlying continuity of types of sexual practices; Halperin and others, persuaded by Foucault, stress instead the extent to which social conventions shape the categories recognized as salient in the assessment, and even the experience of sexual desire and activity. Richard Posner makes a complicated synthesis of the two positions, recognizing the extent to which sexual categories are "socially constructed," but suggesting that within this historical variety we may see certain biological constants. The debate is intellectually fascinating—and it is also urgent, for all too frequently, in our social and legal lives, we have proceeded as if we knew for sure that a person's sexuality is something innate and "natural"; these new inquiries promote self-understanding, and hence justice.

The conservative attack on gay studies, then, is not a defense of classical learning, or of the Western philosophical tradition. It is an attack on that learning and that tradition, disguised as a defense. At root, these critics are saying little about intellectual life and everything about political life: these studies, they are saying, are motivated by the desire of certain people to be included in the academy and to have their way of life recognized as an object of study, and that is precisely what we object to: these people should not be included and their way of life should not be recognized. But why not? What is the argument? Why are these people, and knowledge about them, being pushed away? The Aristophanic answer comes back: because there is something strange about them and they make us very uncomfortable. Never mind that both history and philosophy are, in their very nature, forms of inquiry into the strange and unsettling.

  "Go with me," says the Old Education. "I am manliness. I am tradition. I am reason." But reason is not impenetrable manliness or invulnerable mastery or inflexible adherence to tradition. Reason is, as Plato once said, a soft, slender gold cord, flexibly pulled by the draw of truth and understanding. Unless (he notes), as often happens, it is rudely shoved aside by the iron strings of self-interest, greed, and fear.

# Part Seven

# Desirable Goals
# and Possible Solutions

# 23

# Stateways Can Change Folkways

## Elliot Aronson

In 1954, the United States Supreme Court declared that separate but equal schools were, by definition, unequal. In the words of Chief Justice Earl Warren, when black children are separated from white children on the basis of race alone, it "generates a feeling of inferiority as to their status in the community that may affect their hearts and minds in a way unlikely ever to be undone." Without our quite realizing it, this decision launched our nation into one of the most exciting, large-scale social experiments ever conducted.

In the aftermath of this historic decision, many people were opposed to integrating the schools on "humanitarian" grounds. They predicted a holocaust if the races were forced to mingle in schools. They argued that laws cannot force people to like and respect each other. This echoed the sentiments of the distinguished sociologist William Graham Sumner, who, years earlier, had stated "stateways don't change folkways." What Sumner meant, of course, is you can't legislate morality; you can force people to desegregate, but you can't force them to like one another. A great many people urged that desegregation be delayed until attitudes could be changed.

Social psychologists at that time, of course, believed the way to change behavior is to change attitudes. Thus, if you can get bigoted adults to

228 Part Seven: Desirable Goals and Possible Solutions

become less prejudiced against blacks, then they will not hesitate to allow their children to attend school with blacks. Although they should have known better, many social scientists were relatively confident they could change bigoted attitudes by launching information campaigns. They took a "sixteen-millimeter" approach to the reduction of prejudice: If prejudiced people believe blacks are shiftless and lazy, then all you have to do is show them a *movie*—a movie depicting that blacks are industrious, decent people. The idea is that you can combat misinformation with information. If Shakespeare believes Jews are conniving bloodsuckers because he has been exposed to misinformation about Jews, expose him to a more accurate range of information about Jews, and his prejudice will fade away. If most South Africans believe blacks commit virtually all crimes, show them the white convicts, and they'll change their beliefs. Unfortunately, it is not quite that simple. Whether prejudice is largely a function of economic conflict, conformity to social norms, or deeply rooted personality needs, it is not easily changed by an information campaign. Over the years, most people become deeply committed to their prejudicial behavior. To develop an open, accepting attitude toward minorities when all of your friends and associates are still prejudiced is no easy task. A mere movie cannot undo a way of thinking and a way of behaving that has persisted over the years.

. . . [W]here important issues are involved, information campaigns fail, because people are inclined not to sit still and take in information that is dissonant with their beliefs. Paul Lazarsfeld,[1] for example, described a series of radio broadcasts in the early 1940s designed to reduce ethnic prejudice by presenting information about various ethnic groups in a warm and sympathetic manner. One program was devoted to a description of Polish-Americans, another was devoted to Italian-Americans, and so forth. Who was listening? The major part of the audience for the program about Polish-Americans consisted of Polish-Americans. And guess who made up the major part of the audience for the program on Italian-Americans? Right. Moreover . . . if people are compelled to listen to information uncongenial to their deep-seated attitudes, they will reject it, distort it, or ignore it. . . . For most people, prejudice is too deeply rooted in their own belief systems, is too consistent with their day-to-day behavior, and receives too much support and encouragement from the people around them to be reduced by a book, a film, or a radio broadcast.

## THE EFFECTS OF EQUAL-STATUS CONTACT

Although changes in attitude might induce changes in behavior, as we have seen, it is often difficult to change attitudes through education. What social psychologists have long known, but have only recently begun to understand, is that *changes in behavior can effect changes in attitudes.* On the simplest level, it has been argued that, if blacks and whites could be brought into direct contact, prejudiced individuals would come into contact with the reality of their own experience, not simply a stereotype; eventually, this would lead to greater understanding. Of course, the contact must take place in a situation in which blacks and whites have equal status; throughout history many whites have always had a great deal of contact with blacks, but typically in situations in which the blacks played such menial roles as slaves, porters, dishwashers, shoe-shine boys, washroom attendants, and domestics. This kind of contact only serves to increase stereotyping by whites and thus adds fuel to their prejudice against blacks. It also serves to increase the resentment and anger of blacks. Until recently, equal-status contact has been rare, both because of educational and occupational inequities in our society and because of residential segregation. The 1954 Supreme Court decision was the beginning of a gradual change in the frequency of equal-status contact.

Occasionally, even before 1954, isolated instances of equal-status integration had taken place. The effects tended to support the notion that behavior change will produce attitude change. In a pioneering study, Morton Deutsch and Mary Ellen Collins[2] examined the attitudes of whites toward blacks in public housing projects. Specifically, in one housing project, black and white families were assigned to buildings in a segregated manner—that is, they were assigned to separate buildings in the same project. In another project, the assignment was integrated—black and white families were assigned to the same building. Residents in the integrated project reported a greater positive change in their attitudes toward blacks subsequent to moving into the project than did residents of the segregated project. From these findings, it would appear that stateways *can* change folkways, that you can legislate morality—not directly, of course, but through the medium of equal-status contact. If diverse racial groups can be brought together under conditions of equal status, they stand a chance of getting to know each other better. This can increase understanding and decrease tension, *all other things being equal.**

---

*The study alluded to in this paragraph took place in public housing projects rather than in private residential areas. This is a crucial factor that will be discussed in a moment.

THE VICARIOUS EFFECTS OF DESEGREGATION

It wasn't until much later that social psychologists began to entertain the notion that desegregation can affect the values of people who do not even have the opportunity to have direct contact with minority groups. This can occur through [such] mechanisms . . . as the *psychology of inevitability*. Specifically, if I know that you and I will inevitably be in close contact, and I don't like you, I will experience dissonance. In order to reduce dissonance I will try to convince myself you are not as bad as I had previously thought. I will set about looking for your positive characteristics and will try to ignore, or minimize the importance of, your negative characteristics. Accordingly, the mere fact that I know I must at some point be in *close contact* with you will force me to change my prejudiced attitudes about you, *all other things being equal*. As we saw earlier, laboratory experiments have confirmed this prediction: For example, children who believed they must inevitably eat a previously disliked vegetable began to convince themselves the vegetable wasn't as bad as they had previously thought.[3] Similarly, college women who knew they were going to spend several weeks working intimately with a woman who had several positive and negative qualities developed a great fondness for that woman before they even met her; this did not occur when they were *not* led to anticipate working with her in the future.[4]

Admittedly, it's a far cry from a bowl of vegetables to relations between blacks, Latinos, and whites. Few social psychologists are so naive as to believe that deep-seated racial intolerance can be eliminated if people reduce their dissonance simply through coming to terms with what they believe to be inevitable events. I would suggest that, under ideal conditions, such events *can* begin to unfreeze prejudiced attitudes and produce a *diminution* of hostile feelings in most individuals. I will discuss what I mean by "ideal conditions" in a moment; but first, let us put a little more meat on those theoretical bones. How might the process of dissonance reduction take place?

Turn the clock back to the late 1950s. Imagine a forty-five-year-old white male whose sixteen-year-old daughter attends a segregated school. Let us assume he has a negative attitude toward blacks, based in part on his beliefs that blacks are shiftless and lazy and that all black males are oversexed and potential rapists. Suddenly, the edict is handed down by the Justice Department: The following autumn, his fair-haired, young daughter must go to an integrated school. State and local officials, while perhaps not liking the idea, clearly convey the fact that there's nothing that can be done to prevent it—it's the law of the land and it must be obeyed. The father might, of course, refuse to allow his child to obtain an education, or he could send her to an expensive private school. But such measures are either terribly drastic or terribly costly. So he decides he must send her to an integrated school. His cognition that his fair-haired young daughter must inevitably attend the same school with blacks is dissonant with his cognition that blacks are shiftless rapists. What does he do? My guess is he will begin to reexamine his beliefs about blacks. Are they *really* all that shiftless? Do they *really* go around raping people? He may take another look—this time, with a strong inclination to look for the good qualities in blacks rather than to concoct and exaggerate bad, unacceptable qualities. I would guess that, by the time September rolls around, his attitude toward blacks would have become unfrozen and would have shifted in a positive direction. If this shift can be bolstered by positive events *after* desegregation—for example, if his daughter has pleasant and peaceful interactions with her black schoolmates— a major change in the father's attitudes is likely to result. Again, this analysis is admittedly oversimplifed. But the basic process holds. And look at the advantages this process has over an information campaign. A mechanism has been triggered that *motivated* the father to alter his negative stereotype of blacks.

My analysis strongly suggests that a particular kind of public policy would be most potentially beneficial to society—a policy exactly opposite of what has been generally recommended. As mentioned previously, following the 1954 Supreme Court decision, there was a general feeling that integration must proceed slowly. Most public officials and many social scientists believed that, in order to achieve harmonious racial relations, integration should be delayed until people could be reeducated to become less prejudiced. In short, the general belief in 1954 was that the behavior (integration) must *follow* a cognitive change. My analysis suggests that the best way to produce eventual interracial harmony would be to launch into behavioral change. Moreover, *and most important,* the sooner the individuals realize integration is inevitable, the sooner their prejudiced attitudes will begin to change. On the other hand, this process can be (and has been) sabotaged by public officials through fostering the belief that integration can be circumvented or delayed. This serves to create the illusion that the event is not inevitable. In such circumstances, there will be no attitude change; the result will be an increase in turmoil and disharmony. Let's go back to our previous example: If the father of the fair-haired daughter is led (by the statements and tactics of a governor, a mayor, a school-board chairman, or a local sheriff) to believe there's a way out of integration, he will feel no need to reexamine his negative beliefs about blacks. The result is apt to be violent opposition to integration.

Consistent with this reasoning is the fact that, as desegregation has spread, favorable attitudes toward desegregation have increased. In 1942, only 3 percent of the whites in this country favored desegregated schools; by 1956, the figure rose to 49 percent; in 1970, 75 percent. Finally, in 1980, as it became increasingly clear school desegregation was inevitable, the figure approached 90 percent.[5] The change in the South (taken by itself) is even more dramatic. In 1942, only 2 percent of the whites in the South favored integrated schools; in 1956, while most southerners still believed the ruling could be circumvented, only 14 percent favored desegregation; but by 1970, as desegregation continued, just under 50 percent favored desegregation—and the figures continued to climb in the 1980s. Of course, such statistical data do not constitute absolute proof that the reason people are changing their attitudes toward school desegregation is that they are coming to terms with what is inevitable—but the data are highly suggestive.

In a careful analysis of the process and effects of school desegregation, Thomas Pettigrew raised the question of why, in the early years of desegregation, violence occurred in some communities, such as Little Rock and Clinton, and not in others, such as Norfolk and Winston-Salem. His conclusion, which lends further support to my reasoning, was that "violence has generally resulted in localities where at least some of the authorities give prior hints that they would gladly return to segregation if disturbances occurred; peaceful integration has generally followed firm and forceful leadership."[6] In other words, if people were not given the opportunity to reduce dissonance, there was violence. As early as 1953, Kenneth B. Clark[7] observed the same phenomenon during the desegregation in some of the border states. He discovered that immediate desegregation was far more effective than gradual desegregation. Moreover, violence occurred in those places where ambiguous or inconsistent policies were employed or where community leaders tended to vacillate. The same kind of thing happened when military units began to desegregate during World War II: trouble was greatest where policies were ambiguous.[8]

## BUT ALL OTHER THINGS ARE NOT ALWAYS EQUAL

In the preceding section, I presented an admittedly oversimplified view of a very complex phenomenon. I did this intentionally as a way of indicating how things can proceed theoretically under ideal conditions. But conditions are seldom ideal. There are almost always some complicating circumstances. Let us now look at some of the complications and then proceed to discuss how these complications might be eliminated or reduced.

When I discussed the fact that prejudice was reduced in an integrated housing project, I made special note of the fact it was a *public* housing project. Some complications are introduced if it involves privately owned houses. Primarily, there is a strong belief among whites that, when blacks move into a neighborhood, real-estate values decrease. This belief introduces economic conflict and competition, which militate against the reduction of prejudiced attitudes. Indeed, systematic investigations in integrated *private* housing show an increase in prejudiced attitudes among the white residents.[9]

Moreover, as I mentioned, the experiments on the psychology of inevitability were done in the laboratory, where the dislikes involved in the studies were almost certainly not as intense or as deep-seated as racial prejudice is in the real world. Although it is encouraging to note that these findings were paralleled by the data from actual desegregation efforts, it would be naive and misleading to conclude that the way to desegregation will always be smooth as long as individuals are given the opportunity to come to terms with inevitability. Frequently, trouble begins once desegregation starts. This is often due, in part, to the fact that the contact between white and minority-group children (especially if it is not begun until high school) is usually not equal-status contact. Picture the scene: A tenth-grade boy from a poor black or Latino family, after being subjected to a second-rate education, is suddenly dropped into a learning situation in a predominately white middle-class school taught by white middle-class teachers, where he finds he must compete with white middle-class students who have been reared to hold white middle-class values. In effect, he is thrust into a highly competitive situation for which he is unprepared, a situation in which the rules are not his rules and payoffs are made for abilities he has not yet developed. He is competing in a situation that, psychologically, is far removed from his home turf. Ironically enough, these factors tend to produce a diminution of his self-esteem —the very factor that influenced the Supreme Court decision in the first place.[10] In his careful analysis of the research on desegregation, Walter Stephan[11] found *no* studies indicating significant increases in self-esteem among black students, while 25 percent of the studies he researched showed a significant *drop* in their self-esteem following desegregation. In addition, prejudice was not substantially reduced. Stephan found that it increased in almost as many cases as it decreased.

With these data in mind, it is not surprising to learn that a newly integrated high school is typically a tense place. It is natural for minority-group students to attempt to raise their self-esteem. One way of raising self-esteem is to stick together, lash out at whites, assert their individuality, reject white values and white leadership, and so on.[12]

Let me sum up the discussion thus far: (1) Equal-status contact under the ideal conditions of no economic conflict can and does produce increased understanding and a diminution of prejudice.[13] (2) The psychology of inevitability can and does set up pressures to reduce prejudiced attitudes, and can set the stage for smooth, nonviolent school desegregation, *under ideal conditions.* (3) Where economic conflict is present (as in integrated neighborhoods of private domiciles) there is often an increase in prejudiced attitudes. (4) Where school desegregation results in a competitive situation, especially if there are serious inequities for the minority groups, there is often an increase in hostility of blacks or Latinos toward whites that is at least partially due to an attempt to regain some lost self-esteem.


## INTERDEPENDENCE—A POSSIBLE SOLUTION

School desegregation can open the door to increased understanding among students, but, by itself, it is not the ultimate solution. The issue is not simply getting youngsters of various races and ethnic backgrounds into the same school—it's what happens after they get there that is crucial. As we have seen, if the atmosphere is a highly competitive one, whatever tensions exist initially might actually be increased as a result of contact. . . .

The key factor seems to be *mutual interdependence*—a situation wherein individuals need one another and are needed by one another in order to accomplish their goal. Several researchers have demonstrated the benefits of cooperation in well-controlled laboratory experiments. Morton Deutsch,[14] for example, has shown that problem-solving groups are both friendlier and more attentive when a cooperative atmosphere is introduced than when a competitive atmosphere prevails. Similarly, research by Patricia Keenan and Peter Carnevale has shown that cooperation within groups can also foster cooperation between groups.[15] That is, cooperative relations that are established in one group often carry over when that group is later called upon to interact with a different group. In their study, groups that engaged in a cooperative task were more cooperative in a subsequent negotiation with another group, as compared to groups who had initially worked in a competitive fashion.

Unfortunately, cooperation and interdependence are not characteristic of the process that exists in most school classrooms, even at the elementary level. We have already alluded to the competitive nature of the process; let us take a closer look at it. First, let's define "process." Whenever people interact, two things exist simultaneously. One of these things is the content and the other is the process. By content, I simply mean the substance of their encounter; by process, I mean the dynamics of the encounter. In a classroom, for example, the content could be arithmetic, geography, social studies, or music; the process is the manner in which these lessons are taught. It goes without saying that the content is of great importance. However, the importance of the process is frequently underestimated. But it is through the process that pupils learn a great deal about the world they live in. Indeed, I would even go so far as to say that, in some respects, the process is a more important source of learning than the content itself.

I was provided with a golden opportunity to observe classroom process some years ago when I was called in as a consultant to the Austin, Texas, school system. Desegregation had just taken place; this was followed by a great deal of turmoil and a number of unpleasant incidents. My colleagues and I entered the system, not to smooth over the unpleasantness but, rather, to see if there was anything we might do to help desegregation achieve some of the positive goals envisioned for it. The first thing my colleagues and I did was systematically observe the process. We tried to do this with fresh eyes—as if we were visitors from another planet—and the most typical process we observed was this: The teacher stands in front of the class, asks a question, and waits for the children to indicate that they know the answer. Most frequently, six to ten youngsters strain in their seats and wave their hands to attract the teacher's attention. They seem eager to be called on. Several other students sit quietly with their eyes averted, as if trying to make themselves invisible. When the teacher calls on one of the students, there are looks of disappointment, dismay, and unhappiness on the faces of those students who were eagerly raising their hands but were not called on. If the student who is called on comes up with the right answer, the teacher smiles, nods approvingly, and goes on to the next question. This is a great reward for the child who happens to be called on. At the same time the fortunate student is coming up with the right answer and being smiled upon by the teacher, an audible groan can be heard coming from the children who were striving to be called on but were ignored. It is obvious they are disappointed because they missed an opportunity to show the teacher how smart and quick they are.

Through this process, students learn several things. First, they learn there is one and only one expert in the classroom: the teacher. They also learn there is one and only one correct answer to any question the teacher asks—namely, the answer the teacher has in mind. The students' task is to figure out which answer the teacher expects. The students also learn that the payoff comes from pleasing the teacher by actively displaying how quick, smart, neat, clean, and well behaved they are. If they do this successfully, they will gain the respect and love of this powerful person. This powerful person will then be kind to them and will tell their parents what wonderful children they are. There is no payoff for them in consulting with their peers. Indeed, their peers are their enemies—to be beaten. Moreover, collaboration is frowned upon by most teachers; if it occurs during class time it is seen as disruptive, and if it takes place during an exam, it is called "cheating."

The game is very competitive and the stakes are very high—in an elementary-school classroom, the youngsters are competing for the respect and approval of one of the two or three most important people in their world (important for most students, anyway). If you are a student who knows the correct answer and the teacher calls on one of your peers, it is likely you will sit there hoping and praying he or she will come up with the wrong answer so you will have a chance to show the teacher how smart you are. Those who fail when called on, or those who do not even raise their hands and compete, have a tendency to resent those who succeed. Frequently, the "losers" become envious and jealous of the successful students, perhaps they tease them or ridicule them by referring to them as "teacher's pets." They might even use physical aggression against them in the school yard. The successful students, for their part, often hold the unsuccessful students in contempt; they consider them to be dumb and uninteresting. The upshot of this process—which takes place, to a greater or lesser extent, in most classrooms—is that friendliness and understanding are not promoted among *any* of the children in the same classroom. Quite the reverse. The process tends to create enmity, even among children of the same racial group. When ethnic or racial unfamiliarity is added, or when tension brought about by forced busing flavors the stew of an already unhappy process, the situation can become extremely difficult and unpleasant.

Although competitiveness in the classroom is typical, it is not inevitable. In my research, I found that many classroom teachers were eager to try more cooperative techniques. Accordingly, my colleagues and I developed a simple method wherein children were put into interdependent learning groups; we systematically compared their performance, satisfaction, and liking for one another with that of children in more traditional, competitive classroom situations.[16] We called our method the *jigsaw* technique because it works very much like a jigsaw puzzle.

An example will clarify: In our initial experiment, we entered a fifth-grade classroom of a newly desegregated school. In this classroom, the children were studying biographies of famous Americans. The upcoming lesson happened to be a biography of Joseph Pulitzer, the famous journalist. First, we constructed a biography of Joseph Pulitzer consisting of six paragraphs. Paragraph one was about Joseph Pulitzer's ancestors and how they came to this country; paragraph two was about Joseph Pulitzer as a little boy and how he grew up; paragraph three was about Joseph Pultizer as a young man, his education, and his early employment; paragraph four was about his middle age and how he founded his newspaper; and so forth. Each major aspect of Joseph Pulitzer's life was contained in a separate paragraph. We mimeographed our biography of Joseph Pulitzer, cut each copy of the biography into six one-paragraph sections, and gave every child in each of the six-person learning groups one paragraph about Joseph Pulitzer's life. Thus, each learning group had within it the entire biography of Joseph Pulitzer, but each individual had no more than one-sixth of the story. Like a jigsaw puzzle, each child had one piece of the puzzle, and each child was dependent on the other children in the group for the completion of the big picture. In order to learn about Joseph Pulitzer, each child had to master a paragraph and teach it to the others. Students took their paragraphs and went off by themselves where they could learn them. In learning the paragraph, the children were free to consult with their counterpart in one of the other learning groups. That is, if Johnnie had been dealt Joseph Pulitzer as a young man, he might have consulted with Christina, who was in a different learning group and had also been dealt Pulitzer as a young man. They could use each other to rehearse and clarify for themselves the important aspects of that phase of Joseph Pulitzer's life. A short time later, the students came back into session with their six-person groups. They were informed that they had a certain amount of time to communicate their knowledge to one another. They were also informed that, at the end of the time (or soon thereafter), they were going to be tested on their knowledge.

When thrown on their own resources, the children eventually learned to teach and to listen to one another. The children gradually learned that none of them could do well without the aid of each person in the group—and that each member had a unique and essential contribution to make. Suppose you and I are children in the same group. You've been dealt Joseph Pulitzer as a young man; I've been dealt Pulitzer as an old man. The only way I can learn about Joseph Pulitzer as a young man is to pay close attention to what you are saying. You are a very important resource for me. The teacher is no longer the sole resource— he or she isn't even an important resource; indeed, the teacher isn't even in the group. Instead, every kid in the circle becomes important to me. I do well if I pay attention to other kids; I do poorly if I don't. I no longer get rewarded for trying to please the teacher at your expense. It's a whole new ball game.

But cooperative behavior doesn't happen all at once. Typically, it requires several days before children use this technique effectively. Old habits are difficult to break. The students in our experimental group had grown accustomed to competing during all of their years in school. For the first few days, most of the youngsters tried to compete—even though competitiveness was dysfunctional. Let me illustrate with an actual example typical of the way the children stumbled toward the learning of the cooperative process. In one of our groups there was a Mexican-American boy, whom we will call Carlos. Carlos was not very articulate in English, his second language. He had learned over the years how to keep quiet in class because frequently, when he had spoken up in the past, he was ridiculed. In this instance, he had a great deal of trouble communicating his paragraph to the other children; he was very uncomfortable about it. He liked the traditional way better. This is not surprising, because, in the system we introduced, Carlos was forced to speak, whereas before he could always deindividuate himself and keep a low profile in the classroom. But the situation was even more complex than that—it might even be said the teacher and Carlos had entered into a conspiracy, that they were in collusion. Carlos was perfectly willing to be quiet. In the past, the teacher called on him occasionally; he would stumble, stammer, and fall into an embarrassed silence. Several of his peers would make fun of him. The teacher had learned not to call on him anymore. The decision probably came from the purest of intentions—the teacher simply did not want to humiliate him. But, by ignoring him, she had written him off. The implication was that he was not worth bothering with— at least the other kids in the classroom got that message. They believed there was one good reason why the teacher wasn't calling on Carlos— he was stupid. Indeed, even Carlos began to draw this conclusion. This is part of the dynamic of how desegregation, when coupled with a competitive process, can produce unequal-status contact and can result in even greater enmity between ethnic groups and a loss of self-esteem for members of disadvantaged ethnic minorities.[17]

Let us go back to our six-person group. Carlos, who had to report on Joseph Pulitzer's young manhood, was having a hard time. He stammered, hesitated, and fidgeted. The other kids in the circle were not very helpful. They had grown accustomed to a competitive process and responded out of this old overlearned habit. They knew what to do when a kid stumbles—especially a kid whom they believed to be stupid. They ridiculed him, put him down, and teased him. During our experiment, it was Mary who was observed to say: "Aw, you don't know it, you're dumb, you're stupid. You don't know what you're doing." In our initial experiment, the groups were being loosely monitored by a research assistant who was floating from group to group. When this incident occurred, our assistant made one brief intervention: "OK, you can do that if you want to. It might be fun for you, but it's *not* going to help you learn about Joseph Pulitzer's young manhood. The exam will take place in an hour." Notice how the reinforcement contingencies have shifted. No longer does Mary gain much from putting Carlos down—in fact, she now stands to lose a great deal. After a few days and several similar experiences, it began to dawn on the students in Carlos's group that the *only* way they could learn about Joseph Pulitzer's young manhood was by paying attention to what Carlos had to say. Gradually, they began to develop into pretty good interviewers. Instead of ridiculing Carlos when he was having a little trouble communicating what he knew, they began asking probing questions—the kind of questions that made it easier for Carlos to communicate what was in his head. Carlos began to respond to this treatment by becoming more relaxed; with increased relaxation came an improvement in his ability to communicate. After a couple of weeks, the other children concluded Carlos was a lot smarter than they had thought he was. They began to see things in him they had never seen before. They began to like him. Carlos began to enjoy school more and began to see the Anglo students in his group not as tormenters but as helpful and responsible people. Moreover, as he began to feel increasingly comfortable in class and started to gain more confidence in himself, his academic performance began to improve. The vicious cycle had been reversed; the elements that had been causing a downward spiral were changed—the spiral now began to move upward.

We have now replicated this experiment in scores of classrooms with thousands of students. The results are clear-cut and consistent. Children in the interdependent, jigsaw classrooms grow to like each other better, develop a greater liking for school, and develop greater self-esteem than children in traditional classrooms. The increase in liking among children in the jigsaw classroom crosses ethnic and racial boundaries.[18] The exam performance of members of ethnic minorities is higher in the jigsaw classroom than in the traditional classrooms. For example, in one study[19] my colleagues and I found that, within two weeks of participating in the jigsaw groups, minority-group children increased their performance almost an entire letter grade, without any cost to the performance of the other children. Finally, teachers enjoyed using the technique and found it to be effective. Most of the teachers who agreed to use the jigsaw method as part of our experiment continued to use it *after* the experiment was over.

One of the crucial factors underlying the positive effects of the jigsaw technique is the development of empathy. . . . [I]ncreasing a person's empathy—the ability to put oneself in another's position—is beneficial to human relations, enhancing helping behavior and decreasing aggression. In the classroom, the best way to maximize learning—especially in the jigsaw situation—is to pay close attention to the child who is speaking. For example, if I am in a jigsaw group with Carlos and want to learn what he knows, not only must I listen attentively to him, but I must also put myself in his shoes in order to ask him questions in a clear and nonthreatening manner. In the process, I learn a lot not only about the subject, and not only about Carlos, but about the process of seeing the world through another person's eyes. In a fascinating experiment, Diane Bridgeman demonstrated the positive effects of participating in the jigsaw classroom on the child's ability to take another person's perspective.[20] She administered a series of cartoon sequences to ten-year-old children, half of whom had spent eight weeks participating in jigsaw classes. The cartoons are aimed at measuring a child's ability to empathize. In one sequence of cartoons, for example, a little boy looks sad as he says good-bye to his father at the airport. In the next frame, a mailman delivers a package to the child. When the boy opens it, he finds a toy airplane—and promptly bursts into tears. When Bridgeman asked the children why the little boy cried, almost all of the children told her the reason: The airplane reminded the child of being separated from his father, which made him sad. So far so good. Now for the crucial part. Bridgeman asked the children what the mailman who delivered the package was thinking. Most children that age make a consistent error, based on the egocentric assumption that their knowledge is universal; specifically, they erroneously assume *the mailman* would know the boy was sad because the gift reminded him of his father leaving. The responses of the children who had participated in the jigsaw classes followed a different pattern, however. Because of their jigsaw experience, they were better able to take the mailman's perspective; they knew he was not privy to the same information they were and that he wasn't aware of the scene at the airport. Accordingly, the jigsaw children realized the mailman would experience *confusion* at the sight of a little boy crying over receiving a nice present. In sum, participation in jigsaw groups has a general impact on a child's ability to see the world through another person's eyes; this seems to be a major cause of the beneficial effects described above.

One of the most encouraging ramifications of this increase in empathy is that the usual tendency people have of giving themselves the benefit of the doubt can now be extended to other people, including people who aren't members of their own ethnic or racial group. Let me explain. You will recall that in making attributions about the cause of failure, people tend to give themselves the benefit of the doubt—but rarely extend that benefit to others. Thus, if I do poorly on an exam, I tend to conclude that I was sleepy or that the questions were unfair; but if *you* do poorly on an exam, I would tend to conclude that you were stupid or lazy. In a series of experiments,[21] my colleagues and I corroborated this finding: We found that, in a competitive situation, not only do children attribute their rivals' failures to lack of ability, they also attribute their rivals' successes to luck. But here is the interesting part: We also found that, in a *cooperative* situation (like jigsaw), children are as generous with their partners as they are with themselves; they attribute their partner's success to skill, and failure to an unlucky break. This is exciting because, when we can begin to think of members of other races and ethnic groups with the same generosity we extend to ourselves, the ultimate attribution error breaks down and prejudice is being reduced at a deep level.

Although interdependence—especially through the jigsaw technique —is clearly a promising strategy, it is not a perfect solution. For example, while jigsaw does produce beneficial effects with high-school students,[22] it works *best* with young children, before prejudiced attitudes have an opportunity to become deeply ingrained. Moreover, prejudice is a complex phenomenon; no one solution is *the* solution. As we have seen, many aspects of our society are changing simultaneously—more equitable exposure of ethnic minorities via the mass media, greater educational opportunities, and so on. It is a slow process, and equity is still a long distance away. Yet prejudice is on the wane, and this is encouraging. Recall that, at one time, it was argued that desegregation would be impossible without prior attitude change. It was once generally believed that a good deal of prejudice is generally the result of a deeply rooted personality disorder that must be cured before desegregation can proceed. The evidence indicates that, for the vast majority of individuals, this is not true. The first wedge in the diminution of prejudice is desegregation. . . .

NOTES

1. P. Lazarsfeld, *Radio and the Printed Page* (New York: Duell, Sloan and Pearce, 1940).

2. M. Deutsch and M. E. Collins, *Interracial Housing: A Psychological Evaluation of a Social Experiment* (Minneapolis: University of Minnesota Press, 1951). See also D. Wilner, R. Walkley, and S. Cook, *Human Relations in Interracial Housing* (Minneapolis: University of Minnesota Press, 1955).

3. J. Brehm, "Increasing Cognitive Dissonance by a Fait-accompli," *Journal of Abnormal and Social Psychology* 58 (1959): 379–82.

4. D. Darley and E. Berscheid, "Increased Liking as a Result of the Anticipation of Personal Contact," *Human Relations* 20 (1967): 29–40.

5. National Opinion Research Center, *General Social Surveys, 1972–1980: Cumulative Codebook* (Storrs, Conn.: Roper Public Opinion Research Center, University of Connecticut, 1980).

6. T. F. Pettigrew, "Social Psychology and Desegregation Research," *American Psychologist* 16 (1961): 105–112.

7. K. B. Clark, "Desegregation: An Appraisal of the Evidence," *Journal of Social Issues* 9, no. 4 (1953).

8. S. Stouffer, E. Suchman, L. DeVinney, S. Star, and R. Williams, Jr., "The American Soldier: Adjustment During Army Life," in *Studies in Social Psychology in WWII* (Vol. 1) (Princeton: Princeton University Press, 1949).

9. B. Kramer, "Residential Contact as a Determinant of Attitudes toward Negroes," unpublished Ph.D. dissertation, Harvard University (1951); A. Winder, "White Attitudes towards Negro-white Interaction in an Area of Changing Racial Composition," *American Psychologist* 7 (1952): 330–31.

10. S. Asher and V. Allen, "Racial Preference and Social Comparison Processes," *Journal of Social Issues* 25 (1969): 157–66; W. Stephan and J. Kennedy, "An Experimental Study of Inter-ethnic Competition in Segregated Schools," *Journal of School Psychology* 13 (1975): 234–47; H. Gerard and N. Miller, *School Desegration* (New York: Plenum, 1976).

11. W. G. Stephan, "School Desegregation: An Evaluation of Predictions Made in *Brown* v. *The Board of Education*," *Psychological Bulletin* 85 (1978): 217–38.

12. J. Lester, "Beep! Beep! Bang! Umgawa! Black Bower!" in R. Kytle (ed.), *Confrontation: Issues of the 70s* (New York: Random House, 1971), pp. 162–81.

13. Deutsch and Collins, *Interracial Housing*.

14. M. Sherif and C. Sherif, *An Outline of Social Psychology* (New York: Harper and Bros., 1956). Sherif, Harvey, White, Hood, and Sherif, Intergroup conflict and cooperation.

15. M. Deutsch, "A Theory of Cooperation and Competition," *Human Relations* 2 (1949) 129–52; M. Deutsch, "An Experimental Study of the Effects of Cooperation and Competition upon Group Process," *Human Relations* 2 (1949): 199–232.

16. P. Keenan and P. Carnevale, "Positive Effects of Within-group Competition on Between-group Negotiation," *Journal of Applied Social Psychology* 19 (1989): 977–92.

17. E. Aronson, C. Stephan, J. Sikes, N. Blaney, and M. Snapp, *The Jigsaw Classroom* (Beverly Hills, Calif.: Sage Publications, 1978); E. Aronson and N. Osherow, "Cooperation, Prosocial Behavior, and Academic Performance: Experiments in the Desegregated Classroom," in L. Bickman (ed.), *Applied Social Psychology Annual* (Vol. 1) (Beverly Hills, Calif: Sage Publications, 1980), pp. 163-96.

18. W. Stephan, "An Experimental Study of Inter-ethnic Competition in Segregated Schools," *Journal of School Psychology* 13 (1975): 234–47.

19. R. Geffner, "The Effects of Interdependent Learning on Self-esteem, Inter-ethnic Relations, and Intra-ethnic Attitudes of Elementary School Children: A Field Experiment," unpublished Ph.D. dissertation, University of California, Santa Cruz, 1978; A. Gonzalez, "Classroom Cooperation and Ethnic Balance," unpublished Ph.D. dissertation, University of California, Santa Cruz, 1979.

20. W. Lucker, D. Rosenfield, J. Sikes, and E. Aronson, "Performance in the Interdependent Classroom: A Field Study," *American Education Research Journal* 13 (1977): 115-23.

21. D. Bridgeman, "Enhanced Role-taking through Cooperative Interdependence: A Field Study," *Child Development* 52 (1981): 1231-38.

22. C. Stephan, J. Kennedy, and E. Aronson, "Attribution of Luck or Skill as a Function of Cooperating or Competing with a Friend or Acquaintance," *Sociometry* 40 (1977): 107–111; N. Presser, C. Stephan, J. Kennedy, and E. Aronson, "Attributions to Success and Failure in Cooperative, Competitive, and Interdependent Interaction," *European Journal of Social Psychology* 8 (1978): 269–74; S. Stephan, M. Burnham, and E. Aronson, "Attributions for Success and Failure after Cooperation, Competition, or Team Competition," *European Journal of Social Psychology* 9 (1979): 109-114.

23. A. Gonzalez, "Classroom Cooperation and Ethnic Balance," unpublished Ph.D. dissertation, University of California, Santa Cruz, 1979.

24. T. F. Pettigrew, "Social Psychology and Desegregation Research," *American Psychologist* 15 (1961): 61-71.

# 24

# Toward the Elimination of Racism: The Study of Intergroup Behavior

## Samuel L. Gaertner and John F. Dovidio

Within the literature on intergroup behavior, there is general agreement that factors which increase the salience of group boundaries increase the degree of intergroup bias. . . . Basically, with increased awareness of the intergroup boundary there is enhanced appreciation of ingroup-outgroup or we-they categorizations. This enhanced appreciation transforms a person's perceptions and behavior from an impersonal to an intergroup level of responding. At the intergroup level, people act in terms of their social identity, more faithfully conforming to the group's norms and also treating others in terms of their corresponding group memberships rather than their personal identities. . . . Outgroup members, in particular, become depersonalized, undifferentiated, substitutable entities. . . . In addition, with increased boundary salience, an individual's motivation for maintaining positive self-regard initiates social comparison processes that result in increased positive evaluations for ingroup relative to outgroup members. . . .

Recently, in the context of group mergers, we have been investigating the possibility of replacing the salience of the intergroup boundary with the percent of common membership within a superordinate entity. We

From "Problems, Progress, and Promise," in *Prejudice, Discrimination, and Racism* by Samuel L. Gaertner and John F. Dovidio (San Diego, Calif.: Academic Press, 1986), pp. 322–30. Copyright © 1986 by Academic Press, Inc. Reprinted by permission of the publisher.

suggest that superordinate goals successfully reduce intergroup conflict . . . because they increase the likelihood that members of these groups will perceive themselves as belonging to one group rather than to two. . . . Strategies that increase the salience of a common or superordinate group are hypothesized to reduce the salience of prior group boundaries and thereby contribute to the development of a general sense of unity and identity.

In addition to reducing the salience of the previous group boundaries, increasing the salience of the superordinate group, and each member's identification with and commitment to it, can also harness ingroup forces (both cognitive and motivational) that can further increase the likelihood of more differentiated, personalized, and positive interactions among the members. Thus, it is proposed that features of contact situations that emphasize a common, superordinate entity (e.g., a town, neighborhood, or school) can take advantage of the ingroup forces which would otherwise contribute to the development of intergroup bias and redirect these forces toward the elimination of social conflict. Ingroup membership, for example, influences how the prevailing intergroup events are cognitively processed. Information about ingroup members is coded and stored in memory using more complex, differentiated classifications than is information concerning outgroup members. . . . Therefore, we believe that strategies of intergroup contact that emphasize the salience of the superordinate group can utilize ingroup forces productively to promote intergroup acceptance and personalized interactions between the memberships.

Consistent with this perspective, Slavin and Madden's . . . review of school practices that improve race relations revealed that participating on interracial sports teams and in cooperative learning groups were among the activities most related to positive interracial attitudes. . . . Although it is not clearly understood why cooperative interaction facilitates intergroup acceptance, it is possible that intergroup cooperation not only reduces the salience of the intergroup boundary but also contributes to members' perceiving the existence of one entity rather than two. . . . Although intergroup cooperation has positive benefits, it is not always easy to induce cooperation among groups. Imposing a superordinate group identity, however, has been shown to increase the likelihood of cooperative, self-restrained behavior among individuals . . . and therefore this strategy may have additional potential for changing the nature of intergroup relationships. That is, emphasizing a common, superordinate identity may facilitate the induction of cooperative interaction between groups that may otherwise be independent or competitive.

When interracial behavior is considered, the problems associated with

reducing the salience of intergroup boundaries and increasing the awareness of a superordinate entity are compounded by the number of conver-
gent cultural, social, and physical boundaries that differentiate the groups.
It is not likely that the members would or could forsake their previous
subgroup identities completely or permanently, nor is that necessarily desirable. . . . Nevertheless, an increased salience of the superordinate group
even for temporary periods may permit positive bonds to develop through
the perforated boundary and thus change the basis for future interaction.
Furthermore, subgroup and superordinate group identities can be salient
simultaneously. For example, members of a household constitute a family, but they can also categorize themselves as parents and children without
losing awareness of their superordinate connection. The formation of a
superordinate group thus does not require each constituent subgroup to
forsake its identity entirely.

. . . [I]n integrated settings the adoption of a color-blind perspective
is usually associated with the requirement that the behavior of blacks must
conform to the prevailing norms of white, middle-class culture. Failure
of blacks to adapt to this expectation typically prevents them from attain-
ing their desired rewards from the meritocracy. This requirement to conform devalues black culture, and thus black people, and also precludes
the opportunity for the total aggregate to profit from diversity. . . .

From our superordinate or merged group perspective, the research
challenge is to discover techniques and strategies that induce the members of separate groups to conceive of the aggregate as one entity, and
then to examine whether this perception facilitates cooperativeness, acceptance, and personalized interactions between the memberships in ways
that may even generalize beyond the immediate superordinate group context. An initial test of this approach examined the way physical arrangements of the memberships in space (in terms of the seating patterns) affect
the degree to which two groups perceive themselves as one unit rather
than two. The idea that the arrangements of people or objects in space
can influence the manner in which elements are perceptually organized
is derived from some basic postulates of Gestalt psychology. . . . Perhaps,
in addition to other strategies, approaches that engage the visual system
to induce the perception of one entity would be particularly effective with
groups that are physically differentiated. . . . It was expected that the
manner in which people from different subgroups are dispersed in space
(e.g., around a conference table, classroom, or city) would influence their
conceptual representation of the aggregate as either one group, two groups,
or separate individuals and consequently their degree of intergroup bias.

In this study, two groups of four students (two males and two females) met in separate rooms to reach consensus on the best solution to the Winter Survival Problem. . . . This task requires participants to imagine that their plane had crashed in northern Minnesota in the winter and to rank-order 10 items (e.g., a gun, newspaper, candy bar) in terms of their importance to the group's survival. Following the group discussion and consensus, the two groups (AAAA and BBBB) were merged together in a single room around a hexagonal table. Using color-coded identifications, subjects were arranged in one of three seating patterns: Segregated, Partially Segregated, and Fully Integrated. The subjects were then asked to reach consensus again on the Winter Survival Problem. Next, questionnaires were administered to assess each participant's impression of his or her group experience. For example, subjects were asked whether the merged group felt like one unit, two units, or separate individuals and whom they would vote for to be leader if the survival problem were real rather than hypothetical. It was predicted that as the seating pattern varied from Segregated (a pattern which physically emphasized subgroup boundaries) to Partially Integrated to Fully Integrated (a pattern which physically degraded subgroup boundaries) there would be decreased salience of the premerger group boundaries resulting in a greater sense of unity and decreased intergroup bias.

The results indicated that with greater integration in seating, participants more frequently experienced the merged aggregate as one unit rather than two and showed less ingroup bias in their choice for leader. . . . Similarly, this pattern of reduced ingroup favoritism as a function of seating integration characterized participants' perceptions of the relative value of members' contributions to the solution and their ratings of friendliness between and within subgroups. When the group was used as the unit of analysis, the results also revealed that the Fully Integrated, relative to the Segregated, seating pattern increased feelings that the merged entity was one unit and reduced ingroup bias in leader selection. Furthermore, subjects' individual solutions to the Winter Survival Problem at the end of the experiment suggested that participants in the Fully Integrated condition tended to internalize the merged group's solution more than did subjects in the Segregated condition.

Further evidence of the positive effects of seating arrangement is revealed in an internal analysis that examined the consequences of members conceiving the merged unit as one entity rather than as two groups. In this analysis, the impression of one unit or two was treated as an independent variable. The results revealed that subjects who conceived of the aggregate as one unit perceived the merged group as more cooperative, democratic, pleasant, close, and successful than did subjects who saw the group as two units. In addition, participants who perceived the merged group as one unit were more satisfied with the group atmosphere, believed that members worked better together, and had greater confidence in the group's solution. Although it is not a statistically reliable effect, subjects who perceived the merged group as two units tended to show an ingroup favoritism effect: They liked people who were formerly from their subgroup more than people formerly from the other subgroup. This bias did not exist among subjects who saw the merged group as one unit.

. . . Optimistically, shared group identity and the development of a sense of partnership can eliminate manifestations of even . . . subtle, indirect, and rationalizable forms of racism. . . . [D]espite reasons to be concerned about the progress of race relations, there are also significant reasons for optimism. Progress toward understanding racism has been made at a level of theoretical development that goes significantly beyond mere intuition. By understanding the causes of racism, innovative steps toward the elimination of racism can be taken using strategies and methods that rely on processes that may be as fundamental as those that appear to be involved in the development of prejudice, discrimination, and racism.

# 25

# The Making of an American Democratic Socialist of African Descent

## Cornel West

America is in the midst of a massive social breakdown. Never before in U.S. history has national decline and cultural decay so thoroughly shaken people's confidence in their capacity to respond to present-day problems. America remains the premier military power in the world, yet has a waning influence on the global scene. American big business can no longer compete with that of Japan, West Germany, and others as a result of bad management, myopic profiteering, insufficient productive investments, and a refusal to educate its workers adequately. The mediocrity of American leaders is horrendous. Money-driven elections and packaged politicians (turned fundraisers) have made the political system virtually an ugly joke —whose punchline is on the America people.

Cultural decay is pervasive. The erosion of civil society—shattered families, neighborhoods, schools, and voluntary associations—has contributed to a monumental eclipse of hope and to a collapse of meaning across the country. Civil terrorism—the sheer avalanche of mindless and calculated violence in our social fabric—haunts many urban, suburban, and rural streets. Deteriorating physical infrastructures—unkept highways, subways, bridges, and buildings—are everywhere. Escalating class inequality (including growing gaps between rich and poor), xenophobic violence (especially men against women, whites against people of color and against Jews, straight against lesbians and gays), and ecological devastation frighten most Americans.

Consumer culture—a way of life that spawns addictive personalities and passive citizens—promotes a profound spiritual impoverishment and moral shallowness. The culture industries of TV, radio, film, and video bombard Americans with degrading stereotypes—especially of women and people of color—and saturate leisure time with seductive images of sexual foreplay and orgiastic pleasures. Never before have Americans been so ill-equipped to confront the traumas of despair, dread, and death, even as so many, especially those among the political and economic elite, ignore the social chaos and self-destruction eating at the core of American society.

In short, there is a growing nihilism and cynicism afoot in the country. This nihilism—the lived experience of meaninglessness, hopelessness, and lovelessness—encourages social anomie (drugs, crime) and therapeutic forms of escape (sports, sex). This cynicism, often masquerading as patriotic lore, traditional "common sense," and nostalgic posturing, is a form of paralysis; the body politic shrugs its shoulders while it waddles in private opulence and public squalor.

This present moment of massive social breakdown in America occurs at a time of epochal change in the Soviet Union and Eastern Europe: the revolutionary shift of authoritarian regimes with command economies to parliamentary political systems with capitalist economies. This collapse of bureaucratic elitist forms of communism—encouraged by the courageous and visionary Mikhail Gorbachev of the USSR and enacted by heroic working peoples in these countries—has helped revivify the spirit of revolution in our day. Yet this epochal change warrants both support and suspicion. It is salutary because it reasserts the autonomy and integrity of civil society (e.g., individual liberties to speak, organize, publish, travel, and worship). It also is frightening in that it rekindles ugly xenophobia (such as anti-Semitism and chauvinistic nationalism) and unleashes harsh "free market" forces. To put it crudely, the breathtaking anti-Communist revolutions of 1989 affirm and accent the libertarian—not egalitarian—aspects of the capitalist revolutions of 1776, 1789, and 1848. Like those revolutions of old—and like the present moment of the major capitalist power in the world, the United States—fundamental issues of employment, health care, housing, child care, and education for all are being ignored and overlooked.

The profound tragedy of the epochal change in the [former] Soviet

Union and Eastern Europe may be a turning away from these fundamental issues—a kind of global erasure of egalitarian and democratic concern for jobs, food, shelter, literacy, and health care for all. This would mean that along with the unleashing of capitalist market forces on an international scale goes an unleashing of despair for those caught within or concerned about the world's ill-fed, ill-clad, and ill-housed, especially those in "invisible" Africa, Asia, and Latin America. This tidal wave of popular cynicism and nihilism about the capacities of people to imagine, create, and sustain alternatives to the world-encompassing capitalist order is the specter now haunting the globe.

This enormous obstacle of cynicism and nihilism is the starting point for freedom fighters who defend and promote egalitarian and democratic possibilities in our time. How do we put the fundamental issues of employment, health and child care, housing, ecology, and education on the agenda of the powers that be in a world disproportionately shaped by transnational corporations and nation-state elites in a global multipolar capitalist order? How do we keep a focus on these issues while we fight racism, patriarchy, homophobia, and ecological abuse? What effective forms of progressive politics can emerge in this new moment of history?

The present tasks for the remaking of the left are threefold. First, given the extraordinary power of capitalism and the pervasive cynicism and skepticism toward fundamental social change it breeds, we should try to understand and support all egalitarian and democratic concerns, efforts, and movements that focus on more and better jobs, food, shelter, education, child and health care, and ecological balance. This means, in part, a wholesale critical inventory of ourselves and our communities of struggle. More pointedly, the existential and ethical dimensions of our lives require serious scrutiny. Why do we still fight and hope for social change? What really sustains our faith in struggle and our hope for change in these barbaric times? How do we analyze and account for the egalitarian values and democratic sensibilities we act upon?

I am suggesting here neither moral confession nor personal therapy. Rather, I am calling for a historical assessment and political reading of our morality and morale, in order to shed light on how we can make them more contagious to others captive to the prevailing cynicism and nihilism. This assessment and reading should disclose some of the cultural sources of critique and resistance still extant in a society saturated by market ways of life.

Second, we must confront candidly the intellectual crisis of the left. How do we best analyze and explain our society and world? Which moral visions and values apply? What do we mean by such precious ideals as equality, democracy, freedom, and justice? What are the complex dynamics of such ugly phenomena as racism, patriarchy, ageism, homophobia, class exploitation, bureaucratic domination, and ecological abuse? How do we best mobilize and organize both victims and people of good will? What are the appropriate responses to the collapse of communist regimes, the new developments in southern Africa and Brazil, the economic power of Japan and Europe, and the diverse yet devastated state of most of Africa, Asia, the Middle East, and Latin America?

These crucial questions and urgent challenges require a careful evaluation of past and present efforts of those social theorists, historical sociologists, and cultural critics who have grappled seriously with them. I am convinced that, despite its blindnesses and inadequacies—especially in regard to racism, patriarchy, homophobia, and ecological abuse—Marxist thought is an indispensable tradition for freedom fighters who focus on the fundamental issues of jobs, food, shelter, literacy, health, and child care for all. One of the major ironies of our time is that Marxist thought becomes even more relevant after the collapse of communism in the Soviet Union and Eastern Europe than it was before. The explosion of capitalist market forces on a global scale—concomitant with open class conflict, aggressive consumerism, rapacious individualism, xenophobic tribalism, and chauvinistic nationalism—makes Marxist thought an inescapable part of the intellectual weaponry for present-day freedom fighters.

Third, we have to specify the kind of credible strategies and tactics for progressive politics in the United States. The existential and ethical dimensions of struggle—linked to subtle analyses and sophisticated explanations of power, wealth, status, and prestige—must yield concrete ways that people's pressure can be brought to bear to change American society. This entails a fresh examination of the crisis of leadership, mobilization, and organization of the left. I shall now elaborate on each of the three tasks for the remaking of the left in the present global capitalist epoch in light of my own critical self-inventory over time and space.

A wholesale critical inventory of ourselves and our communities of struggle is neither self-indulgent autobiography nor self-righteous reminiscence. Rather, it is a historical situating and locating of our choices, sufferings, anxieties, and efforts in light of the circumscribed options and alternatives available to us. We are all born into and build on circumstances, traditions, and situations not of our own choosing; yet we do make certain choices that constitute who we are and how we live in light of these fliud circumstances, traditions, and situations.

The most significant stage-setting for my own life pilgrimage has been neither academic life nor political organizations, but rather my closely knit family and overlapping communities of church and friends. These pillars of civil society—my loving parents, siblings, and communities—transmitted to me ideals and images of dignity, integrity, majesty, and humility. These ideals and images—couched within Christian narratives, symbols, rituals, and, most importantly, concrete moral examples—provided existential and ethical equipment to confront the crises, terrors, and horrors of life. The three major components of this equipment were a Christian ethic of love-informed service to others, ego-deflating humility about oneself owing to the precious yet fallible humanity of others, and politically engaged struggle for social betterment. This Christian outlook, as exemplified in our time by Martin Luther King, Jr., serves as the basis for my life vocation. As a youth, I resonated with the sincere black militancy of Malcolm X, the defiant rage of the Black Panther party, and the livid black theology of James Cone. Yet I did not fully agree with them. I always felt that they lacked the self-critical moment of humility I discerned in the grand example of Martin Luther King, Jr. Such humility has always been a benchmark of genuine love for, and gratitude to, ordinary people whose lives one is seeking to enhance. I witnessed this same kind of integrity and dignity in the humble attitude of black folk of my early heroes: the Godfather of Soul, James Brown; the legendary baseball player, Willie Mays; my pastor, Rev. Willie P. Cooke (of Shiloh Baptist Church in Sacramento, California); my grandfather, Rev. C. L. West, of Metropolitan Baptist Church in Tulsa, Oklahoma; and my older brother, Clifton L. West III, to me an exemplary human being. In this way, Martin Luther King, Jr., has always been not so much a model to imitate but *the* touchstone for personal inspiration, moral wisdom, and existential insight. I heard him speak in person only once—when I was ten years old (1963)— and I remember not his words but his humble spirit and sense of urgency. . . .

I became part of the first generation of young black people to attend prestigious lily-white institutions of higher learning in significant numbers —institutions still coping with the new wave of Jewish faculty and students who had confronted an earlier tribal civility, snobbish gentility, and institutional loyalty of primarily well-to-do white Anglo-Saxon Protestants. Owing to my family, church, and the black social movements of the 1960s, I arrived at Harvard unashamed of my African, Christian, and militant decolonized outlooks. More pointedly, I acknowledged and accented the empowerment of my black styles, mannerisms, and viewpoints, my Christian values of service, love, humility, and struggle, and my anti-colonial sense of self-determination for oppressed people and nations around the world. But I soon discovered that this positive black identity, these persuasive Christian values, and this deep commitment to struggles for freedom were not enough. Given my privileged position (as a student—only about 18 percent of black young people were enrolled in college at the time) and grand opportunities, I needed a more profound understanding of history, a deeper grasp of the complex, conflict-ridden dynamics of societies and cultures, and a more flexible perspective on human life.

My passionate interest in philosophy was—and remains—primarily motivated by the radical historical *conditionedness* of human existence and the ways in which possibilities and potentialities are created, seized, and missed by individuals and communities within this ever changing conditionedness, including our inescapable death, illness, and disappointment. This attention to the historical character of all thought and action has led me to be suspicious of intellectual quests for truth unwilling to be truthful about themselves, including my own. So though I find delight in the life of the mind—inseparable from, yet not identical with, struggles for freedom—I do not put primary value on intelligence or book knowledge. Rather, I believe we have a moral obligation—for the quality of human life and protection of the environment—to be wise, especially about the pitfalls and shortcomings of mere intelligence and book knowledge. . . .

It was during the two short years at Princeton that I became convinced that the values of individuality—the sanctity and dignity of all individuals shaped in and by communities—and of democracy—as a way of life and mode of being-in-the-world, not just a form of governance—were most precious to me. This is why, when I returned to Harvard as a DuBois Fellow to write my dissertation, I turned first to T. H. Green, the British neo-Hegelian of the late nineteenth century, and then to the ethical dimensions of Marxist thought. Marx's own debts to the Romantics' preoccupation with many-sided personality and full-fledged individuality (as in Friedrich Schiller's *Letters on Aesthetic Education*) and to the early socialists' focus on universal suffrage, women's rights, abolitionism, and workplace democracy intrigued me. I became convinced that Marx's own intellectual development should be understood in terms of this fascinating tension between the moral conviction of the flowering of individuality under wholesale democratic socioeconomic and political conditions and the theoretical concern of explaining scientifically the dynamics and tendencies of profit-driven capitalist societies that foster a narrow individualism and a truncated political democracy.

. . . *The Ethical Dimensions of Marxist Thought*—written over a decade ago when I was in my mid-twenties—was my first attempt to understand Marxist thought as one grand stream, among others, of the larger modern articulation of historical consciousness, an articulation fanned by

Romantic quests for harmony and wholeness and fueled by concrete revolutionary and reformist movements for freedom, equality, and democracy. Such quests and movements may result in aborted authoritarian arrangements or be crushed by powerful capitalist powers. Yet the precious values of individuality and democracy that can guide and regulate such quests and movements sit at the center of Marx's own thought. . . .

[D]espite the deep tensions in Marx's thought, there are other and better versions of Marxism put forward by Marx himself in his best moments. My point here is not that Marx's social theory fully accounts for all social and historical phenomena; rather, it is that social theory wedded in a nuanced manner to concrete historical analyses must be defended in our present moment of epistemic skepticism, explanatory agnosticism, political impotence (among progressives), and historical cynicism.

So it is necessary to discredit the fashionable trashing of Marxist thought in the liberal academy. Besides predictable caricatures of Marxist thought by conservatives, this trashing principally proceeds from ironic skeptics and aesthetic historicists. The former shun any theory that promotes political action with purpose; for them, any social project of transformation reeks of authoritarian aims. The latter highlight wholesale contingency and indeterminacy, with little concern with how and why change and conflict take place. . . .

Needless to say, crude Marxist perspectives warrant scrutiny and rejection. Yet in these days of Marxist-bashing, it is often assumed that vulgar Marxist thought exhausts the Marxist tradition—as if monocausal accounts of history, essentialist conceptions of society, or reductionist readings of culture are all Marxist thought has to offer. One wonders whether any such critics have read Marx's *Eighteenth Brumaire, Class Struggles in France,* or the *Grundrisse.*

Faddish ironic skepticism and aesthetic historicism are contemporary assaults on the twin pillars of Marxist social theory: historically specific accounts of structures such as modes of production, state apparatuses and bureaucracies, and socially detailed analyses of how such structures shape and are shaped by cultural agents. These pillars require that one's understanding of history, society, and culture highlight latent and manifest multifarious human struggles for identity, power, status, and resources. More pointedly, it demands that one bite the explanatory bullet and give analytical priority to specific forms of struggle over others. For sophisticated Marxists, this does not mean that class explains every major event in the past or present, or that economic struggles supersede all others. It simply suggests that in capitalist societies, the dynamic processes of capital accumulation and the commodification of labor condition social and cultural practices in an *inescapable* manner. How such practices are played out in various countries and regions for different races, classes, and genders in light of the fundamental capitalist processes will be determined in an experimental and empirical manner. Like other refined forms of historical sociology, Marxist theory proceeds within the boundaries of warranted assertable claims and rationally acceptable conclusions. Its assertions can be wrong in part because they are believed to be right.

The high intellectual moments of Marxist theory . . . are those that bring together explanatory power, analytical flexibility, and a passion for social freedom. Yet certain critical phenomena of the modern world—nationalism, racism, gender oppression, homophobia, ecological devastation—have not been adequately understood by Marxist theorists. My rejoinder simply is that these complex phenomena cannot be grasped, or changed, without the insights of Marxist theory, although we do need other theories to account for them fully. . . .

I am suggesting that we focus on the oppositional cultures of oppressed peoples that extend far beyond their workplaces. In other words, we need a serious *Simmelian* moment (as in Georg Simmel's *The Philosophy of Money*) in Marxist theory that probes into the lived experiences of people in light of fundamental capitalist processes. The aim here is not to reduce cultural efforts to ideological battles, but rather to discern and determine the distinctive elements of the structures of feeling, structures of meaning, ways of life and struggle under dynamic circumstances not of people's own choosing. In this way, Marxist theory can give social substance and political content to postmodern themes of otherness, difference, and marginality. And limited epistemological debates about foundationalism and skepticism, realism and pragmatism can give way to more fruitful exchanges about clashing methodological, theoretical, and political conceptions of how to understand and change contemporary cultures and societies.

I am a non-Marxist socialist in that as a Christian, I recognize certain irreconcilable differences between Marxists of whatever sort and Christians of whatever sort. Since my conception of Christian faith is deeply, though not absolutely, historical, this disagreement is not primarily a metaphysical issue; rather, it is a basic existential difference in the weight I put on certain biblical narratives, symbols, and rituals that generate sanity and meaning for me. My Christian perspective—mediated by the rich traditions of the Black Church that produced and sustains me—embraces depths of despair, layers of dread, encounters with the sheer absurdity of the human condition, and ungrounded leaps of faith alien to the Marxist tradition. Like so much of black music Christian insights speak on existential and visceral levels neglected by the Marxist tradition. This is not so because the Marxist tradition is Eurocentric—for there are traditions and figures in Europe that do speak to existential issues, e.g., Samuel Beckett, T. S. Eliot, Martin Buber, Susanne Langer. Rather, the Marxist tradition is silent about the existential meaning of death, suffering, love, and friendship owing to its preoccupation with improving the social circumstances under which people pursue love, revel in friendship, and confront death. I share this concern.

Yet like both Russian novelists and blues singers, I also stress the concrete lived experience of despair and tragedy and the cultural equipment requisite for coping with the absurdities, anxieties, and frustrations, as well as the joys, laughter, and gaiety of life. In this deep sense Marxism is not and cannot serve as a religion. And if it is cast as a religion, it is a shallow secular ideology of social change that fails to speak to us about the ultimate facts of human existence. To put it charitably, Marxist thought does not purport to be existential wisdom—of how to live one's life day by day. Rather, it claims to be a social theory of histories, societies, and cultures. Social theory is not the same as existential wisdom. Those theories that try to take the place of wisdom disempower people on existential matters, just as those wisdoms that try to shun theory usually subordinate people to the political powers that be.

My writings constitute a perennial struggle between my African and American identities, my democratic socialist convictions, and my Christian sense of the profound tragedy and possible triumph in life and history. I am a prophetic Christian freedom fighter principally because of distinctive Christian conceptions of what it is to be human, how we should act toward one another, and what we should hope for. These conceptions —put forward in a variety of diverse streams and strains of the Christian tradition stretching back over centuries—has to do with the indispensable yet never adequate capacities of human beings to create error-proof or problem-free situations, theories, or traditions—hence the strong anti-dogmatic or fallible character of prophetic Christian thought and practice which encourage relentless critical consciousness; the moral claim to view each and every individual as having equal status as warranting dignity, respect, and love, especially those who are denied such dignity, respect, and love by individuals, families, groups, social structures, economic systems, or political regimes—hence the prophetic Christian identification and solidarity with the downtrodden and disinherited, the degraded and dispossessed; and lastly, the good news of Jesus Christ which lures and links human struggles to the coming of the kingdom—hence the warding off of disempowering responses to despair, dread, disappoint-ment, and death.

Prophetic Christianity has a distinctive, though not exclusive, capacity to highlight critical, historical, and universal consciousness that yields a vigilant disposition toward prevailing forms of individual and institutional evil, an unceasing suspicion of ossified and petrified forms of dogmatism, and a strong propensity to resist various types of cynicism and nihilism.

Prophetic Christian conceptions of what it is to be human, how we should act, and what we should hope for are neither rationally demonstra-ble nor empirically verifiable in a necessary and universal manner. Rather, they are embedded and enacted in a form of life—a dynamic set of com-munities that constitute a diverse tradition—that mediates how I inter-pret my experiences, sufferings, joys, and undertakings. There are indeed good reasons to accept prophetic Christian claims, yet they are good not because they result from logical necessity or conform to transcendental criteria. Rather, these reasons are good (persuasive to some, nonsense to others) because they are rationally acceptable and existentially enabling for many self-critical finite and fallible creatures who are condemned to choose traditions under circumstances not of our own choosing. To choose a tradition (a version of it) is more than to be convinced by a set of arguments; it is also to decide to live alongside the slippery edge of life's abyss with the support of the dynamic stories, symbols, interpretations, and insight bequeathed by communities that came before.

I have always shunned the role of theologian because I have little interest in systematizing the dogmas and doctrines, insights and intuitions of the Christian tradition. Nor do I think that they can be rendered coherent and consistent. The theological task is a noteworthy endeavor—especially for the life of the church—yet my vocation uses Christian resources, among others, to speak to the multilayered crises of contemporary society and culture. So I am more a cultural critic with philosophic training who works out of the Christian tradition than a theologian who focuses on the syste-matic coherency or epistemic validity of Christian claims.

This vocation puts social theory, historiography, cultural criticism, and political engagement at the center of my prophetic Christian outlook. I do not believe that there are such things as Christian social theory, Chris-tian historiography, Christian cultural criticism, or Christian politics—just as there are no such things as Christian mathematics, Christian physics, or Christian economics. Rather, there is prophetic Christian thought and practice informed by the best of these disciplines that highlights and en-hances the plight of the loveless, luckless, landless, and other victims of social structural arrangements. In this way, my prophetic vocation overlaps insignificant ways with such Marxists as Harry Magdoff and Paul Sweezy. In the present methodological debate against ironic skeptics, aesthetic historicists, political cynics, and explanatory agnostics, we stand together in defense of Marxist theory and socialist politics—even as we may disagree on how we conceive of Marxist theory or the kind of socialism we promote. . . .

The crisis of leadership in black and progressive communities is symptomatic of the paucity of credible strategies and tactics for social change in the United States. It also reflects the relative inability of the left to mobilize and organize over time and space. Needless to say, there is no easy way out of this impasse.

The effort is more difficult due to the pervasive disarray of the progressive movement in the United States. Never before in our history has the U.S. left been so bereft of courageous leaders of vision, intelligence, and integrity. We simply do not have formidable figures that the public identifies with progressive causes. Aside from those preoccupied with electoral politics and admirable local activists with little national attention, there are no major leaders who articulate in bold and defiant terms—with genuine passion and analytical clarity—the moral imperative to address the maldistribution of resources, wealth, and power, escalating xenophobia, ecological devastation, national decline, and spiritual impoverishment we are facing. This crisis of leadership adds to the balkanization of U.S. progressive politics—its fragmentation, isolation, and insularity. Given the power of big business and cultural conservatism, the U.S. left has potency primarily when strong leadership—rooted in extraparliamentary organizational activity—energizes and galvanizes demoralized progressives and liberals across racial, class, regional, age, and gender lines. This usually does not last long —so the propitious moment must be seized.

We find it hard to seize this moment not only because of the establishment's strategies of repression and incorporation but also owing to the consumer culture—with its addictive seductions and pacifying pastimes— that often saps and disperses our energies for collective struggle. Market morality engulfs us in such a way that it is difficult to arrange our lives so that communal activity supersedes personal pursuits. Market mentality makes it hard for us to believe our sacrificial progressive efforts will make a real difference in our busy and short lives. And since there can be no substantive progressive politics without oppositional subcultures, institutions, and networks, the predominant "market way of life" presents a—maybe *the*—major challenge for progressive politics.

At the moment, the most *explosive* issues in U.S. society revolve around black bodies and women's wombs—race and abortion. And, in a fundamental sense, the starting points—though not landing grounds —for progressive politics in the 1990s may be *enhancement* of the poor, especially those of color, and protection of women's rights. Yet reform measures such as progressive taxation and appointment of liberal judges fall far short of what is required. We also need a progressive cultural renaissance that reshapes our values, restructures how we live, and puts struggle and sacrifice closer to the center of what we think and do. Only then will our fight to turn back a market-driven, conservative United States—already far down the road to social chaos and self-destruction— be not only desirable but also credible. The defense of the relevance of Marxist thought, including its ethical dimensions, after the Cold War is an indispensable weapon in this fight. . . .

[T]he future of U.S. progressive politics lies in the capacity of a collective leadership to energize, mobilize, and organize working and poor people. Democratic socialists can play a crucial role in projecting an all-embracing moral vision of freedom, justice, and equality, and making social analyses that connect and link activists together. In this way we can be a socialist leaven in a larger progressive loaf. Yet this loaf will never get baked if we remain separate, isolated, insular, and fragmented. America's massive social breakdown requires that we come together— for the sake of our lives, our children, and our sacred honor.

# 26

# Human Rights, Rationality, and Sentimentality

## Richard Rorty

In a report from Bosnia, David Rieff said, "To the Serbs, the Muslims are no longer human. . . . Muslim prisoners, lying on the ground in rows, awaiting interrogation, were driven over by a Serb guard in a small delivery van."[1] This theme of dehumanization recurred when Rieff said:

> A Muslim man in Bosansi Petrovac . . . [was] forced to bite off the penis of a fellow-Muslim. . . . If you say that a man is not human, but the man looks like you and the only way to identify this devil is to make him drop his trousers— Muslim men are circumcised and Serb men are not—it is probably only a short step, psychologically, to cutting off his prick. . . . There has never been a campaign of ethnic cleansing from which sexual sadism has gone missing.

The moral to be drawn from Rieff's stories is that Serbian murderers and rapists do not think of themselves as violating human rights. For they are not doing these things to fellow human beings, but to *Muslims*. They are not being inhuman, but rather are discriminating between true humans and pseudo-humans. They are making the same sort of distinction the Crusaders made between humans and infidel dogs, and Black Muslims make between humans and blue-eyed devils. The founder of my university was able both to own slaves and to think it self-evident that all men were endowed by their creator with certain inalienable rights. This was because he had convinced himself that the consciousness of blacks, like that of animals, "participates more of sensation than of reflection."[2] Like the Serbs, Mr. Jefferson did not think of himself as violating human rights.

Serbs take themselves to be acting in the interests of true humanity by purifying the world of pseudo-humanity. In this respect, their self-image resembles that of moral philosophers who hope to cleanse the world of prejudice and superstition. This cleansing will permit us to rise above our animality by becoming, for the first time, wholly rational and thus wholly human. Serbs, moralists, Jefferson, and Black Muslims all use the term "men" to mean "people like us." They all think that the line between humans and animals is not simply the line between featherless bipeds and the rest. Rather, this line divides some featherless bipeds from others: there are animals walking about in humanoid form. We and those like us are paradigm cases of humanity, but those too different from us in behavior or custom are, at best, borderline cases. As Clifford Geertz puts it, "Men's most importunate claims to humanity are cast in the accents of group pride."[3]

We here in the safe, rich democracies feel about Serbian torturers and rapists as they feel about their Muslim victims: they are more like animals than like us. But we are not doing anything to help the Muslim women who are being gang-raped or the Muslim men who are being castrated, any more than we did anything in the 1930s when the Nazis were amusing themselves by torturing Jews. Here in the safe countries we find ourselves saying things like "That's how things have always been in the Balkans," suggesting that, unlike us, those people are used to being raped and castrated. The contempt we always feel for losers—Jews in the 1930s, Muslims now—combines with our disgust at the winners' behavior to produce the semiconscious attitude: "a pox on both your houses." We think of Serbs or Nazis as animals, because ravenous beasts of prey are animals. We think of Muslims or Jews being herded into concentration camps as animals, because cattle are animals. Neither sort of animal is very much like us, and there seems no point in human beings getting involved in quarrels between animals.

The human-animal distinction, however, is only one of three main ways in which we paradigmatic humans distinguish ourselves from borderline cases. A second is by invoking the distinction between adults and children. Ignorant and superstitious people, we say, are like children; they will attain true humanity only if raised up by proper education. If they seem incapable of such education, that shows that they are not really the same kind of being as we educable people are. Blacks, the whites in the United States and in South Africa used to say, are like children; that is why it is appropriate to address black males, of whatever age, as "boy." Women, men used to say, are permanently childlike; that is why it is appropriate to spend no money on their education and to refuse them access to power.

When it comes to women, however, there are simpler ways of excluding them from true humanity: for example, using "man" as a synonym of "human being." As feminists have pointed out, such usages reinforce the average male's thankfulness that he was not born a woman, as well as his fear of the ultimate degradation: feminization. The extent and depth of the latter fear are evidenced by the particular sort of sexual sadism Rieff describes. His point that such sadism is never absent from attempts to purify the species or cleanse the territory confirms Catharine MacKinnon's claim that, for most men, being a woman does not count as one way of being human. Being a nonmale is the third main way of being nonhuman.

Philosophers have tried to help straighten out this confusion by specifying what is special about featherless bipeds, explaining what is essential to being human. Plato suggested that there is a big difference between us and animals, a difference worthy of respect and cultivation. He thought that human beings have a special added ingredient that puts them in a different ontological category than brutes. Respect for this ingredient provides a reason for people to be nice to each other. Anti-Platonists like Nietzsche reply that attempts to get people to stop murdering, raping, and castrating one another are, in the long run, doomed to failure—for the real truth about human nature is that we are a uniquely nasty and dangerous kind of animal. When contemporary admirers of Plato claim that all featherless bipeds—even the stupid and childlike, even the women, even the sodomized—have the same inalienable rights, admirers of Nietzsche reply that the very idea of "inalienable human rights" is, like the idea of a special added ingredient, a laughably feeble attempt by the weaker members of the species to fend off the stronger members.

As I see it, one important intellectual advance that has been made in our century is the steady decline in interest in this quarrel between Plato and Nietzsche about what we are really like. There is a growing willingness to neglect the question "What is our nature?" and to substitute the question "What can we make of ourselves?" We are much less inclined than our ancestors were to take "theories of human nature" seriously, much less inclined to take ontology or history or ethology as a guide to life. We are much less inclined to pose the ontological question "What *are* we?" because we have come to see that the main lesson of both history and anthropology is our extraordinary malleability. We are coming to think of ourselves as the flexible, protean, self-shaping animal rather than as the rational animal or the cruel animal.

One of the shapes we have recently assumed is that of a human rights culture. I borrow the term "human rights culture" from the Argentinean jurist and philosopher Eduardo Rabossi. In an article called "Human Rights Naturalized"

Rabossi argues that philosophers should think of this culture as a new, welcome fact of the post-Holocaust world. Rabossi wants them to stop trying to get behind or beneath this fact, stop trying to detect and defend its so-called philosophical presuppositions. On Rabossi's view, philosophers like Alan Gewirth are wrong to argue that human rights cannot depend upon historical facts. "My basic point," Rabossi says, is that "the world has changed, that the human rights phenomenon renders human rights foundationalism outmoded and irrelevant."[4]

Human rights foundationalism is the continuing attempt by quasi-Platonists to win, at last, a final victory over their opponents. Rabossi's claim that this attempt is *outmoded* seems to me both true and important; it is my principal topic in this essay. I shall enlarge upon, and defend, Rabossi's claim that the question of whether human beings really *have* the rights enumerated in the Helsinki Declaration is not worth raising. In particular, I shall defend the claim that nothing relevant to moral choice separates human beings from animals except historically contingent facts of the world, cultural facts.

This claim is sometimes called "cultural relativism" by those who indignantly reject it. One reason they reject it is that such relativism seems to them incompatible with the fact that our human rights culture is morally superior to other cultures. I quite agree that ours is morally superior, but I do not think that this superiority counts in favor of the existence of a universal human nature. It would only do so if we assumed that a claim of moral superiority entails a claim to superior knowledge—assumed that such a claim is ill-founded if not backed up by knowledge of a distinctively human attribute. But it is not clear why "respect for human dignity"—our sense that the differences between Serb and Muslim, Christian and infidel, gay and straight, male and female should not matter—must presuppose the existence of any such attribute.

Traditionally, the name of the shared human attribute that supposedly "grounds" morality is "rationality." Cultural relativism is associated with irrationalism because it denies the existence of morally relevant transcultural facts. To agree with Rabossi one must, indeed, be irrationalist in that sense. But one need not be irrationalist in the sense of ceasing to make one's web of belief as coherent, and as perspicuously structured, as possible. Philosophers like myself, who think of rationality as simply the attempt at such coherence, agree with Rabossi that foundationalist projects are outmoded. We see our task as a matter of making our own culture—the human rights culture—more self-conscious and more powerful, rather than of demonstrating its superiority to other cultures by an appeal to something transcultural.

We think that the most philosophy can hope to do is to summarize our culturally influenced intuitions about the right thing to do in various situations. The summary is effected by formulating a generalization from which these intuitions can be deduced, with the help of noncontroversial lemmas. That generalization is not supposed to ground our intuitions, but rather to summarize them. John Rawls's "Difference Principle" and the U.S. Supreme Court's construction, in recent decades, of a constitutional "right to privacy" are examples of this kind of summary. We see the point of formulating such summarizing generalizations as increasing the predictability, and thus the power and efficiency, of our institutions, thereby heightening the sense of shared moral identify that brings us together in a moral community.

Foundationalist philosophers, such as Plato, Aquinas, and Kant, have hoped to provide independent support for such summarizing generalizations. They would like to infer these generalizations from further premises, premises capable of being known to be true independently of the truth of the moral intuitions that have been summarized. Such premises *are* supposed to justify our intuitions, by providing premises from which the content of those intuitions can be deduced. I shall lump all such premises together under the label "claims to knowledge about the nature of human beings." In this broad sense, claims to know that our moral intuitions are recollections of the Form of the Good, or that we are the disobedient children of a loving God, or that human beings differ from other kinds of animal by having dignity rather than mere value are all claims about human nature. So are such counterclaims as that human beings are merely vehicles for selfish genes or merely eruptions of the will to power. To claim such knowledge is to claim to know something that, though not itself a moral intuition, can *correct* moral intuitions. It is essential to this idea of moral knowledge that a whole community might come to *know* that most of its most salient intuitions about the right thing to do were wrong.

But now suppose we ask: *is* there this sort of knowledge? What kind of question is *that*? On the traditional view, it is a philosophical question, belonging to a branch of epistemology known as "metaethics." But on the pragmatist view I favor, it is a question of efficiency: a question about how best to grab hold of history—how best to bring about the utopia sketched by the Enlightenment. If the activities of those who attempt to achieve this sort of knowledge seem of little use in actualizing this utopia, that is a reason to think there is no such knowledge. If it seems that most of the work of changing moral intuitions is being done by manipulating our feelings rather than by increasing our knowledge, that is a reason to think there is no knowledge of the sort that philosophers like Plato, Aquinas, and Kant hoped to get.

This pragmatist argument against the Platonist has the same form as an argument for cutting off payment to the priests who perform purportedly war-winning sacrifices—an argument which says that all the real work of winning the war seems to be done by generals and admirals, not to mention foot soldiers. This argument does not say: since there seem to be no gods, there is probably no need to support the priests. It says instead: since there is apparently no need to support the priests, there probably are no gods. We pragmatists argue from the fact that the emergence of the human rights culture seems to owe nothing to increased moral knowledge, and everything to hearing sad and sentimental stories, to the conclusion that there is probably no knowledge of the sort Plato envisaged. We go on to argue that since no useful work seems to be done by insisting on a purportedly ahistorical human nature, there probably is no such nature, or at least nothing in that nature that is relevant to our moral choices.

In short, my doubts about the effectiveness of appeals to moral knowledge are doubts about causal efficacy, not about epistemic status. My doubts have nothing to do with any of the theoretical questions discussed under the heading of "metaethics": questions about the relation between facts and values, or between reason and passion, or between the cognitive and the noncognitive, or between descriptive statements and action-guiding statements. Nor do they have anything to do with questions about realism and antirealism. The difference between the moral realist and the moral antirealist seems to pragmatists a difference that makes no practical difference. Further, such metaethical questions presuppose the Platonic distinction between inquiry that aims at efficient problem solving and inquiry that aims at a goal called "truth for its own sake." That distinction collapses if one follows Dewey in thinking of all inquiry—in physics as well as ethics—as practical problem solving or if one follows Peirce in seeing *every* belief as action-guiding.[5]

Even after the priests have been pensioned off, however, the memories of certain priests may still be cherished by the community—especially the memories of their prophecies. We remain profoundly grateful to philosophers like Plato and Kant, not because they discovered truths but because they prophesied cosmopolitan utopias—utopias most of whose details they may have gotten wrong, but utopias we might never have struggled to reach had we not heard their prophecies. As long as our ability to know and in particular to discuss the question "What is man?" seemed the most important thing about us human beings, people like Plato and Kant accompanied utopian prophecies with claims to know something deep and important—something about the parts of the soul or the transcendental status of the common moral consciousness. But this ability and those questions have, in the past two hundred years, come to seem much less important. It is this cultural sea change that Rabossi summarizes in his claim that human rights foundationalism is *outmoded*. In the remainder of this essay, I want to take up the following questions: *Why* has knowledge become much less important to our self-image than it was two hundred years ago? Why does the attempt to found culture on nature, and moral obligation on knowledge of transcultural universals, seem so much less important to us than it seemed in the Enlightenment? Why is there so little resonance, and so little point, in the question "Do human beings in fact *have* the rights listed in the Helsinki Declaration"? Why, in short, has moral philosophy become such an inconspicuous part of our culture?

A simple answer to these questions is: because between Kant's time and ours, Darwin argued most intellectuals out of the view that human beings contained a special added ingredient. He convinced most of us that we were exceptionally talented animals, animals clever enough to take charge of our own evolution. I think this answer is right as far as it goes. But it leads to a further question: Why did Darwin succeed, relatively speaking, so very easily? Why did he not cause the creative philosophical ferment that was caused by Galileo and Newton?

The revival by the New Science of the seventeenth century of Democritean-Lucretian corpuscularian picture of nature scared Kant into inventing transcendental philosophy, inventing a brand-new kind of knowledge, one that could demote the corpuscularian world picture to the status of "appearance." Kant's example encouraged the idea that the philosopher, as an expert on the nature and limits of knowledge, can serve as a supreme cultural arbiter.[6] But by the time of Darwin this idea was already beginning to seem quaint. The historicism that dominated the intellectual world of the early nineteenth century had created an antiessentialist mood. So when Darwin came along, he fit into the evolutionary niche that Herder and Hegel had begun to colonize. Intellectuals who populate this niche look to the future rather than to eternity. They prefer new ideas about how to change things over stable criteria for determining the desirability of change. They are the ones who think much of both Plato and Nietzsche outmoded.

The best explanation both of Darwin's relatively easy triumph and of our own increasing willingness to substitute hope for knowledge is that the nineteenth and twentieth centuries saw, among Europeans and Americans, an extraordinary increase in wealth, literacy, and leisure. This increase made possible an unprecedented acceleration in the rate of moral progress. Such events as the French Revolution and the ending of the transatlantic slave trade helped nineteenth-century intellectuals in the rich democracies to say: It is enough for us to know that we live in an age in which human beings can make things better for ourselves.[7] We do not need to dig behind this historical fact to nonhistorical facts about what we really are.

In the two centuries since the French Revolution, we have learned that human beings are far more malleable than Plato or Kant had dreamed. The more we are impressed by this malleability, the less interested we become in questions about our ahistorical nature. The more we see a chance to recreate ourselves, the more we shall read Darwin not as offering one more theory about what we really are but as providing reasons why we do not need to ask what we really are. Nowadays, to say that we are clever animals is not to say something philosophical and pessimistic but something political and hopeful—namely, if we can work together, we can make ourselves into whatever we are clever and courageous enough to imagine ourselves becoming. This is to set aside Kant's question "What is man?" and to substitute the question "What sort of world can we prepare for our greatgrandchildren?"

The question "What is man?" in the sense of "What is the deep ahistorical nature of human beings?" owed its popularity to the standard answer to that question: we are the *rational* animal, the one that can *know* as well as merely feel. The residual popularity of this answer accounts for the residual popularity of Kant's astonishing claim that sentimentality has nothing to do with morality, that there is something distinctively and transculturally human called "the sense of moral obligation" which has nothing to do with love, friendship, trust, or social solidarity. As long as we believe *that*, people like Rabossi are going to have a tough time convincing us that human rights foundationalism is an outmoded project.

To overcome this idea of a sui generis sense of moral obligation, it would help to stop answering the question "What makes us different from other animals?" by saying, "We can know and they can merely feel." We should substitute "We can feel *for each other* to a much greater extent than they can." This substitution would let us disentangle Christ's suggestion that love matters more than knowledge from the neo-Platonic suggestion that knowledge of the truth will make us free. For as long as we think there is an ahistorical power that makes for righteousness—a power called truth or rationality—we will not be able to put foundationalism behind us.

The best, and probably the only, argument for putting foundationalism behind us is the one I have already suggested: it would be more efficient to do so, because it would let us concentrate our energies on manipulating sentiments, on sentimental education. That sort of education gets people of different kinds sufficiently well acquainted with one another that they are less tempted to think of those different from themselves as only quasi-human. The goal of this sort of manipulation of sentiment is to expand the reference of the terms "our kind of people" and "people like us."

All I can do to supplement this argument from increased efficiency is to offer a suggestion about how Plato managed to convince us that knowledge of universal truths mattered as much as he thought it did. Plato thought that the philosopher's task was to answer questions like "Why should I be moral? Why is it rational to be moral? Why is it in my interest to be moral? Why is it in the interest of human beings as such to be moral?" He thought this because he thought that the best way to deal with people like Thrasymachus and Gorgias was to demonstrate to them that they had an interest of which they were unaware, an interest in being rational, in acquiring self-knowledge. Plato thereby saddled us with a distinction between the true and the false self. That distinction was, by the time of Kant, transmuted into a distinction between categorical, rigid moral obligation and flexible, empirically determinable self-interest. Contemporary moral philosophy is still lumbered with this opposition between self-interest and morality, an opposition which makes it hard to realize that my pride in being a part of the human rights culture is no more external to my self than my desire for financial or sexual success.

It would have been better if Plato had decided, as Aristotle was to decide, that there was nothing much to be done with people like Thrasymachus and Callicles and that the problem was how to avoid having children who would be like Thrasymachus and Callicles. By insisting that he could reeducate people who had matured without acquiring appropriate moral sentiments by invoking a higher power than sentiment, the power of reason, Plato got moral philosophy off on the wrong foot. He led moral philosophers to concentrate on the rather rare figure of the psychopath, the person who has no concern for any human being other than himself. Moral philosophy has systematically neglected the much more common case: the person whose treatment of a rather narrow range of featherless bipeds is morally impeccable, but who remains indifferent to the suffering of those outside this range, the ones he thinks of as pseudo-humans.[8]

Plato set things up so that moral philosophers think they have failed unless they convince the rational egotist that he should not be an egotist—convince him by telling him about his true, unfortunately neglected self. But the rational egotist is not the problem. The problem is the gallant and honorable Serb who sees Muslims as circumcised dogs. It is the brave soldier and good comrade who loves and is loved by his mates, but who thinks of women as dangerous, malevolent whores and bitches.

Plato thought that the way to get people to be nicer to each other was to point out what they all had in common—rationality. But it does little good to point out, to the people I have just described, that many Muslims and women are good at mathematics or engineering or jurisprudence. Resentful young Nazi toughs were quite aware that many Jews were clever and learned, but this only added to the pleasure they took in beating such Jews. Nor does it do much good to get such people to read Kant and agree that one should not treat rational agents simply as means. For everything turns on who counts as a fellow human being, as a rational agent in the only relevant sense—the sense in which national agency is synonymous with membership in *our* moral community.

For most white people, until very recently, most black people did not so count. For most Christians, until the seventeenth century or so, most heathen did not so count. For the Nazis, Jews did not count. For most males in countries in which the average annual income is less than two thousand pounds, most females still do not so count. Whenever tribal and national rivalries become important, members of rival tribes and nations will not so count. Kant's account of the respect due to rational agents tells you that you should extend the respect you feel for the people like yourself to all featherless bipeds. This is an excellent suggestion, a good formula for secularizing the Christian doctrine of the brotherhood of man. But it has never been backed up by an argument based on neutral premises, and it never will be. Outside the circle of post-Enlightenment European culture, the circle of relatively safe and secure people who have been manipulating one another's sentiments for two hundred years, most people are simply unable to understand why membership in a biological species is supposed to suffice for membership in a moral community. This is not because they are insufficiently rational. It is, typically, because they live in a world in which it would be just too risky—indeed, would often be insanely dangerous—to let one's sense of moral community stretch beyond one's family, clan, or tribe.

To get whites to be nicer to blacks, males to females, Serbs to Muslims, or straights to gays, to help our species link up into what Rabossi calls a "planetary community" dominated by a culture of human rights, it is of no use whatever to say, with Kant: notice that what you have in common, your humanity, is more important than these trivial differences. For the people we are trying to convince will rejoin that they notice nothing of the sort. Such people are *morally* offended by the suggestion that they should treat someone who is not kin as if he were a brother, or a nigger as if he were white, or a queer as if he were normal, or an infidel as if she were a believer. They are offended by the suggestion that they treat people whom they do not think of as human as if they were human. When utilitarians tell them that all pleasures and pains felt by members of our biological species are equally relevant to moral deliberation, or when Kantians tell them that the ability to engage in such deliberation is sufficient for membership in the moral community, they are incredulous. They rejoin that these philosophers seem oblivious to blatantly obvious moral distinctions, distinctions any decent person would draw.

This rejoinder is not just a rhetorical device, nor is it in any way irrational. It is heartfelt. The *identity* of these people, the people whom we should like to convince to join our Eurocentric human rights culture, is bound up with their sense of who they are *not*. Most people—especially people relatively untouched by the European Enlightenment—simply do not think of themselves as, first and foremost, a human being. Instead, they think of themselves as being a certain good sort of human being—a sort defined by explicit opposition to a particularly bad sort. What is crucial for their sense of who they are is that they are *not* an infidel, *not* a queer, *not* a woman, *not* an untouchable. Just insofar as they are impoverished, and as their lives are perpetually at risk, they have little else than pride in not being what they are not to sustain their self-respect. Since the days when the term "human being" was synonymous with "member of our tribe," we have always thought of human beings in terms of *paradigm* members of the species. We have contrasted us, the *real* humans, with rudimentary or perverted or deformed examples of humanity.

We Eurocentric intellectuals like to suggest that we, the paradigm humans, have overcome this primitive parochialism by using that paradigmatic human faculty, reason. So we say that failure to concur with us is due to "prejudice." Our use of these terms in this way may make us nod in agreement when Colin McGinn tells us, in the introduction to his recent book,[9] that learning to tell right from wrong is not as hard as learning French. The only obstacles to agreeing with his moral views, McGinn explains, are prejudice and superstition.

One can, of course, see what McGinn means: if, like many of us, you teach students who have been brought up in the shadow of the Holocaust, brought up believing that prejudice against racial or religious groups is a terrible thing, it is not very hard to convert them to standard liberal views about abortion, gay rights, and the like. You may even get them to stop eating animals. All you have to do is to convince them that all the arguments on the other side appeal to "morally irrelevant" considerations. You do this by manipulating their sentiments in such a way that they imagine themselves in the shoes of the despised and oppressed. Such students are already so nice that they are eager to define their identity in nonexclusionary terms. The only people such students find any trouble being nice to are the ones they consider irrational—the religious fundamentalist, the smirking rapist, or the swaggering skinhead.

Producing generations of nice, tolerant, well-off, secure, other-respecting students of this sort in all parts of the world is just what is needed—indeed, *all* that is needed—to achieve an Enlightenment utopia. The more youngsters like this we can raise, the stronger and more global our human rights culture will become. But it is not a good idea to encourage these students to label "irrational" the intolerant people they have trouble tolerating. For that Platonic-Kantian epithet suggests that with only a little more effort, the good and rational part of these other people's souls could have triumphed over the bad and irrational part. It suggests that we good people know something these bad people do not know and that it is probably their own silly fault that they do not know it. All they had to do, after all, was to think a little harder, be a little more self-conscious, a little more rational.

But the bad people's beliefs are not more or less "irrational" than the belief that race, religion, gender, and sexual preference are all morally irrelevant—that these are all trumped by membership in the biological species. As used by moral philosophers like McGinn, the term "irrational behavior" means no more than "behavior of which we disapprove so strongly that our spade is turned when asked *why* we disapprove of it." So it would be better to teach our students that these bad people are no less rational, no less clear-headed, no more prejudiced than we good people who respect Otherness. The bad people's problem is, rather, that they were not as lucky in the circumstances of their upbringing as we were. Instead of treating all those people out there who are trying to find and kill Salman Rushdie as irrational, we should treat them as deprived.

Foundationalists think of these people as deprived of truth, of moral knowledge. But it would be better—more concrete, more specific, more suggestive of possible remedies—to think of them as deprived of two more concrete things: security and sympathy. By "security" I mean conditions of life sufficiently risk-free as to make one's difference from others inessential to one's self-respect, one's sense of worth. These conditions have been enjoyed by North Americans and Europeans—the people who dreamed up the human rights culture—much more than they have been enjoyed by anyone else. By "sympathy" I mean the sort of reactions Athenians had more of after seeing Aeschylus's *The Persians* than before, the sort that whites in the United States had more of after reading *Uncle Tom's Cabin* than before, the sort we have more of after watching television programs about the genocide in Bosnia. Security and sympathy go together, for the same reasons that peace and economic productivity go together. The tougher things are, the more you have to be afraid of, the more dangerous your situation, the less you can afford the time or effort to think about what things might he like for people with whom you do not immediately identify. Sentimental education works only on people who can relax long enough to listen.

If Rabossi and I are right in thinking human rights foundationalism outmoded, then Hume is a better adviser than Kant about how we intellectuals can hasten the coming of the Enlightenment utopia for which both men yearned. Among contemporary philosophers, the best adviser seems to me to be Annette Baier. Baier describes Hume as "the woman's moral philosopher" because Hume held that "corrected (sometimes rule-corrected) sympathy, not law-discerning reason, is the fundamental moral capacity."[10] Baier would like us to get rid of both the Platonic idea that we have a true self and the Kantian idea that it is rational to be moral. In aid of this project, she suggests that we think of "trust" rather than "obligation" as the fundamental moral notion. This substitution would mean thinking of the spread of the human rights culture not as a matter of our becoming more aware of the requirements of the moral law, but rather as what Baier calls "a progress of sentiments."[11] This progress consists in an increasing ability to see the similarities between ourselves and people very unlike us as outweighing the differences. It is the result of what I have been calling "sentimental education." The relevant similarities are not a matter of sharing a deep true self that instantiates true humanity, but are such little, superficial similarities as cherishing our parents and our children—similarities that do not distinguish us in any interesting way from many nonhuman animals.

To accept Baier's suggestions, however, we have to overcome our sense that sentiment is too weak a force and that something stronger is required. This idea that reason is "stronger" than sentiment, that only an insistence on the unconditionality of moral obligation has the power to change human beings for the better, is very persistent. I think this persistence is due mainly to a semicon-

scious realization that if we hand our hopes for moral progress over to senti-
ment, we are in effect handing them over to *condescension*. For we shall be
relying on those who have the power to change things—people like the rich
New England abolitionists or rich bleeding hearts like Robert Owen and
Friedrich Engels—rather than relying on something that has power over *them*.
We shall have to accept the fact that the fate of the women of Bosnia depends
on whether television journalists manage to do for them what Harriet Beecher
Stowe did for black slaves—whether these journalists can make us, the audience
back in the safe countries, feel that these women are more like us, more like real
human beings, than we had realized.

To rely on the suggestions of sentiment rather than on the commands of
reason is to think of powerful people gradually ceasing to oppress others, or to
countenance the oppression of others, out of mere niceness rather than out of
obedience to the moral law. But it is revolting to think that our only hope for a
decent society consists in softening the self-satisfied hearts of a leisure class. We
want moral progress to burst up from below, rather than waiting patiently upon
condescension from the top. The residual popularity of Kantian ideas of "unconditional moral obligation"—obligation imposed by deep ahistorical noncontingent forces—seems to me almost entirely due to our abhorrence of the idea that
the people on top hold the future in their hands, that everything depends on them,
that there is nothing more powerful to which we can appeal against them.

Like everyone else, I too would prefer a bottom-up way of achieving utopia,
a quick reversal of fortune that will make the last first. But I do not think this is
how utopia will in fact come into being. Nor do I think our preference for this
way lends any support to the idea that the Enlightenment project lies in the
depths of every human soul.

So why does this preference make us resist the thought that sentimentality
may be the best weapon we have? I think Nietzsche gave the right answer to this
question: we resist out of resentment. We *resent* the idea that we shall have to
wait for the strong to turn their piggy little eyes to the suffering of the weak,
slowly open their dried-up little hearts. We desperately hope there is something
stronger and more powerful that will *hurt* the strong if they do *not* do these
things—if not a vengeful God, then a vengeful aroused proletariat or, at least, a
vengeful superego or, at the very least, the offended majesty of Kant's tribunal
of pure practical reason. The desperate hope for a noncontingent and powerful
ally is, according to Nietzsche, the common core of Platonism, of religious
insistence on divine omnipotence, and of Kantian moral philosophy.[12]

Nietzsche was, I think, right on the button when he offered this diagnosis.
What Santayana called "supernaturalism," the confusion of ideals and power, is
*all* that lies behind the Kantian claim that it is not only nicer, but more *rational*,
to include strangers within our moral community than to exclude them. If we

agree with Nietzsche and Santayana on this point, however, we do not thereby acquire any reason to turn our backs on the Enlightenment project, as Nietzsche did. Nor do we acquire any reason to be sardonically pessimistic about the chances of this project, in the manner of such admirers of Nietzsche as Santayana, Ortega, Heidegger, Strauss, and Foucault.

For even though Nietzsche was quite right to see Kant's insistence on unconditionality as an expression of resentment, he was quite wrong to treat Christianity and the age of the democratic revolutions as signs of human degeneration. He and Kant, alas, shared something with each other that neither shared with Harriet Beecher Stowe—something that Iris Murdoch has called "dryness" and Jacques Derrida has called "phallogocentrism." The common element in the thought of both men was a desire for purity. This sort of purity consists in being not only autonomous, in command of oneself, but also in having the kind of self-conscious self-sufficiency that Sartre describes as the perfect synthesis of the in-itself and the for-itself. This synthesis could be attained, Sartre pointed out, only if one could rid oneself of everything sticky, slimy, wet, sentimental, and womanish.

Although this desire for virile purity links Plato to Kant, the desire to bring as many different kinds of people as possible into a cosmopolis links Kant to Stowe. Kant represents, in the history of moral thinking, a transitional stage between the hopeless attempt to convict Thrasymachus of irrationality and the hopeful attempt to see every new featherless biped who comes along as one of us. Kant's mistake was to think that the only way to have a modest, damped-down, nonfanatical version of Christian brotherhood after letting go of the Christian faith was to revive the themes of pre-Christian philosophical thought. He wanted to make knowledge of a core self do what can be done only by the continual refreshment and recreation of the self, through interaction with selves as unlike itself as possible.

Kant performed the sort of awkward balancing act that is required in transitional periods. His project mediated between a dying rationalist tradition and a vision of a new, democratic world, the world of what Rabossi calls "the human rights phenomenon." With the advent of this phenomenon, Kant's balancing act has become outmoded and irrelevant. We are now in a good position to put aside the last vestiges of the idea that human beings are distinguished by the capacity to know rather than by the capacities for friendship and intermarriage, distinguished by rigorous rationality rather than by flexible sentimentality. If we do so, we shall have dropped the idea that assured knowledge of a truth about what we have in common is a prerequisite for moral education, as well as the idea of a specifically moral motivation. If we do all these things, then we shall see Kant's *Foundations of the Metaphysics of Morals* as a placeholder for *Uncle Tom's Cabin*—a concession to the expectations of an intellectual epoch in which the quest for quasi-scientific knowledge seemed the best response to religious exclusionism.[13]

Unfortunately, many philosophers, especially in the English-speaking world, are still trying to hold on to the Platonic insistence that the principal duty of human beings is to know. That insistence was the lifeline to which Kant and Hegel thought we had to cling.[14] Just as German philosophers in the period between Kant and Hegel saw themselves as saving reason from Hume, many English-speaking philosophers now see themselves as saving reason from Derrida. But with the wisdom of hindsight, and with Baier's help, we have learned to read Hume not as a dangerously frivolous iconoclast but as the wettest, most flexible, least phallogocentric thinker of the Enlightenment. Someday, I suspect, our descendants may wish that Derrida's contemporaries had been able to read him not as a frivolous iconoclast, but rather as a sentimental educator, as another of "the women's moral philosophers."[15]

If one follows Baier's advice, one will see it as the moral educator's task not to answer the rational egotist's question "Why should I be moral?" but rather to answer the much more frequently posed question "Why should I care about a stranger, a person who is no kin to me, a person whose habits I find disgusting?" The traditional answer to the latter question is "Because kinship and custom are morally irrelevant, irrelevant to the obligations imposed by the recognition of membership in the same species." This has never been very convincing, since it begs the question at issue: whether mere species membership is, in fact, a sufficient surrogate for closer kinship. Furthermore, that answer leaves one wide open to Nietzsche's discomfiting rejoinder: that universalistic notion, Nietzsche will sneer, would have crossed the mind of only a slave—or, perhaps, an intellectual, a priest whose self-esteem and livelihood both depend on getting the rest of us to accept a sacred, unarguable, unchallengeable paradox.

A better sort of answer is the sort of long, sad, sentimental story that begins, "Because this is what it is like to be in her situation—to be far from home, among strangers," or "Because she might become your daughter-in-law," or "Because her mother would grieve for her." Such stories, repeated and varied over the centuries, have induced us, the rich, safe, powerful people, to tolerate and even to cherish powerless people—people whose appearance or habits or beliefs at first seemed an insult to our own moral identity, our sense of the limits of permissible human variation.

To people who, like Plato and Kant, believe in a philosophically ascertainable truth about what it is to be a human being, the good work remains incomplete as long as we have not answered the question "Yes, but am I under a *moral obligation* to her?" To people like Hume and Baier, it is a mark of intellectual immaturity to raise that question. But we shall go on asking that question as long as we agree with Plato that it is our ability to *know* that makes us human.

Plato wrote quite a long time ago, in a time when we intellectuals had to pretend to be successors to the priests, had to pretend to know something rather esoteric. Hume did his best to josh us out of that pretense. Baier, who seems to me both the most original and the most useful of contemporary moral philosophers, is still trying to josh us out of it. I think Baier may eventually succeed, for she has the history of the past two hundred years of moral progress on her side. These two centuries are most easily understood not as a period of deepening understanding of the nature of rationality or of morality, but rather as one in which there occurred an astonishingly rapid progress of sentiments, in which it has become much easier for us to be moved to action by sad and sentimental stories.

NOTES

1. David Rieff, "Letter from Bosnia," *New Yorker*, November 23, 1992, 82–95.

2. "Their griefs are transient. Those numberless afflictions, which render it doubtful whether heaven has given life to us in mercy or in wrath, are less felt, and sooner forgotten with them. In general, their existence appears to participate more of sensation than reflection. To this must be ascribed their disposition to sleep when abstracted from their diversions, and unemployed in labor. An animal whose body is at rest, and who does not reflect must be disposed to sleep of course." Thomas Jefferson, "Notes on Virginia," *Writings*, ed. Andrew A. Lipscomb and Albert Ellery Bergh (Washington, D.C., 1905), 1: 194.

3. Clifford Geertz, "Thick Description," in his *The Interpretation of Culture* (New York: Basic Books, 1973), p. 22.

4. See Eduardo Rabossi, "La teoria de los derechos humanos naturalizada," *Revista del Centro de Estudios Constitucionales* (Madrid), no. 5 (January–March 1990): 159–79. Rabossi also says that he does not wish to question "the idea of a rational foundation of morality." I am not sure why he does not. Rabossi may perhaps mean that in the past—e.g., at the time of Kant—this idea still made a kind of sense, but makes sense no longer. That, at any rate, is my own view. Kant wrote in a period when the only alternative to religion seemed to be something like science. In such a period, inventing a pseudo-science called "the system of transcendental philosophy" setting the stage for the show-stopping climax in which one pulls moral obligation out of a transcendental hat— might plausibly seem the only way of saving morality from the hedonists on one side and the priests on the other.

5. The present state of metaethical discussion is admirably summarized by Stephen Darwall, Allan Gibbard, and Peter Railton, "Toward Fin de Siècle Ethics: Some Trends," *Philosophical Review* 101 (January 1992): 115–89. This comprehensive and judicious article takes for granted that there is a problem about "vindicating the objectivity of morality" (127), that there is an interesting question as to whether ethics is "cognitive" or "noncognitive," that we need to figure out whether we have a "cognitive

capacity" to detect moral properties (148), and that these matters can be dealt with ahistorically.

When these authors consider historicist writers such as Alasdair MacIntyre and Bernard Williams, they conclude that they are *"[meta]théoriciens malgré eux"* who share the authors' own "desire to understand morality, its preconditions and its prospects" (183). They make little effort to come to terms with suggestions that there may be no ahistorical entity called "morality" to be understood. The final paragraph of the article does suggest that it might be helpful if moral philosophers knew some more anthropology or psychology or history. But the penultimate paragraph makes clear that, with or without such assists, "contemporary metaethics moves ahead, and positions gain in complexity and sophistication."

It is instructive, I think, to compare this article with Annette Baier's "Some Thoughts on the Way We Moral Philosophers Live Now" (*Monist* 67, no. 4 [1984], 490–97). There Baier suggests that moral philosophers should 'at least occasionally, like Socrates, consider why the rest of society should not merely tolerate but subsidize our activity." She goes on to ask, "Is the large proportional increase of professional philosophers and moral philosophers a good thing, morally speaking? Even if it scarcely amounts to a plague of gadflies, it may amount to a nuisance of owls." The kind of metaphilosophical and historical self-consciousness and self-doubt displayed by Baier seems to me badly needed, but it is conspicuously absent in *Philosophy in Review* (the centennial issue of the *Philosophical Review* in which "Toward Fin de Siècle Ethics" appears). The contributors to this issue are convinced that the increasing sophistication of a philosophical subdiscipline is enough to demonstrate its social utility and are entirely unimpressed by murmurs of "decadent scholasticism."

6. Fichte's *Vocation of Man* is a useful I reminder of the need that was felt, circa 1800, for a cognitive discipline called philosophy that would rescue utopian hope from natural science. It is hard to think of an analogous book written in reaction to Darwin. Those who couldn't stand what Darwin was saying tended to go straight back behind the Enlightenment to traditional religious faith. The unsubtle, unphilosophical opposition. In nineteenth-century Europe, between science and faith suggests that most intellectuals could no longer believe that philosophy might produce some sort of superknowledge, knowledge that might trump the results of physical and biological inquiry.

7. Some contemporary intellectuals, especially in France and Germany, take it as obvious that the Holocaust made it clear that the hopes for human freedom which arose in the nineteenth century are obsolete—that at the end of the twentieth century we postmodernists know that the Enlightenment project is doomed. But even these intellectuals, in their less preachy and sententious moments, do their best to further that project. So they should, for nobody has come up with a better one. It does not diminish the memory of the Holocaust to say that our response to it should not be a claim to have gained a new understanding of human nature or of human history, but rather a willingness to pick ourselves up and try again.

8. Nietzsche was right to remind us that "these same men who, amongst themselves, are so strictly constrained by custom, worship, ritual gratitude and by mutual surveillance and jealousy, who are so resourceful in consideration, tenderness, loyalty,

pride, and friendship, when once they step outside their circle become little better than uncaged beasts of prey" (*The Genealogy of Morals*, trans. Francis Golffing [Garden City, N.Y.: Doubleday, 1956], 174).

9. Colin McGinn, *Moral Literacy: Or, How to Do the Right Thing* (London: Duckworth, 1992), p. 16.

10. Annette Baier, "Hume, the Women's Moral Theorist?" in *Women and Moral Theory*, eds. Eva Kitay and Diana Meyers (Totowa, N.J.: Rowman & Littlefield, 1987), p. 40

11. Baier's book on Hume is entitled *A Progress of Sentiments: Reflections an Hume's Treatise* (Cambridge, Mass.: Harvard University Press, 1991). Baier's view of the inadequacy of most attempts by contemporary moral philosophers to break with Kant comes out most clearly when she characterizes Allan Gibbard (in his book *Wise Choices, Apt Feelings*) as focusing "on the feelings that a patriarchal religion has bequeathed to us" and says that "Hume would judge Gibbard to be, as a moral philosopher, basically a divine disguised as a fellow expressivist" (312).

12. Nietzsche's diagnosis is reinforced by Elizabeth Anscombe's famous argument that atheists are not entitled to the term "moral obligation."

13. See Jane Tompkins, *Sensational Designs: The Cultural Work of American Fiction, 1790–1860* (New York: Oxford University Press, 1985), for a treatment of the sentimental novel that chimes with the point I am trying to make here. In her chapter on Stowe, Tompkins says that she is asking the reader "to set aside some familiar categories for evaluating fiction—stylistic intricacy, psychological subtlety, epistemological complexity—and to see the sentimental novel not as an artifice of eternity answerable to certain formal criteria and to certain psychological and philosophical concerns, but as a political enterprise, halfway between sermon and social theory, that both codifies and attempts to mold the values of its time" (126).

The contrast that Tompkins draws between authors like Stowe and "male authors such as Thoreau, Whitman, and Melville, who are celebrated as models of intellectual daring and honesty" (124), parallels the contrast I tried to draw between public utility and private perfertion in my *Contingency, Irony, and Solidarity* (Cambridge University Press, 1989). I see *Uncle Tom's Cabin* and *Moby Dick* as equally brilliant achievements, achievements we should not attempt to rank hierarchically, because they serve such different purposes. Arguing about which is the better novel is like arguing about which is the superior philosophical treatise: Mill's *On Liberty* or Kierkegaard's *Philosophical Fragments*.

14. Technically, of course, Kant denied knowledge in order to make room for moral faith. But what is transcendental moral philosophy if not the assurance that the noncognitive imperative delivered via the common moral consciousness shows the existence of a "fact of reason"—a fact about what it is to be a human being, a rational agent, a being that is something more than a bundle of spatiotemporal determinations? Kant was never able to explain how the upshot of transcendental philosophy could be knowledge, but he was never able to give up the attempt to claim such knowledge. On the German project of defending reason against Hume, see Fred Reiser, *The Fate of Reason: German Philosophy from Kant to Fichte* (Cambridge, Mass.: Harvard University Press, 1987).

15. I have discussed the relation between Derrida and feminism in "Deconstruction, Ideology and Feminism: A Pragmatist View," *Hypatia* 8 (1993): 96–103, and also in my reply to Alexander Nehamas in *Lire Rorty* (Paris: Eclat, 1992). Richard Bernstein is, I think basically right in reading Derrida as a moralist, even though Thomas McCarthy is also right in saying that "deconstruction" is of no political use.

# 27

# An Exercise in Civility

## Martin E. Marty

Here is a nightmare for those who hate conflict: take a not very large or airy room in Washington, D.C., and jam it full of tables and microphones, chairs, and cameras. Put a document on the table to test at a "public airing." Now invite to the table representatives of groups who are rarely in the same room together. Tell these antagonists that you would like them to talk about four issues that divide Americans, especially religious Americans: reproductive rights (which, to no one's surprise, quickly gets reduced to abortion); the rights of homosexuals; world population; and church and state.

Ordinarily one would want quickly to wake up from such a nightmare. But at a recent meeting sponsored by a group of scholars from Chicago's Park Ridge Center for the Study of Health, Faith, and Ethics, the company was intelligent, interesting, and at times even playful enough to assure a good day. People were disarmed by the very act of accepting the invitation to attend, a fact that their hosts kept in mind by offering an implicit covenant not to exploit them should they choose to be open and vulnerable. In their ordinary state, these people belong to coalitions, as in the Christian Coalition, or in alliances, as in the Interfaith Alliance, from which they stare across the no-man's land between trenches, or march ahead to vanquish the foe—or at least to lobby for their own cause.

Whoever has seen such partisans frighten away moderates from a school board or preempt a precinct meeting knows why we were afraid our gathering might become a nightmare. The Park Ridge Center was trying out a new document, *To Speak and Be Heard: Principles of Religious Discourse*, on these frequent antagonists. Working with a grant from the Pew Charitable Trusts, we—especially colleagues David Guinn and Larry Greenfield—had spent many days on the road and at the conference table in order to prepare the document.

Participating were leaders from the National Conference of Catholic Bishops, Catholics for a Free Choice, National Association of Evangelicals, National Council of Churches, Family Research Council, People for the American Way, Heritage Foundation, Human Rights Campaign, Ethics and Public Policy Center, Religious Coalition for Reproductive Choice, Christian Legal Society, Interfaith Alliance, Religions Action Center of Reform Judaism, Baptist Joint Committee on Public Affairs, First Amendment Center of Freedom Forum, and spokespersons for various agencies concerned with population and "reproductive choice."

Though inviting leaders of these diverse organizations into a small space might have looked like planning a religiopolitical version of the Jerry Springer television show, the intention was just the opposite. If the "principles and guidelines of our document worked here, it could signal a better way to handle conflict. That better way could not require debaters to leave their convictions, passions, and intensities at the door. It could not make tolerance the highest virtue or ask that relativism rule. Only a utopian would expect participants to resolve in a couple of hours what wise people have not accomplished in decades or centuries.

Some among those who attended the meeting were battle-scarred veterans of the controversial 1994 International Conference on Population and Development at Cairo, where informal alliances between the Vatican and hardline Muslim groups had dominated the debate on reproductive rights and overpopulation. To some that conference had been a disaster, and they wanted to learn why things had gone so wrong. Their antagonists, also represented at the Washington table, had walked away triumphant and were spoiling for the next round of battle at a future, second such Cairo event. Would they now, in the carefully-thought-out circumstances of our Washington meeting, be able to speak frankly with one another, showing how their positions were based on profound religious, convictions? Would they be able to hear voices they usually outshout or block? They would, could, and did.

None of the participants needed prodding. Many are old pros at representing their causes; some knew their opponents well and are civil to have coffee together before or after their contentious encounters. But being seasoned spokespeople for their positions tends to make people even more committed than the rank and file, and to have more at stake than others in the outcomes of arguments and conversations.

What the organizers hope will come from efforts like these include at least the following: helping to keep the republic healthy; restoring public confidence that religion—at the root of the most volatile causes but often excluded from discussion—really belongs in the public debate; helping contending groups to keep their searches and conversations going as they seek various levels of common ground and revise agendas to promote causes on which they come to some consensus; developing personal relations among those too often isolated from each other.

The word "civility" has come into favor because it refers both to the civil order and to polite behavior. So many groups are studying and encouraging civility that trendspotters have begun to yawn. Some backlashers have begun to call for more incivility, as if the world were becoming too civil. Yet how much we need civility to guide discourse on issues that threaten the very core of community and efforts to improve the world.

Some of the most moving exchanges at our meeting came when prolife people tried to explain why they cry over daily deaths-by-abortion, and pro-choice people looked into the eyes of their opponents—and, yes, they were and are opponents—and gave voice to the agonies of women who must make desperate choices. The exchanges between representatives of homosexual rights and those who, adhering to their conscience, see homosexual activity as against scriptures, natural law, and the good of the country, all but threatened the peace of the occasion. But no one left the table, and we are confident that we were all changed by the experience.

Some of the polarized parties arranged to have face-to-face meetings the next day at which they would listen to each other as if for the first time. They could continue to learn what offends each other and to respect each other as persons.

The guideline that evoked the most discussion was a "covenant of conversation."

> Those who participate . . . pledge to act and speak with integrity and to regard others as doing so. . . . Members of all faith communities regard their religious as being grounded in integrity and demanding integrity when their adherents speak or act. Many have difficulty, however, understanding that those outside their faith possess and represent the same kind of integrity. . . . Nonetheless, it is possible to establish ground rules and modes of understanding that can help all to manifest integrity and mutual respect. The result of following or acting upon these will not mean that contenders must avoid delicate or explosive topics or that there will always be satisfying agreements or an emerging consensus. But communication need not break down and the process of addressing social issues for human good can continue even in such circumstance.

All who spoke confessed that they strove to have and to manifest integrity, and most confessed that they had difficulty believing their antagonists had or showed it. But it was clear that participants made advances in understanding on this point; communication did not break down, and "the process of addressing social issues for human good" was refreshed.

Once again we learned that the troubling disputes in our republic are grounded in vastly differing world views and responses to texts and leaders; we learned that people cannot and will not lightly give up their stands. Their whole lives are wrapped up in them. Their jobs of representation are not mere jobs; they are ways of life that others have trouble understanding.

Some suggested that help is needed to implement such conversations in local communities. Others voiced frustration that the network of people in religious groups and communities who regularly work at "civil discourse" is alarmingly small and weak. Some cautioned that people of power can use the concepts of civil discourse and civility to manipulate processes and people. But the same voices expressed the conviction that the faith traditions also have often-unplumbed resources for helping people both to love the truth and to speak the truth in love.

# Select Bibliography

Allport, Gordon W. *The Nature of Prejudice*. Special ed. Reading, Mass.: Addison-Wesley. 1979.

Aronson, Elliot. *The Social Animal*. 6th ed. New York: W. H. Freeman, 1991.

Barash, David P. *Sociobiology and Behavior*. 2d ed. New York: Elsevier, 1982,

Dawkins, Richard, *Extended Phenotype*. New York: Oxford University Press, 1959.

———. *The Selfish Gene*. 2d ed. New York: Oxford University Press, 1990.

Dovidio, John F., and Samuel L. Gaertner. *Prejudice, Discrimination, and Racism*. Plympton, Mass.: Academy Publishing, 1986.

Gadamer, Hans George. *Reason in the Age of Science*. Trans. by Frederick G. Lawrence. Cambridge, Mass.: MIT Press, 1982.

Gould, Stephen Jay. *The Mismeasure of Man*. New York: W. W. Norton, 1983.

Lewontin, R. C., Steven Rose, and Leon J. Kamen. *Not in Our Genes: Biology, Ideology, and Human Nature*. New York: Pantheon Books, 1984.

Lorenz, Konrad. *On Aggression*. Trans. by Marjorie K. Wilson. San Diego, Calif: Harcourt-Brace Jovanovich, 1974.

Marcus, George E. *With Malice Toward Some: How People Make Civil Liberties Judgments*. New York: Cambridge University Press, 1995.

Murphy, Jeffrie G. *Evolution, Morality, and the Meaning of Life*. Latham, Md.: Rowman and Allenheld, 1982.

Noel, Lise. *Intolerance: The Parameters of Oppression*. Trans. by Arnold Bennett. McGill, Queens University Press, 1994

Trivers, Robert. *Social Evolution*. Redwood City, Calif: Benjamin-Cummings, 1985.

Van den Berghe, Pierre L. *The Ethnic Phenomenon*. Westport, Conn.: Greenwood Publishing, 1987.

Walzer, Michael. *On Toleration*. New Haven, Conn.: Yale University Press, 1997.

Wilson, Edward O. *Consilience: The Unity of Knowledge*. New York: Alfred A. Knopf Incorporated, 1998.

———. *On Human Nature*. Cambridge, Mass.: Harvard University Press, 1978.

# Contributors

GORDON W. ALLPORT was a member of the Harvard University Department of Psychology from 1930 until his death in 1967.

ELLIOT ARONSON is professor of psychology at the University of California, Santa Cruz.

JOHN DEWEY (1859–1952) is America's most prominent philosopher. He finished his career as a professor of philosophy at Columbia University and produced during his lifetime the thirty-seven volumes of *The Collected Works of John Dewey* published by the Southern Illinois University Press.

JOHN F. DOVIDIO is professor of psychology and Director of the Division of Natural Science and mathematics at Colgate University, Hamilton, New York.

SAMUEL L. GAERTNER is professor of psychology at the University of Delaware.

RICHARD GOLDSTEIN is coexecutive editor of the *Village Voice*.

DAVID GRANN is a senior editor of the *New Republic*.

ABRAHAM KAPLAN is professor of philosophy at the University of Haifa, Israel.

RICHARD D. MOHR is professor of philosophy at the University of Illinois, Urbana-Champaign.

FRANK KOGAN is a contributor at *Popped*, an on-line news site.

TONY KUSHNER is a playwright.

SHARON LERNER is a contributor to the *Village Voice*.

MARTIN MARTY is a Lutheran minister, University of Chicago professor emeritus, senior editor of the *Christian Century*, and director of the Pew Foundation's Public Religion Project.

MICHAEL MUSTO is a gossip columnist at *E-Online* and a contributor to the *Village Voice*.

MARTHA C. NUSSBAUM is professor of law at the University of Chicago.

RICHARD RORTY is professor of comparative literature at Stanford University, California.

PAULA ROTHENBERG is professor of English at William Paterson College in Wayne, New Jersey.

JEAN-PAUL SARTRE, French existentialist philosopher, dramatist, and novelist, died in 1980.

PETER SINGER is Director of the Center for Human Bioethics at Monash University, Clayton, Victoria, Australia.

RAYMOND W. SMITH is chairman of Bell Atlantic Corporation.

PIERRE L. VAN DEN BERGE is professor of sociology and anthropology at the University of Washington, Seattle.

BRICE R. WACHTERHAUSER is associate professor of philosophy at Saint Joseph's University, Philadelphia.

CORNEL WEST is the Alphonse Fletcher Jr. University Professor at Harvard Divinity School.

PATRICIA J. WILLIAMS is professor of law at Columbia University.

EDWARD O. WILSON is the Mellon Professor of the Sciences, Pellegrino University Professor Emeritus, and honorary curator in Entomology in the Museum of Comparative Zoology at Harvard University.